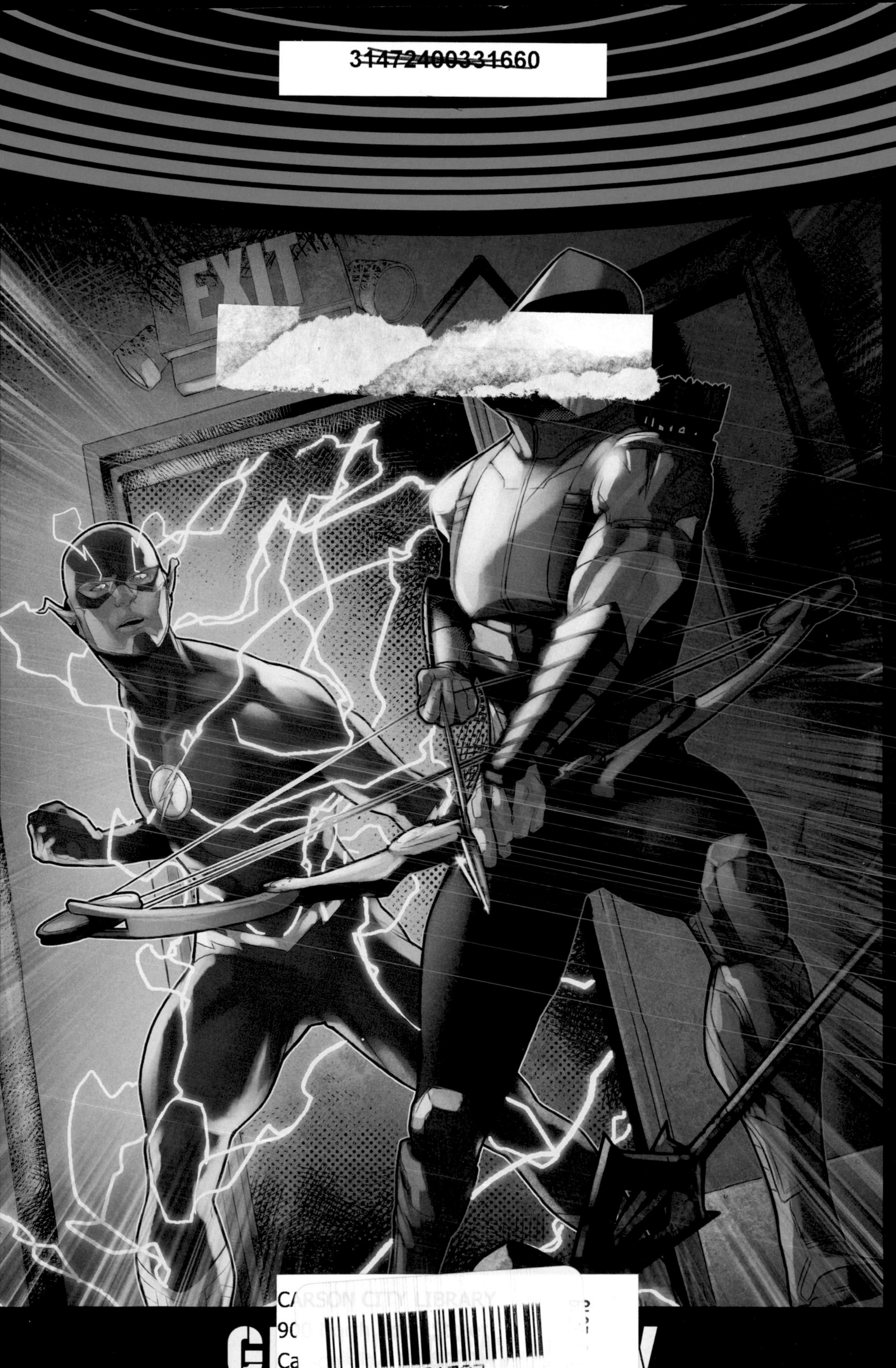
EXIT



G W

VOL.5 ERO

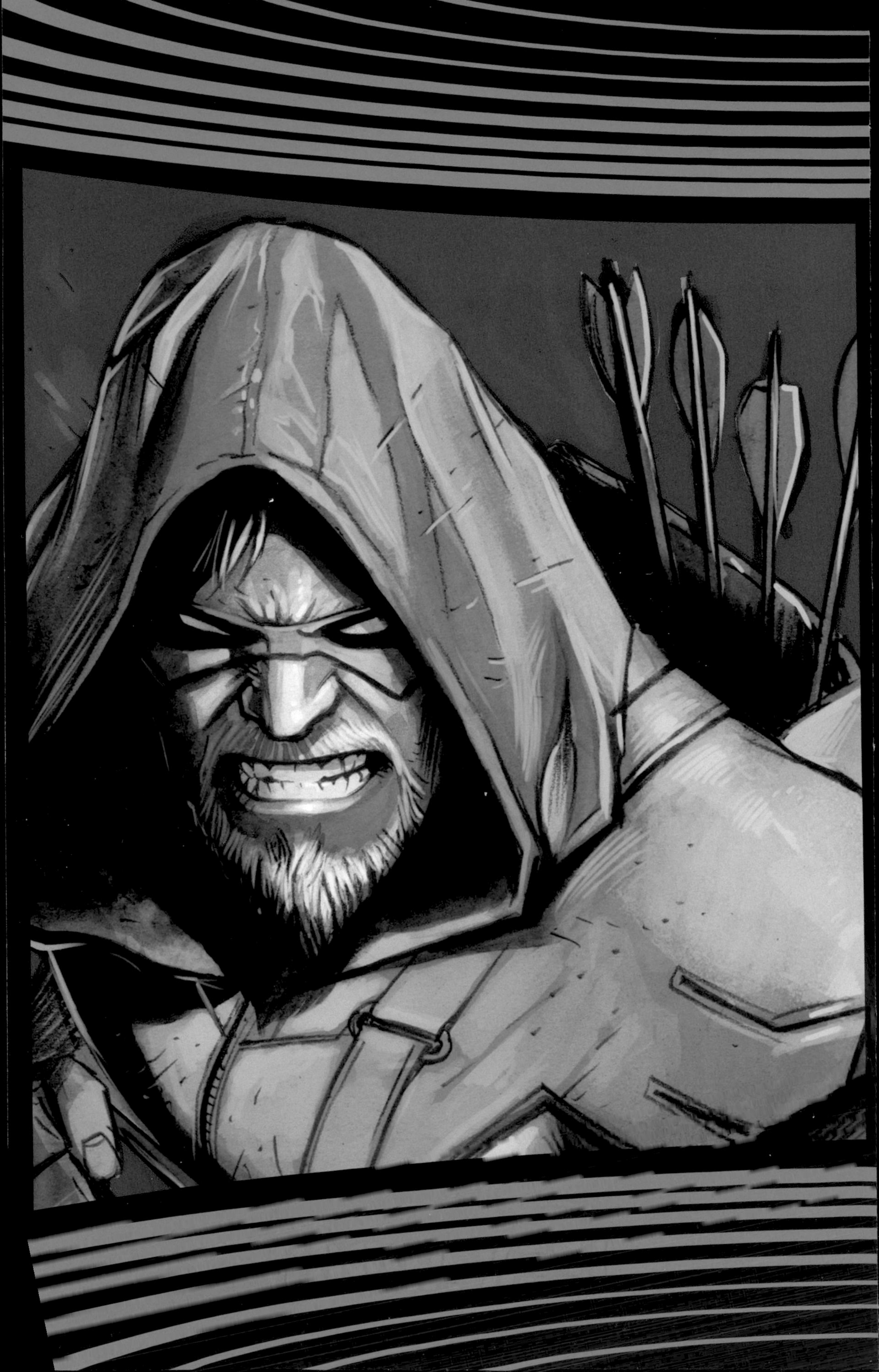

# GREEN ARROW

## VOL.5 HARD-TRAVELING HERO

**BENJAMIN PERCY**
wrlter

**OTTO SCHMIDT**
**JUAN FERREYRA**
**STEPHEN BYRNE**
**JAMAL CAMPBELL**
artists and colorists

**NATE PIEKOS of BLAMBOT ™**
letterer

**OTTO SCHMIDT**
series and collection cover artist

**SUPERMAN** created by **JERRY SIEGEL** and **JOE SHUSTER**.
By special arrangement with the Jerry Siegel family.

**ANDY KHOURI** Editor - Original Series * **HARVEY RICHARDS** Associate Editor - Original Series
**JEB WOODARD** Group Editor - Collected Editions * **ERIKA ROTHBERG** Editor - Collected Edition
**STEVE COOK** Design Director - Books * **MEGEN BELLERSEN** Publication Design

**BOB HARRAS** Senior VP - Editor-in-Chief, DC Comics
**PAT McCALLUM** Executive Editor, DC Comics

**DIANE NELSON** President * **DAN DiDIO** Publisher * **JIM LEE** Publisher * **GEOFF JOHNS** President & Chief Creative Officer
**AMIT DESAI** Executive VP - Business & Marketing Strategy, Direct to Consumer & Global Franchise Management
**SAM ADES** Senior VP & General Manager, Digital Services * **BOBBIE CHASE** VP & Executive Editor, Young Reader & Talent Development
**MARK CHIARELLO** Senior VP - Art, Design & Collected Editions * **JOHN CUNNINGHAM** Senior VP - Sales & Trade Marketing
**ANNE DePIES** Senior VP - Business Strategy, Finance & Administration * **DON FALLETTI** VP - Manufacturing Operations
**LAWRENCE GANEM** VP - Editorial Administration & Talent Relations * **ALISON GILL** Senior VP - Manufacturing & Operations
**HANK KANALZ** Senior VP - Editorial Strategy & Administration * **JAY KOGAN** VP - Legal Affairs * **JACK MAHAN** VP - Business Affairs
**NICK J. NAPOLITANO** VP - Manufacturing Administration * **EDDIE SCANNELL** VP - Consumer Marketing
**COURTNEY SIMMONS** Senior VP - Publicity & Communications * **JIM (SKI) SOKOLOWSKI** VP - Comic Book Specialty Sales & Trade Marketing
**NANCY SPEARS** VP - Mass, Book, Digital Sales & Trade Marketing * **MICHELE R. WELLS** VP - Content Strategy

GREEN ARROW VOL. 5: HARD-TRAVELING HERO

DC Comics, 2900 West Alameda Ave., Burbank, CA 91505
Printed by LSC Communications, Kendallville, IN, USA. 3/30/18. First Printing.
ISBN: 978-1-4012-7853-3

Library of Congress Cataloging-in-Publication Data is available.

**PEFC Certified**

Printed on paper from
sustainably managed
forests and controlled
sources

PEFC/29-31-337    www.pefc.org

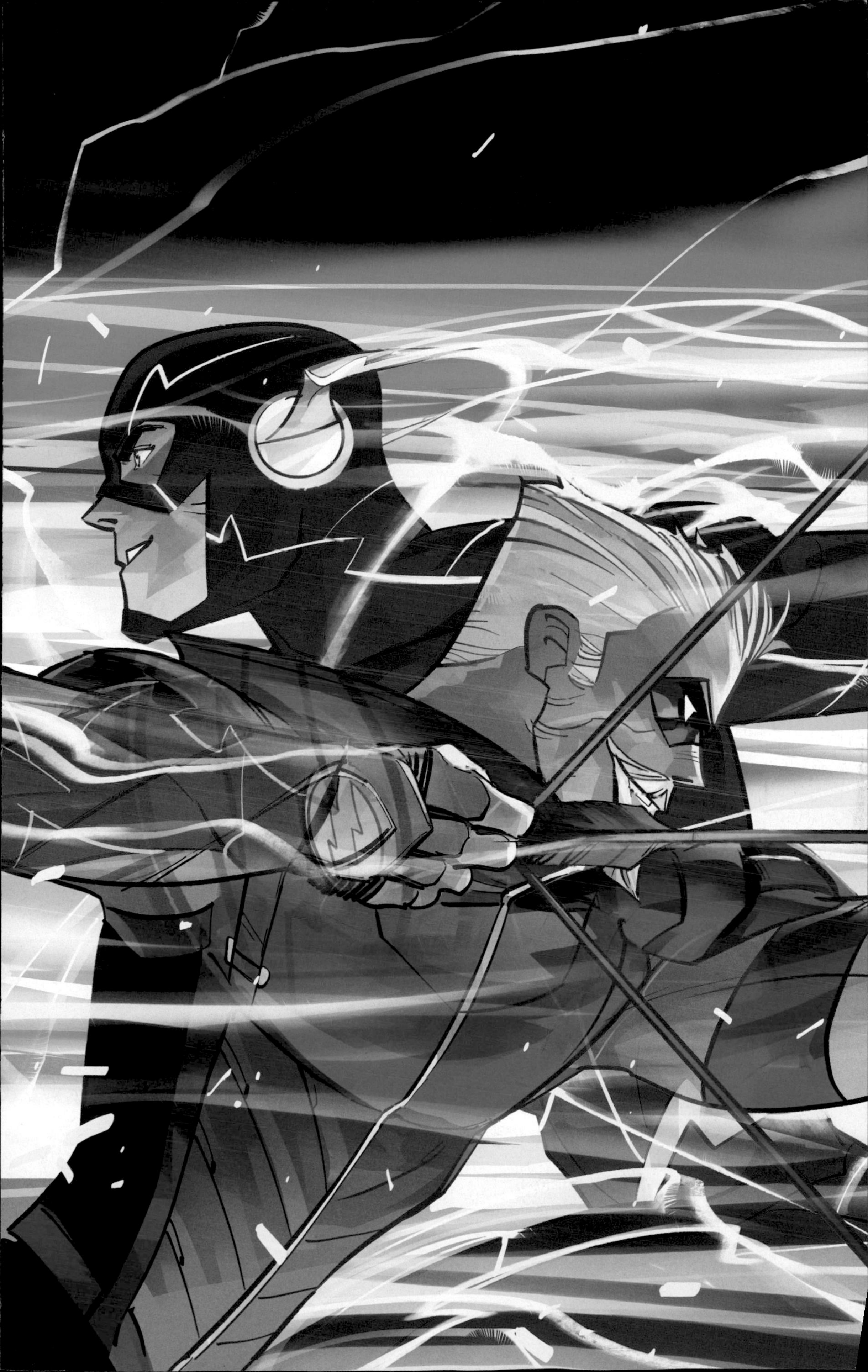

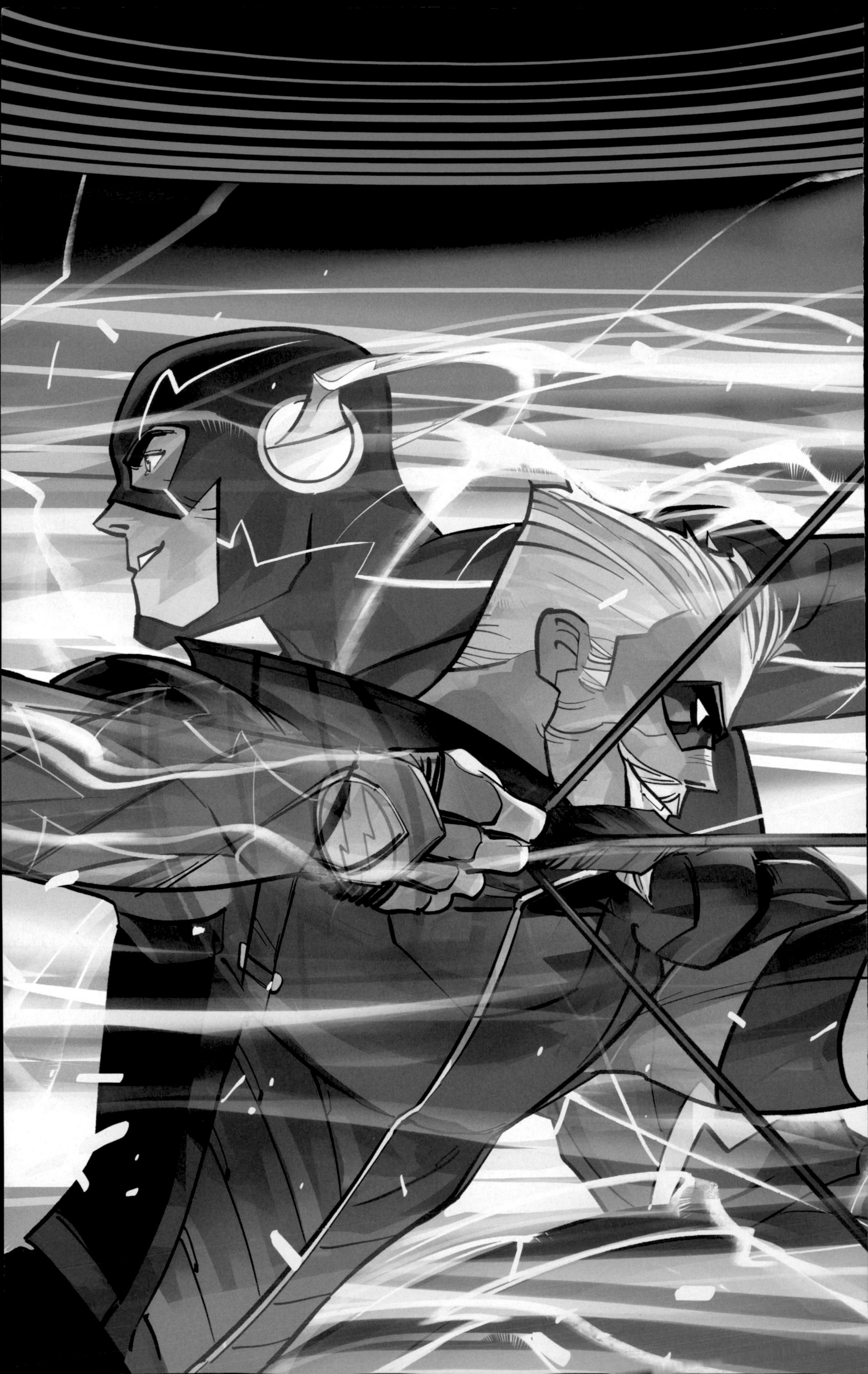

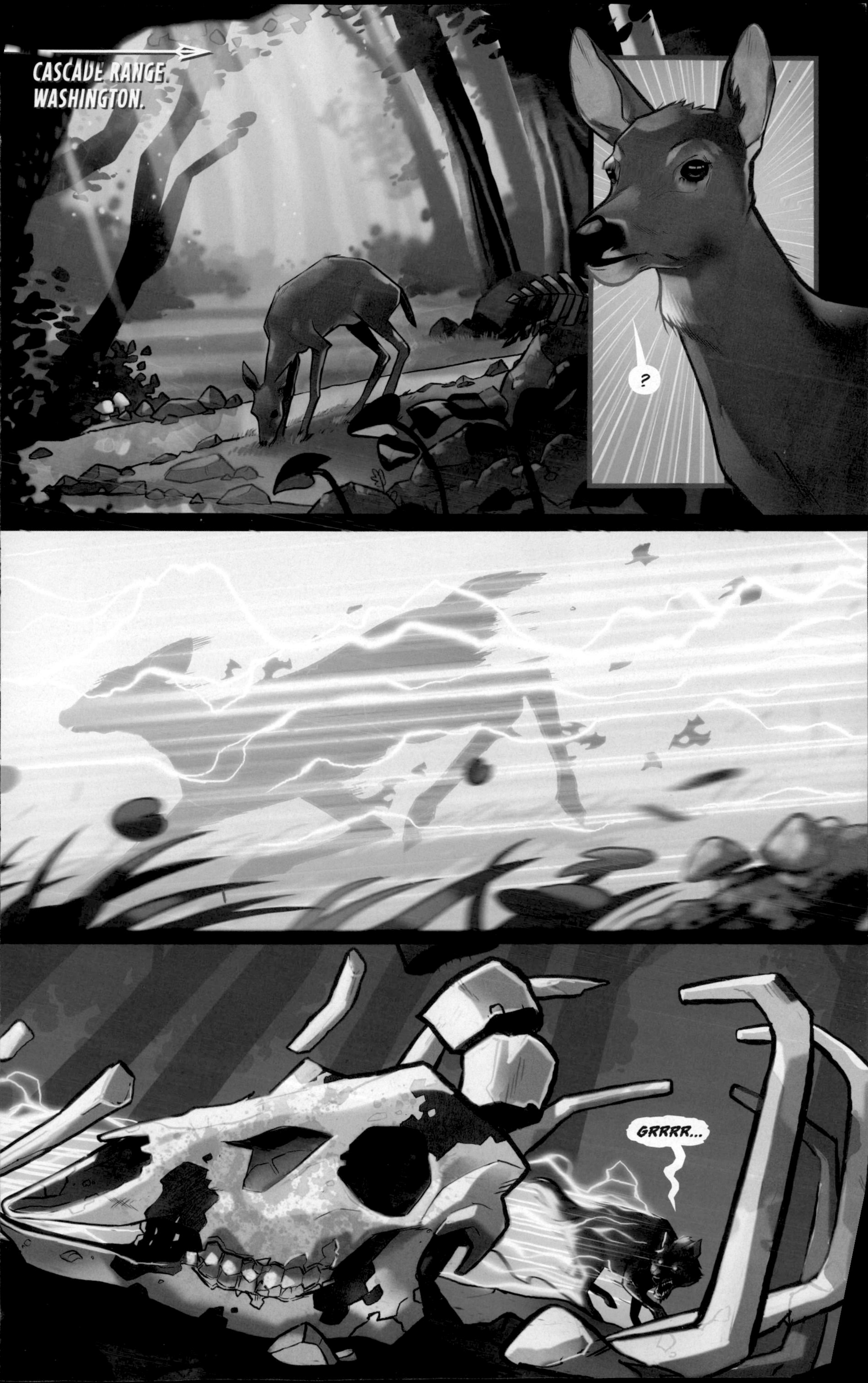
CASCADE RANGE.
WASHINGTON.
?
GRRRR...

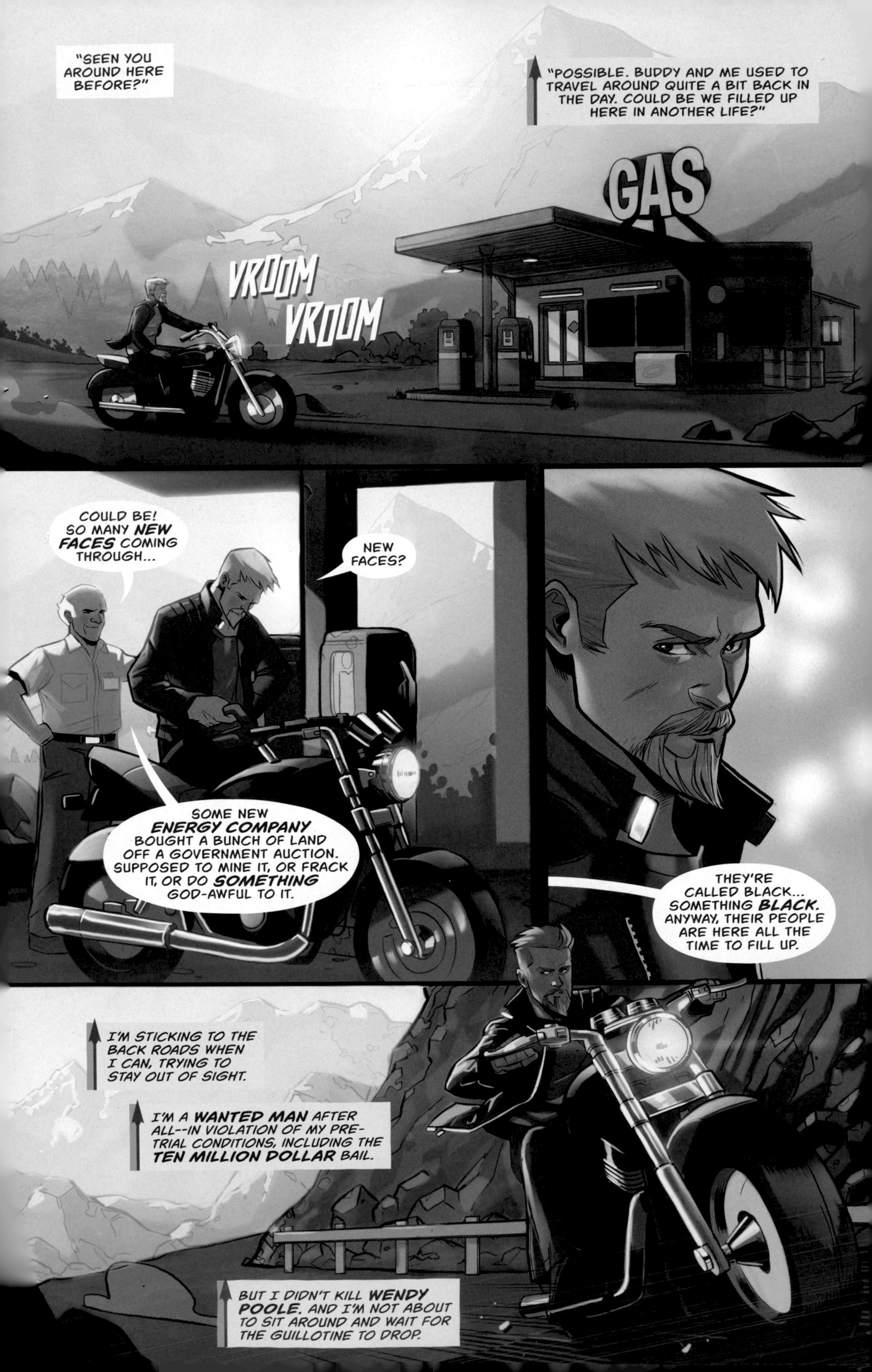
"SEEN YOU AROUND HERE BEFORE?"
"POSSIBLE. BUDDY AND ME USED TO TRAVEL AROUND QUITE A BIT BACK IN THE DAY. COULD BE WE FILLED UP HERE IN ANOTHER LIFE?"
GAS
VROOM VROOM
COULD BE! SO MANY NEW FACES COMING THROUGH...
NEW FACES?
SOME NEW ENERGY COMPANY BOUGHT A BUNCH OF LAND OFF A GOVERNMENT AUCTION. SUPPOSED TO MINE IT, OR FRACK IT, OR DO SOMETHING GOD-AWFUL TO IT.
THEY'RE CALLED BLACK... SOMETHING BLACK. ANYWAY, THEIR PEOPLE ARE HERE ALL THE TIME TO FILL UP.
I'M STICKING TO THE BACK ROADS WHEN I CAN, TRYING TO STAY OUT OF SIGHT.
I'M A WANTED MAN AFTER ALL--IN VIOLATION OF MY PRE-TRIAL CONDITIONS, INCLUDING THE TEN MILLION DOLLAR BAIL.
BUT I DIDN'T KILL WENDY POOLE. AND I'M NOT ABOUT TO SIT AROUND AND WAIT FOR THE GUILLOTINE TO DROP.

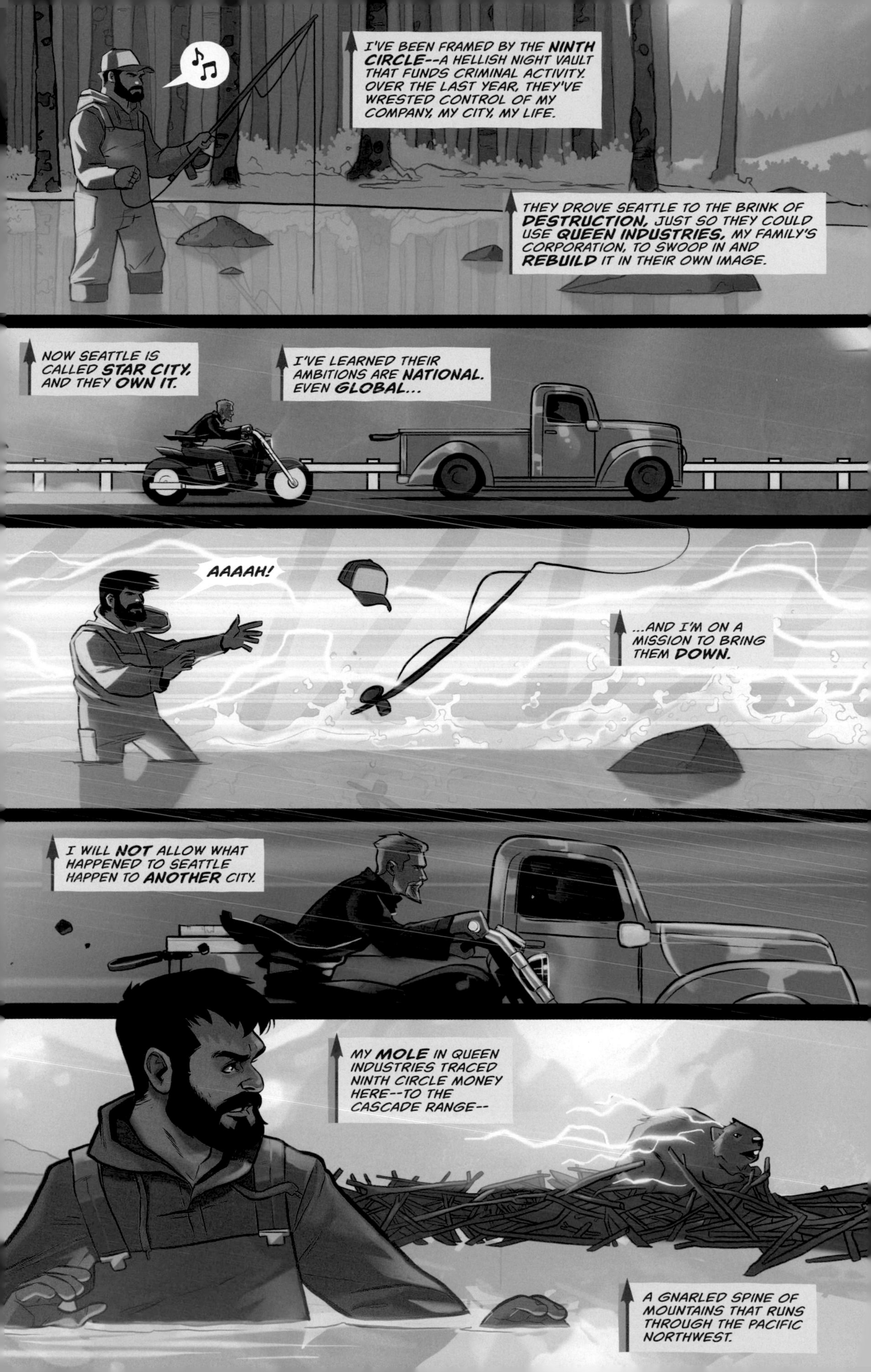
I'VE BEEN FRAMED BY THE NINTH CIRCLE--A HELLISH NIGHT VAULT THAT FUNDS CRIMINAL ACTIVITY. OVER THE LAST YEAR, THEY'VE WRESTED CONTROL OF MY COMPANY, MY CITY, MY LIFE.
THEY DROVE SEATTLE TO THE BRINK OF DESTRUCTION, JUST SO THEY COULD USE QUEEN INDUSTRIES, MY FAMILY'S CORPORATION, TO SWOOP IN AND REBUILD IT IN THEIR OWN IMAGE.
NOW SEATTLE IS CALLED STAR CITY, AND THEY OWN IT.
I'VE LEARNED THEIR AMBITIONS ARE NATIONAL. EVEN GLOBAL...
AAAAH!
...AND I'M ON A MISSION TO BRING THEM DOWN.
I WILL NOT ALLOW WHAT HAPPENED TO SEATTLE HAPPEN TO ANOTHER CITY.
MY MOLE IN QUEEN INDUSTRIES TRACED NINTH CIRCLE MONEY HERE--TO THE CASCADE RANGE--
A GNARLED SPINE OF MOUNTAINS THAT RUNS THROUGH THE PACIFIC NORTHWEST.

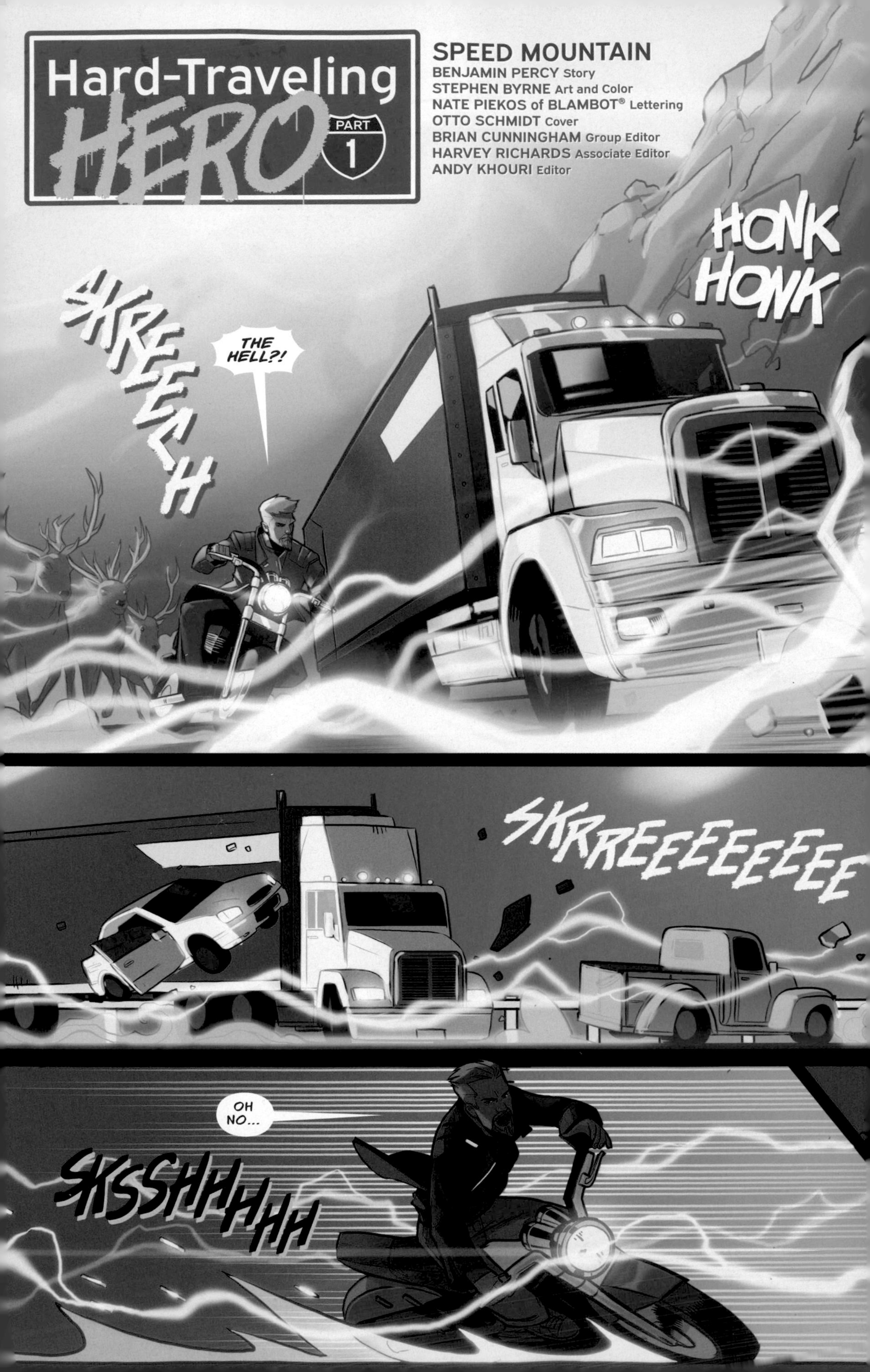
Hard-Traveling HERO
PART 1
SPEED MOUNTAIN
BENJAMIN PERCY Story
STEPHEN BYRNE Art and Color
NATE PIEKOS of BLAMBOT® Lettering
OTTO SCHMIDT Cover
BRIAN CUNNINGHAM Group Editor
HARVEY RICHARDS Associate Editor
ANDY KHOURI Editor
HONK HONK
SKREEECH
THE HELL?!
SKRREEEEEEEE
OH NO...
SKSSHHHHH

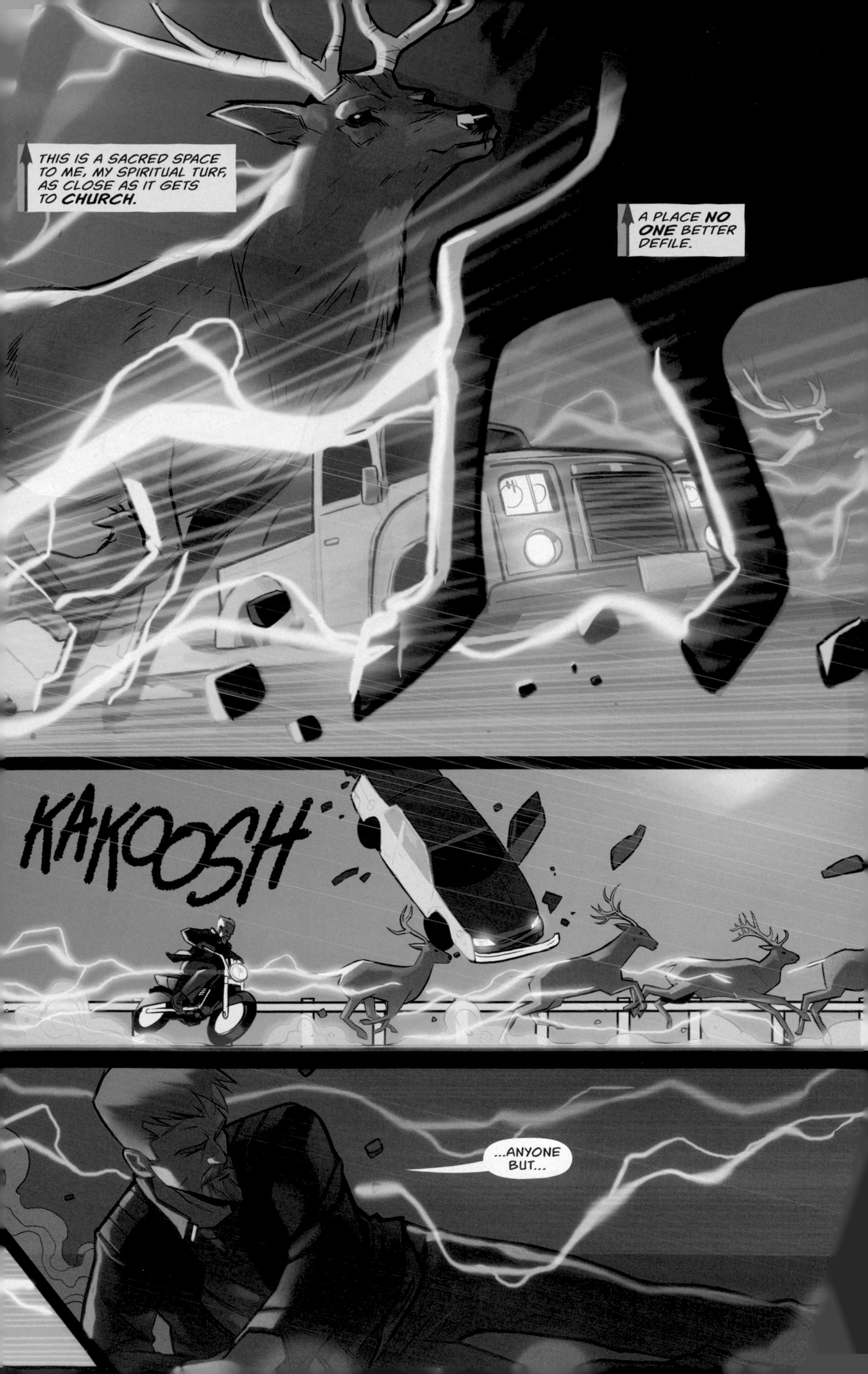
THIS IS A SACRED SPACE TO ME, MY SPIRITUAL TURF, AS CLOSE AS IT GETS TO CHURCH.
A PLACE NO ONE BETTER DEFILE.
KAKOOSH
...ANYONE BUT...

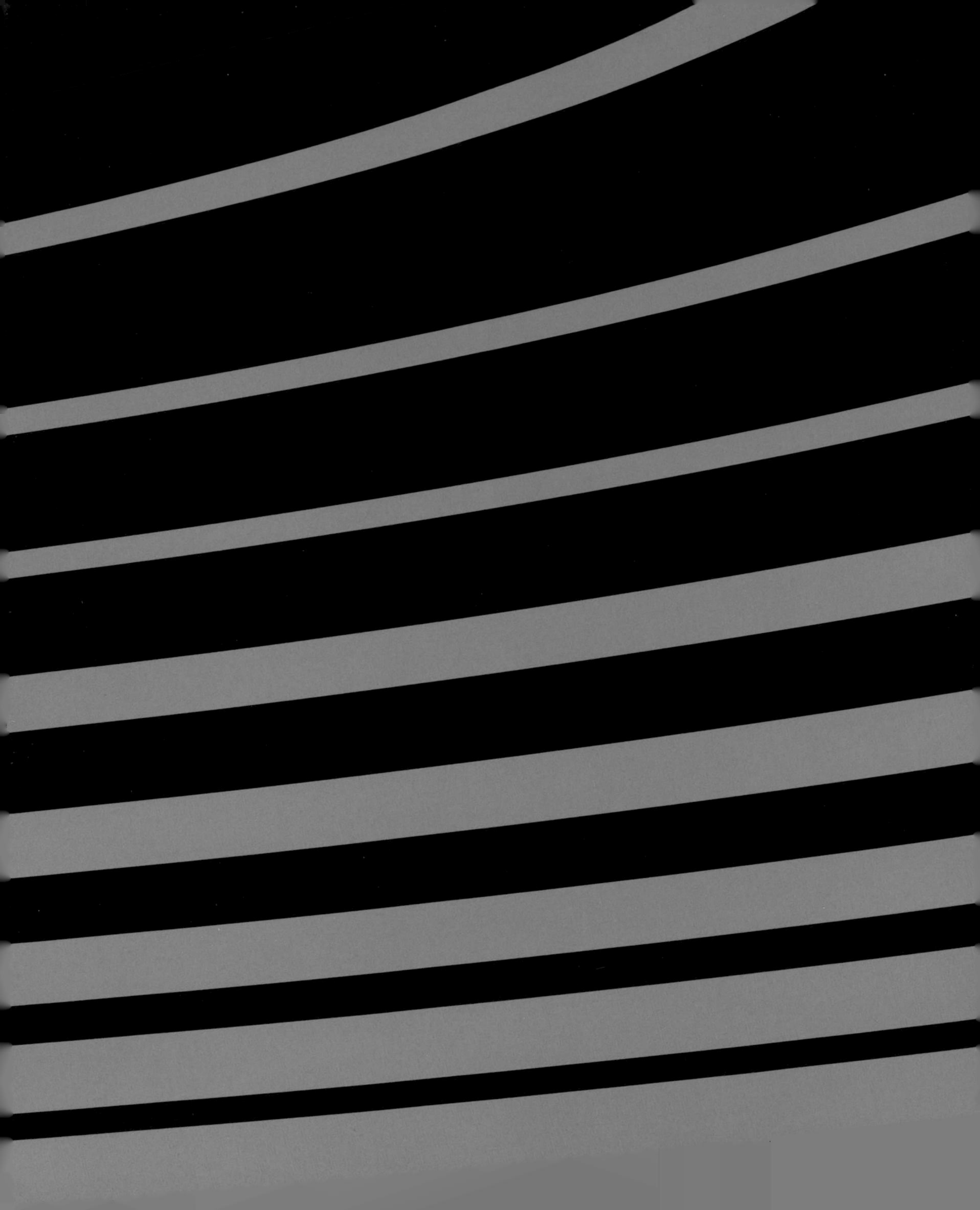

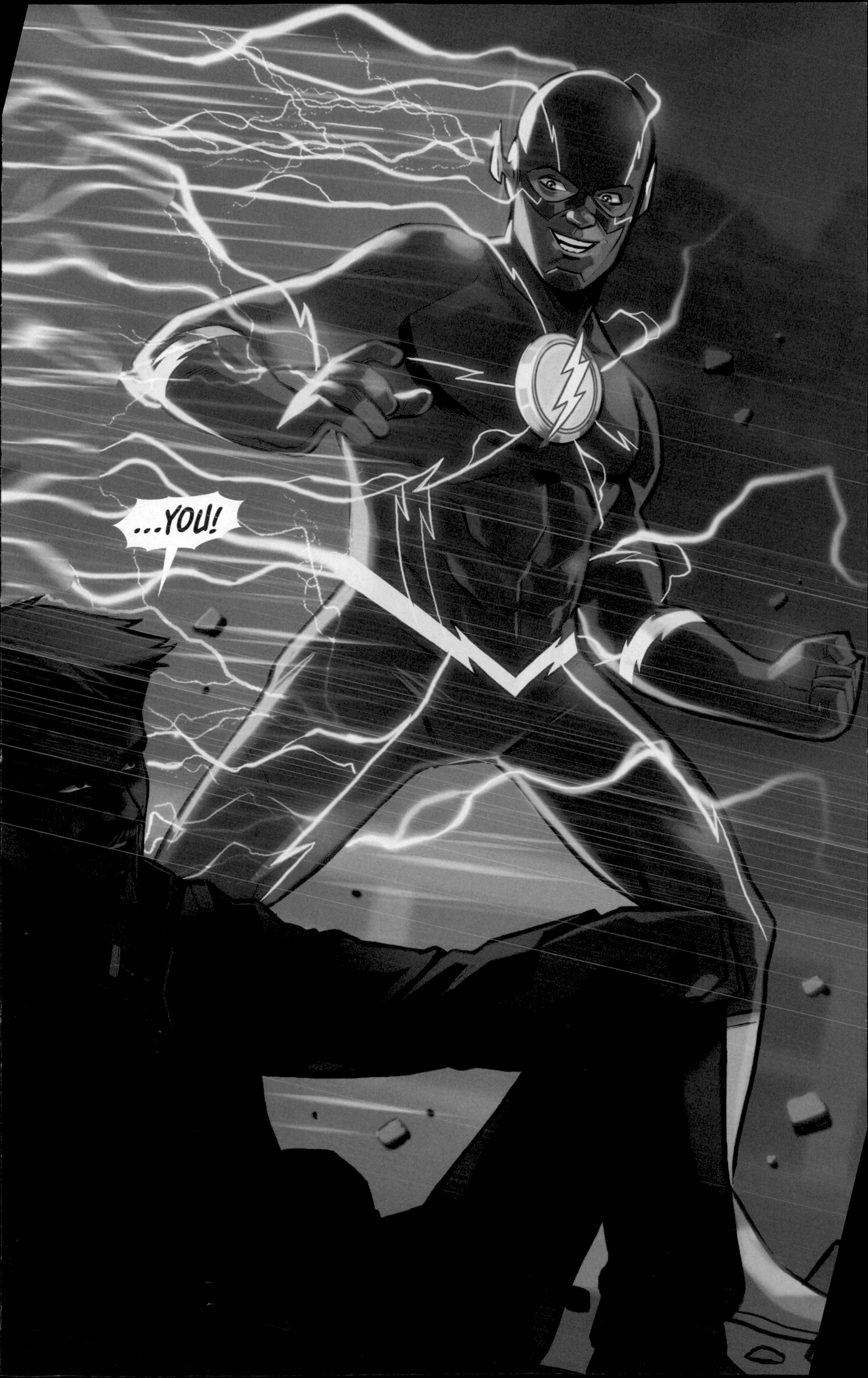
...YOU!

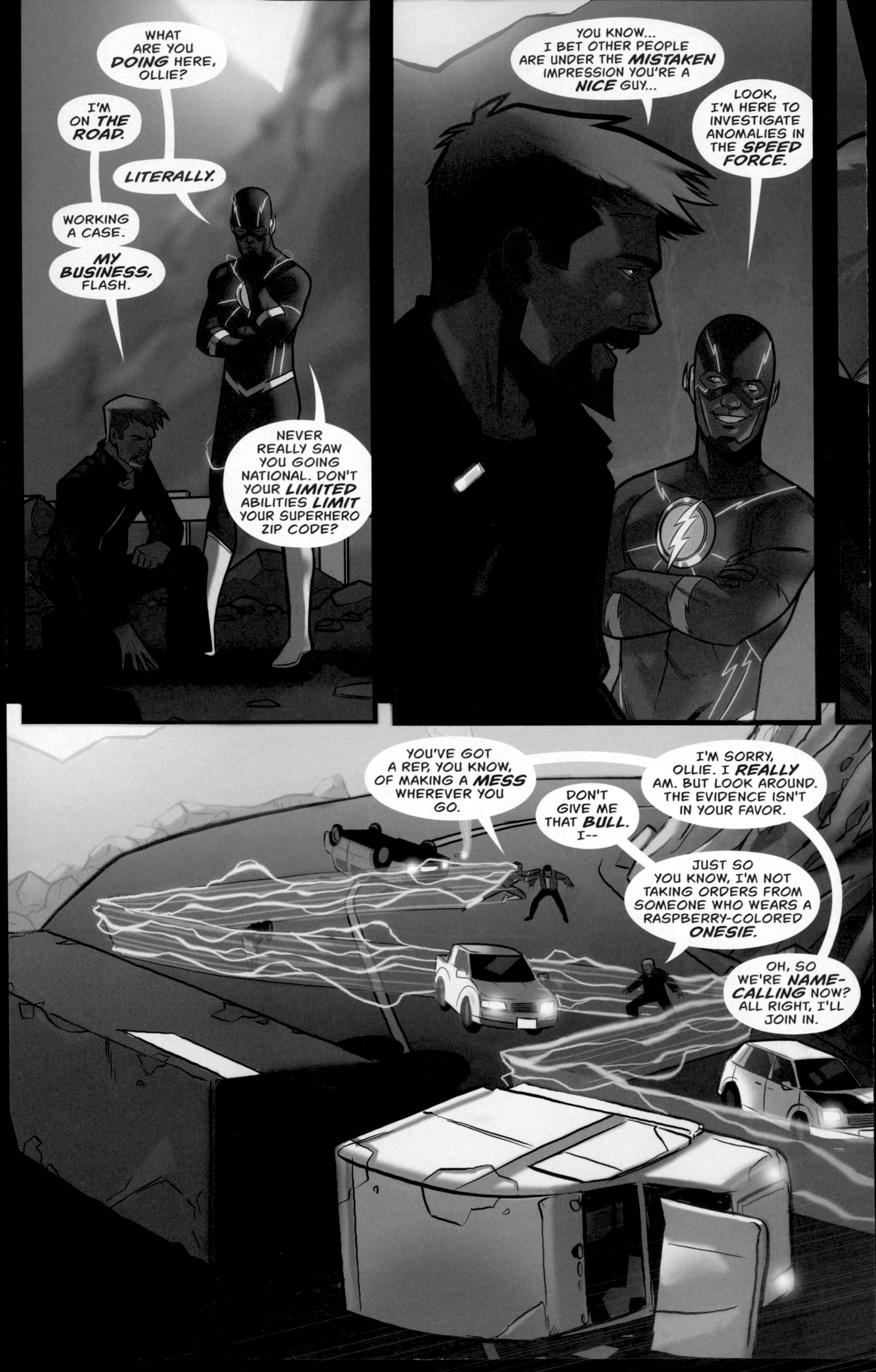
WHAT ARE YOU *DOING* HERE, OLLIE?
I'M ON *THE ROAD.*
*LITERALLY.*
WORKING A CASE.
*MY BUSINESS,* FLASH.
NEVER REALLY SAW YOU GOING NATIONAL. DON'T YOUR *LIMITED* ABILITIES *LIMIT* YOUR SUPERHERO ZIP CODE?
YOU KNOW... I BET OTHER PEOPLE ARE UNDER THE *MISTAKEN* IMPRESSION YOU'RE A *NICE* GUY...
LOOK, I'M HERE TO INVESTIGATE ANOMALIES IN THE *SPEED FORCE.*
YOU'VE GOT A REP, YOU KNOW, OF MAKING A *MESS* WHEREVER YOU GO.
I'M SORRY, OLLIE. I *REALLY* AM. BUT LOOK AROUND. THE EVIDENCE ISN'T IN YOUR FAVOR.
DON'T GIVE ME THAT *BULL.* I--
JUST SO YOU KNOW, I'M NOT TAKING ORDERS FROM SOMEONE WHO WEARS A RASPBERRY-COLORED *ONESIE.*
OH, SO WE'RE *NAME-CALLING* NOW? ALL RIGHT, I'LL JOIN IN.

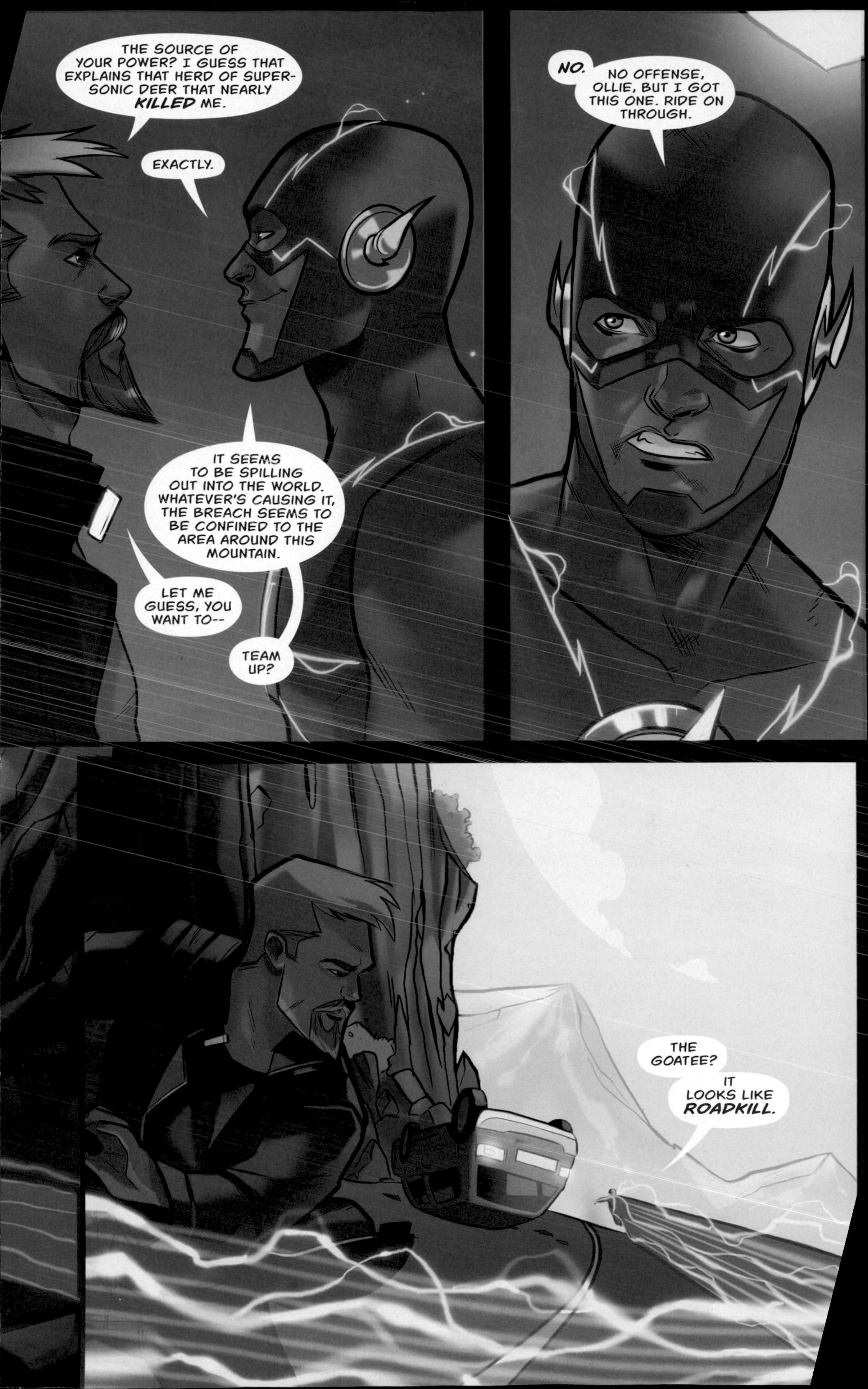
THE SOURCE OF YOUR POWER? I GUESS THAT EXPLAINS THAT HERD OF SUPER-SONIC DEER THAT NEARLY KILLED ME.
EXACTLY.
IT SEEMS TO BE SPILLING OUT INTO THE WORLD. WHATEVER'S CAUSING IT, THE BREACH SEEMS TO BE CONFINED TO THE AREA AROUND THIS MOUNTAIN.
LET ME GUESS, YOU WANT TO--
TEAM UP?
NO.
NO OFFENSE, OLLIE, BUT I GOT THIS ONE. RIDE ON THROUGH.
THE GOATEE?
IT LOOKS LIKE ROADKILL.

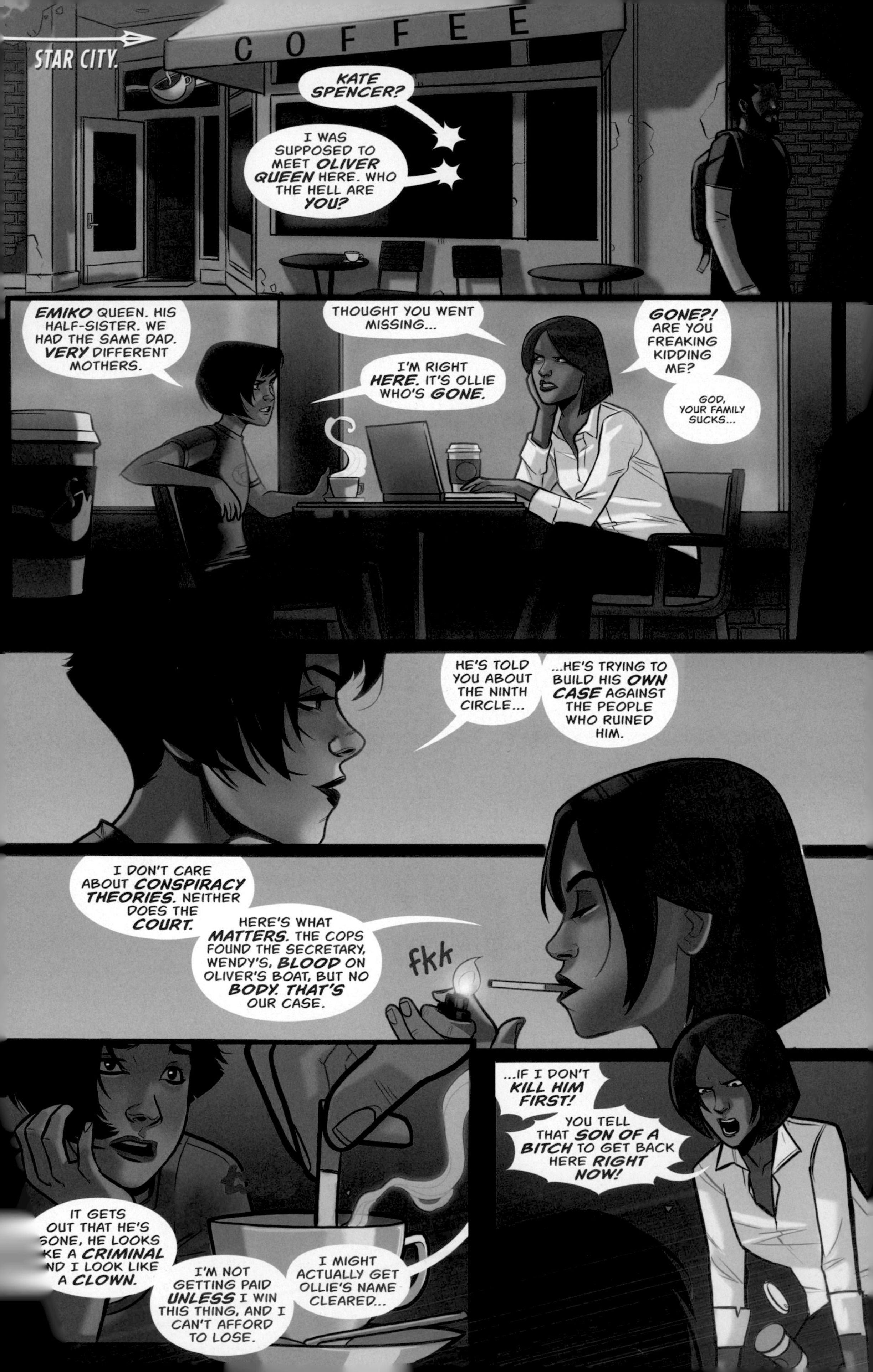
STAR CITY.
COFFEE
KATE SPENCER?
I WAS SUPPOSED TO MEET OLIVER QUEEN HERE. WHO THE HELL ARE YOU?
EMIKO QUEEN. HIS HALF-SISTER. WE HAD THE SAME DAD. VERY DIFFERENT MOTHERS.
THOUGHT YOU WENT MISSING...
I'M RIGHT HERE. IT'S OLLIE WHO'S GONE.
GONE?! ARE YOU FREAKING KIDDING ME?
GOD, YOUR FAMILY SUCKS...
HE'S TOLD YOU ABOUT THE NINTH CIRCLE...
...HE'S TRYING TO BUILD HIS OWN CASE AGAINST THE PEOPLE WHO RUINED HIM.
I DON'T CARE ABOUT CONSPIRACY THEORIES. NEITHER DOES THE COURT.
HERE'S WHAT MATTERS. THE COPS FOUND THE SECRETARY, WENDY'S, BLOOD ON OLIVER'S BOAT, BUT NO BODY. THAT'S OUR CASE.
fkk
IT GETS OUT THAT HE'S GONE, HE LOOKS LIKE A CRIMINAL AND I LOOK LIKE A CLOWN.
I'M NOT GETTING PAID UNLESS I WIN THIS THING, AND I CAN'T AFFORD TO LOSE.
I MIGHT ACTUALLY GET OLLIE'S NAME CLEARED...
...IF I DON'T KILL HIM FIRST!
YOU TELL THAT SON OF A BITCH TO GET BACK HERE RIGHT NOW!

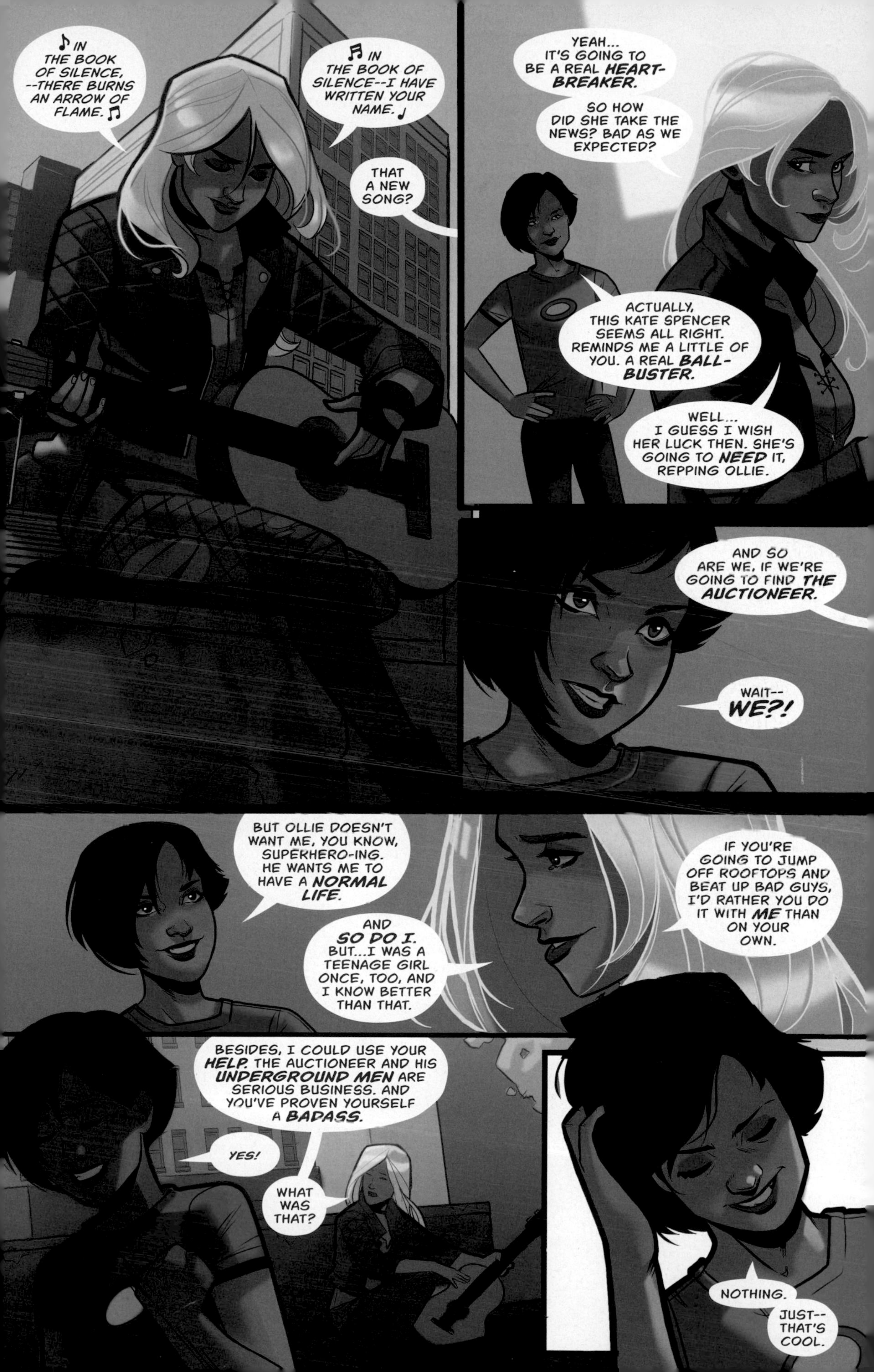
♪ IN THE BOOK OF SILENCE, --THERE BURNS AN ARROW OF FLAME. ♫
♫ IN THE BOOK OF SILENCE--I HAVE WRITTEN YOUR NAME. ♩
THAT A NEW SONG?
YEAH... IT'S GOING TO BE A REAL HEART-BREAKER.
SO HOW DID SHE TAKE THE NEWS? BAD AS WE EXPECTED?
ACTUALLY, THIS KATE SPENCER SEEMS ALL RIGHT. REMINDS ME A LITTLE OF YOU. A REAL BALL-BUSTER.
WELL... I GUESS I WISH HER LUCK THEN. SHE'S GOING TO NEED IT, REPPING OLLIE.
AND SO ARE WE, IF WE'RE GOING TO FIND THE AUCTIONEER.
WAIT-- WE?!
BUT OLLIE DOESN'T WANT ME, YOU KNOW, SUPERHERO-ING. HE WANTS ME TO HAVE A NORMAL LIFE.
AND SO DO I. BUT...I WAS A TEENAGE GIRL ONCE, TOO, AND I KNOW BETTER THAN THAT.
IF YOU'RE GOING TO JUMP OFF ROOFTOPS AND BEAT UP BAD GUYS, I'D RATHER YOU DO IT WITH ME THAN ON YOUR OWN.
BESIDES, I COULD USE YOUR HELP. THE AUCTIONEER AND HIS UNDERGROUND MEN ARE SERIOUS BUSINESS. AND YOU'VE PROVEN YOURSELF A BADASS.
YES!
WHAT WAS THAT?
NOTHING.
JUST-- THAT'S COOL.

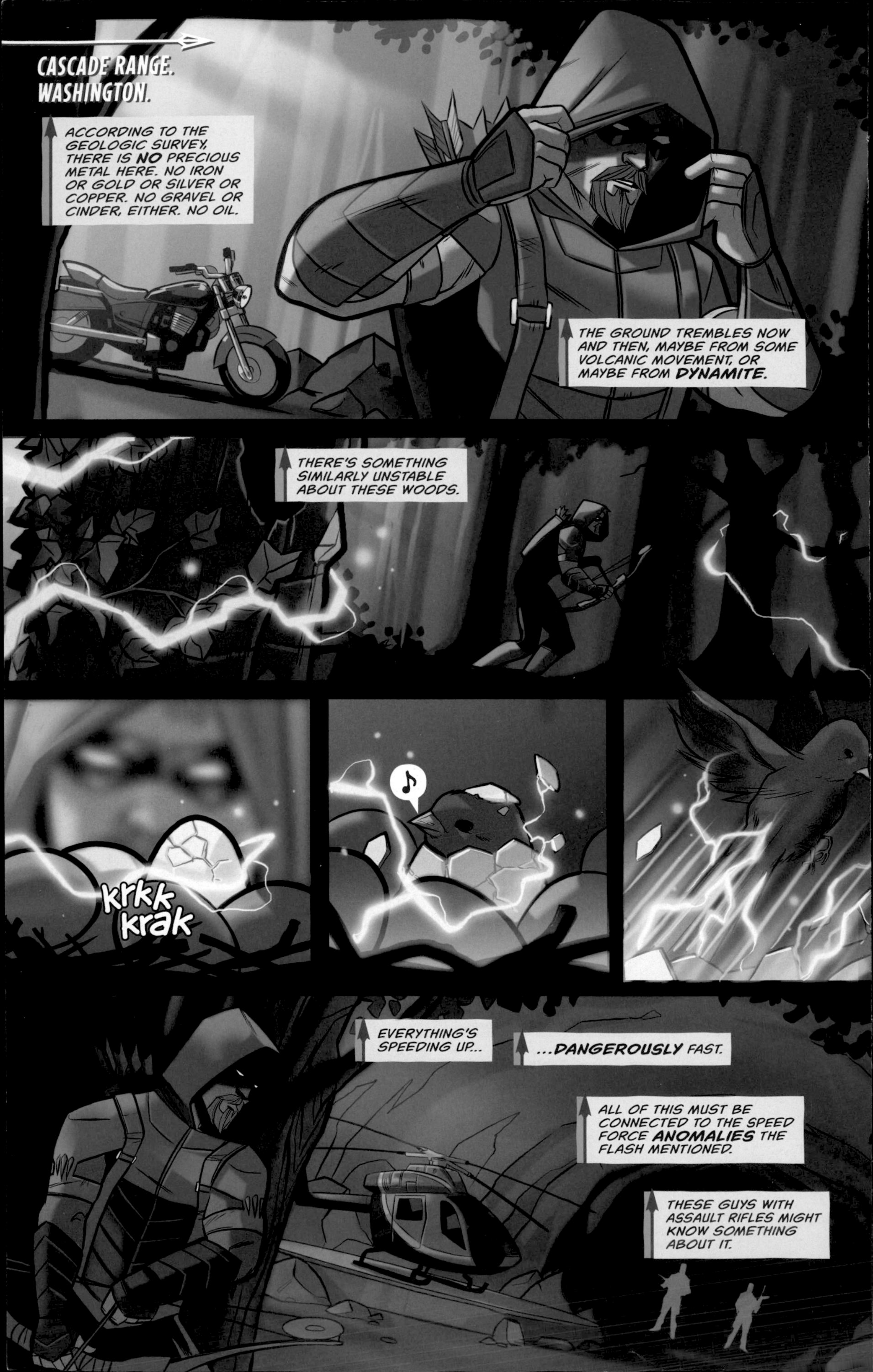
CASCADE RANGE. WASHINGTON.
ACCORDING TO THE GEOLOGIC SURVEY, THERE IS NO PRECIOUS METAL HERE. NO IRON OR GOLD OR SILVER OR COPPER. NO GRAVEL OR CINDER, EITHER. NO OIL.
THE GROUND TREMBLES NOW AND THEN, MAYBE FROM SOME VOLCANIC MOVEMENT, OR MAYBE FROM DYNAMITE.
THERE'S SOMETHING SIMILARLY UNSTABLE ABOUT THESE WOODS.
krkk krak
♪
EVERYTHING'S SPEEDING UP...
...DANGEROUSLY FAST.
ALL OF THIS MUST BE CONNECTED TO THE SPEED FORCE ANOMALIES THE FLASH MENTIONED.
THESE GUYS WITH ASSAULT RIFLES MIGHT KNOW SOMETHING ABOUT IT.

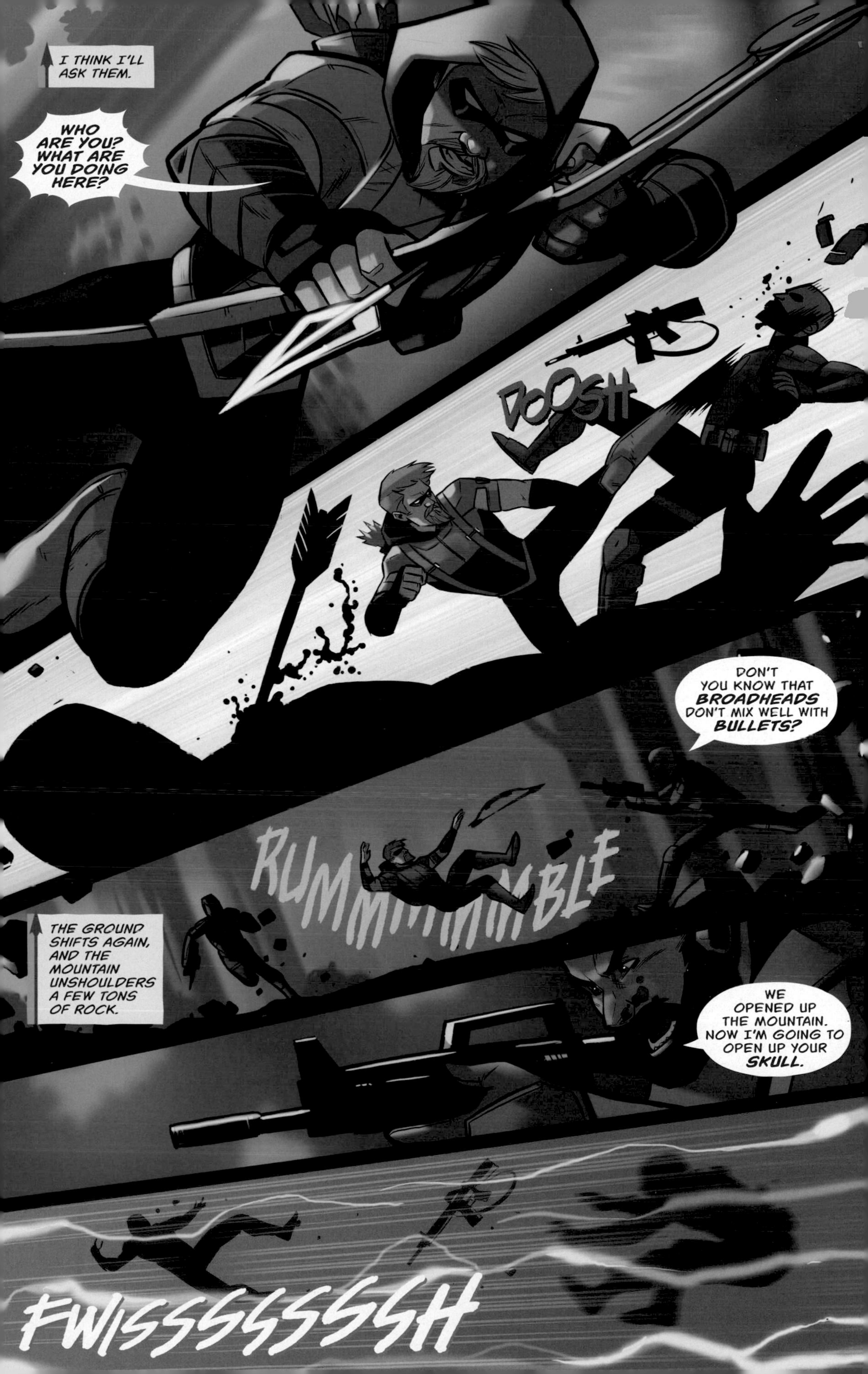
I THINK I'LL ASK THEM.
WHO ARE YOU? WHAT ARE YOU DOING HERE?
DOOSH
DON'T YOU KNOW THAT BROADHEADS DON'T MIX WELL WITH BULLETS?
RUMMMMMMBLE
THE GROUND SHIFTS AGAIN, AND THE MOUNTAIN UNSHOULDERS A FEW TONS OF ROCK.
WE OPENED UP THE MOUNTAIN. NOW I'M GOING TO OPEN UP YOUR SKULL.
FWISSSSSSSH

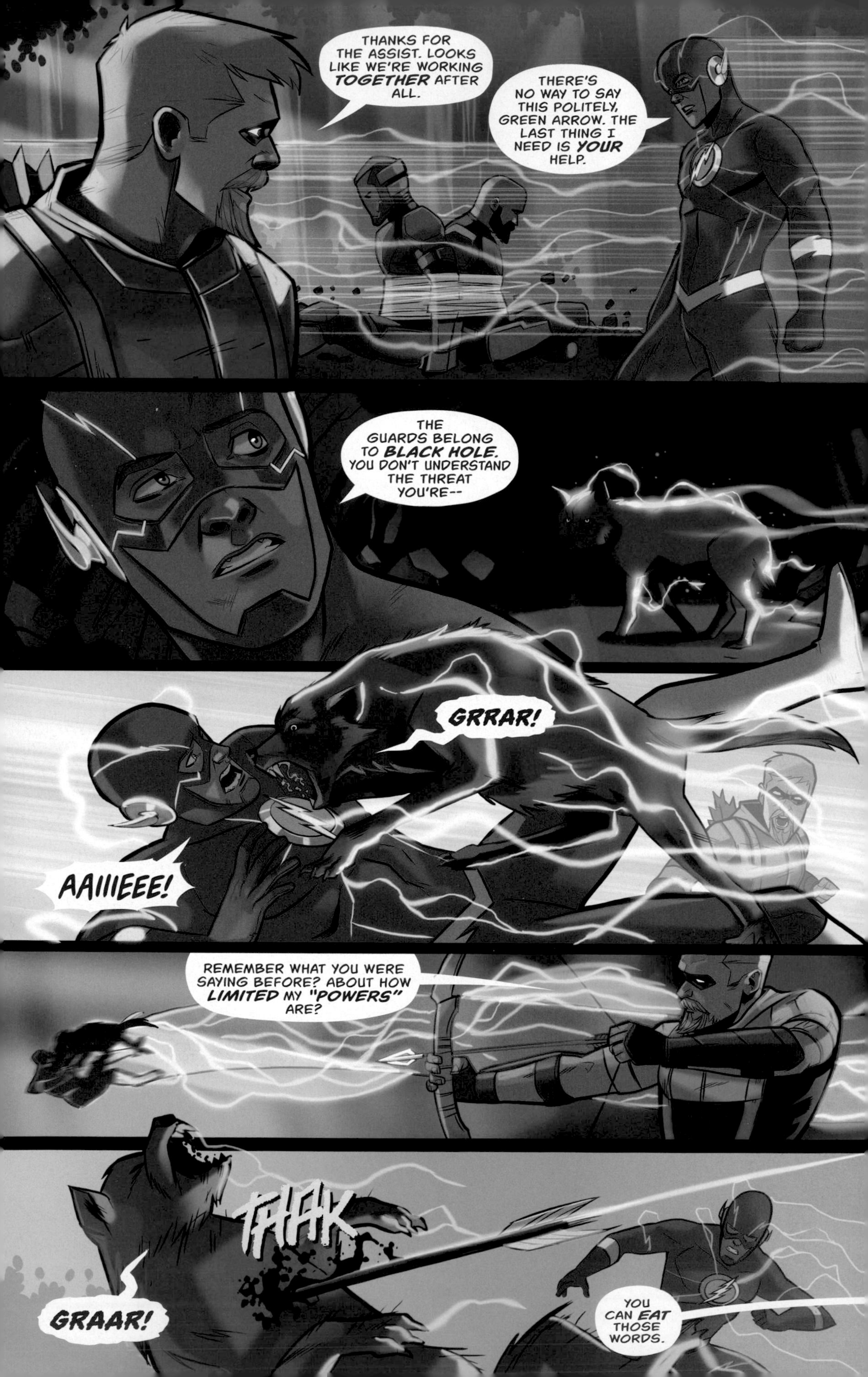
THANKS FOR THE ASSIST. LOOKS LIKE WE'RE WORKING TOGETHER AFTER ALL.
THERE'S NO WAY TO SAY THIS POLITELY, GREEN ARROW. THE LAST THING I NEED IS YOUR HELP.
THE GUARDS BELONG TO BLACK HOLE. YOU DON'T UNDERSTAND THE THREAT YOU'RE--
GRRAR!
AAIIIEEE!
REMEMBER WHAT YOU WERE SAYING BEFORE? ABOUT HOW LIMITED MY "POWERS" ARE?
THAK
GRAAR!
YOU CAN EAT THOSE WORDS.

NOW WHAT THE HELL IS **BLACK HOLE?**

YOU HEARD OF **S.T.A.R. LABS?**

YEAH.

THEY'RE, LIKE, **EVIL** S.T.A.R. LABS.

THEN WHY ARE THEIR GUARDS WEARING THE INSIGNIA OF THE **NINTH CIRCLE?**

A BANK THAT FUNDS ALL THE SUPER-CRIMINAL ENTERPRISE YOU'VE EVER HEARD OF. THEY'RE THE REASON I'M HERE.

NEWS **FLASH--**IF THE NINTH CIRCLE'S **INVESTED** IN BLACK HOLE, THEN HOWEVER DANGEROUS THEY WERE BEFORE... THINGS ARE ABOUT TO GET **WORSE.**

WHAT ARE YOU LOOKING AT ME LIKE THAT FOR?

I DON'T KNOW... THERE'S JUST SOMETHING DIFFERENT ABOUT YOU.

BESIDES THE **"ROADKILL"** GOATEE, YOU MEAN.

 "IF YOU'RE CRAZY ENOUGH TO FOLLOW ME INTO THIS **MOUNTAIN** OF TROUBLE, THEN YOU'RE WELCOME TO JOIN ME! BUT YOU SHOULD LET ME TAKE THE **LEAD** ON THIS."

"NEVER BEEN THE **FOLLOWER.** THAT'S WHY **THE BAT** AND THE **BOY SCOUT** WON'T ALLOW ME INTO THE **JUSTICE LEAGUE** CLUBHOUSE."

 "NO, IT'S ACTUALLY BECAUSE YOU'RE A **JERK.**"

"ENOUGH WITH THE SWEET TALK. WE'VE FOUND THE SOURCE OF YOUR SPEED FORCE ANOMALIES. WHAT'S GOING ON HERE, **SCIENCE-BOY?**"

"THE CASCADES ARE A SUBDUCTION ZONE. AN OCEANIC AND CONTINENTAL PLATE ARE CRASHING AGAINST EACH OTHER..."

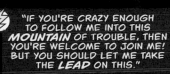

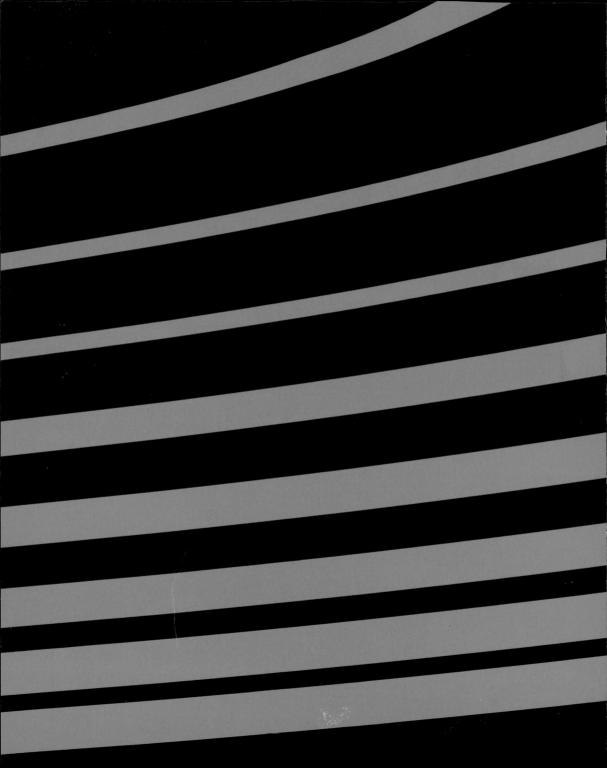

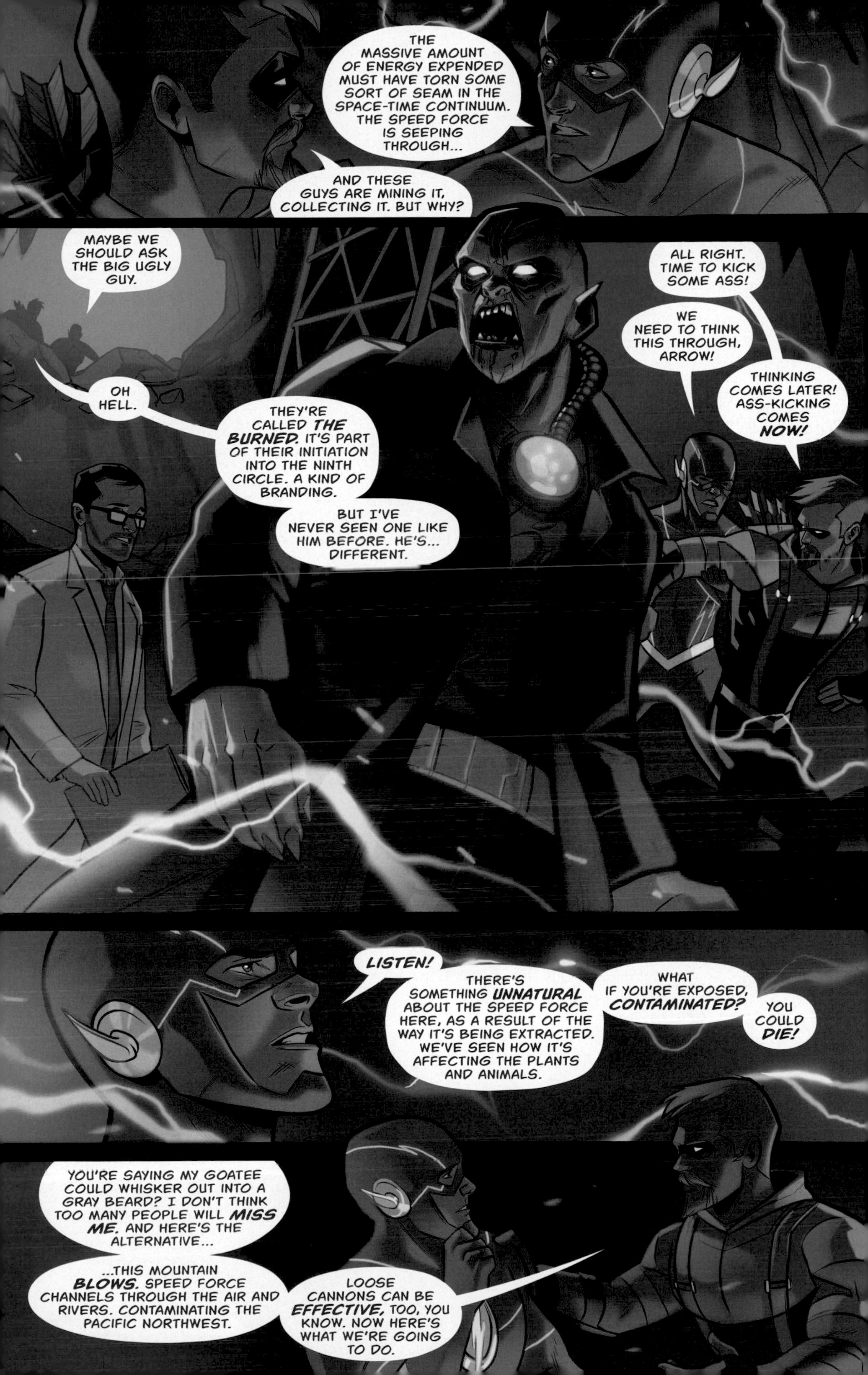
THE MASSIVE AMOUNT OF ENERGY EXPENDED MUST HAVE TORN SOME SORT OF SEAM IN THE SPACE-TIME CONTINUUM. THE SPEED FORCE IS SEEPING THROUGH...
AND THESE GUYS ARE MINING IT, COLLECTING IT. BUT WHY?
MAYBE WE SHOULD ASK THE BIG UGLY GUY.
OH HELL.
THEY'RE CALLED THE BURNED. IT'S PART OF THEIR INITIATION INTO THE NINTH CIRCLE. A KIND OF BRANDING.
BUT I'VE NEVER SEEN ONE LIKE HIM BEFORE. HE'S... DIFFERENT.
ALL RIGHT. TIME TO KICK SOME ASS!
WE NEED TO THINK THIS THROUGH, ARROW!
THINKING COMES LATER! ASS-KICKING COMES NOW!
LISTEN!
THERE'S SOMETHING UNNATURAL ABOUT THE SPEED FORCE HERE, AS A RESULT OF THE WAY IT'S BEING EXTRACTED. WE'VE SEEN HOW IT'S AFFECTING THE PLANTS AND ANIMALS.
WHAT IF YOU'RE EXPOSED, CONTAMINATED?
YOU COULD DIE!
YOU'RE SAYING MY GOATEE COULD WHISKER OUT INTO A GRAY BEARD? I DON'T THINK TOO MANY PEOPLE WILL MISS ME. AND HERE'S THE ALTERNATIVE...
...THIS MOUNTAIN BLOWS. SPEED FORCE CHANNELS THROUGH THE AIR AND RIVERS. CONTAMINATING THE PACIFIC NORTHWEST.
LOOSE CANNONS CAN BE EFFECTIVE, TOO, YOU KNOW. NOW HERE'S WHAT WE'RE GOING TO DO.

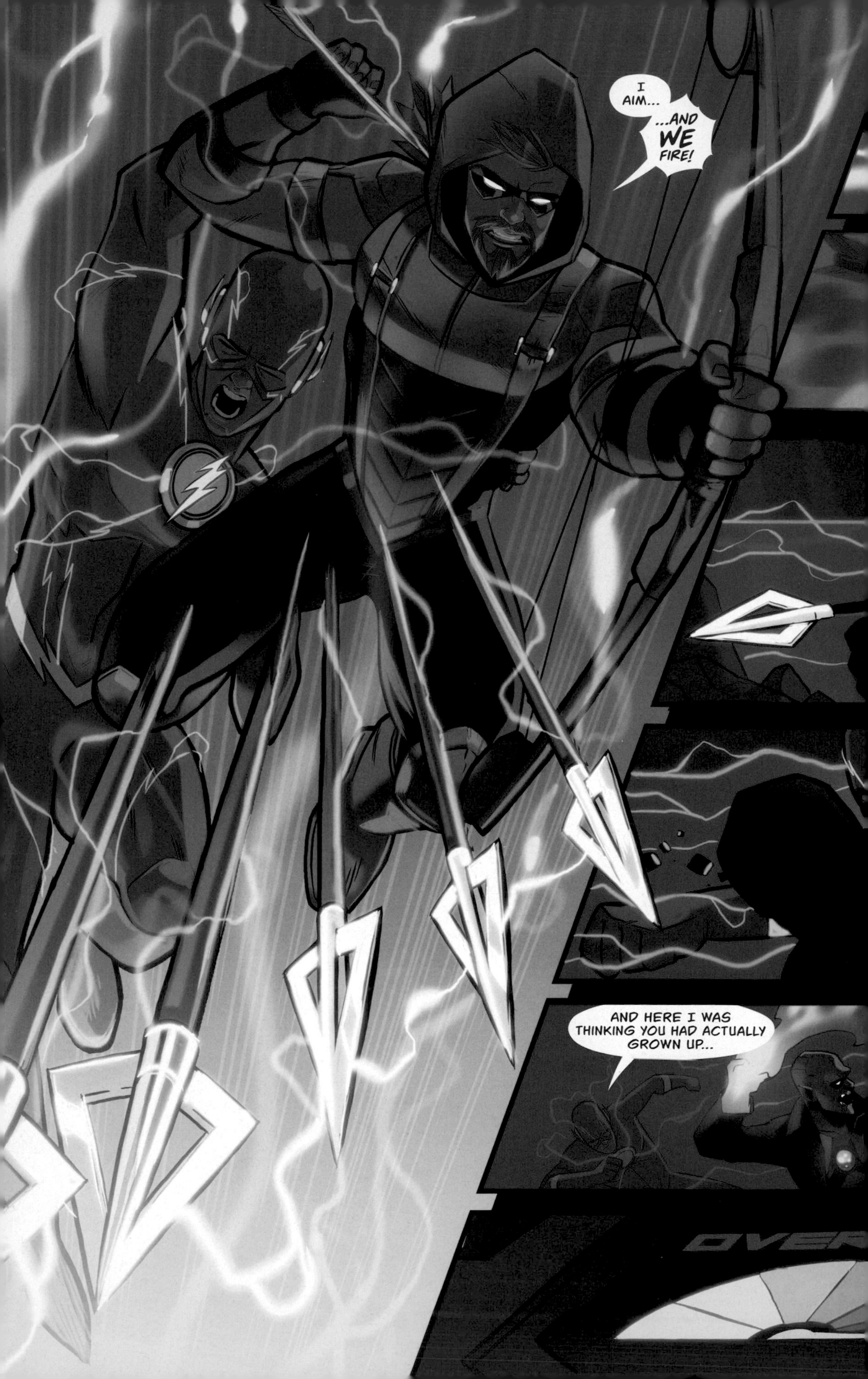
I AIM...
...AND WE FIRE!
AND HERE I WAS THINKING YOU HAD ACTUALLY GROWN UP...

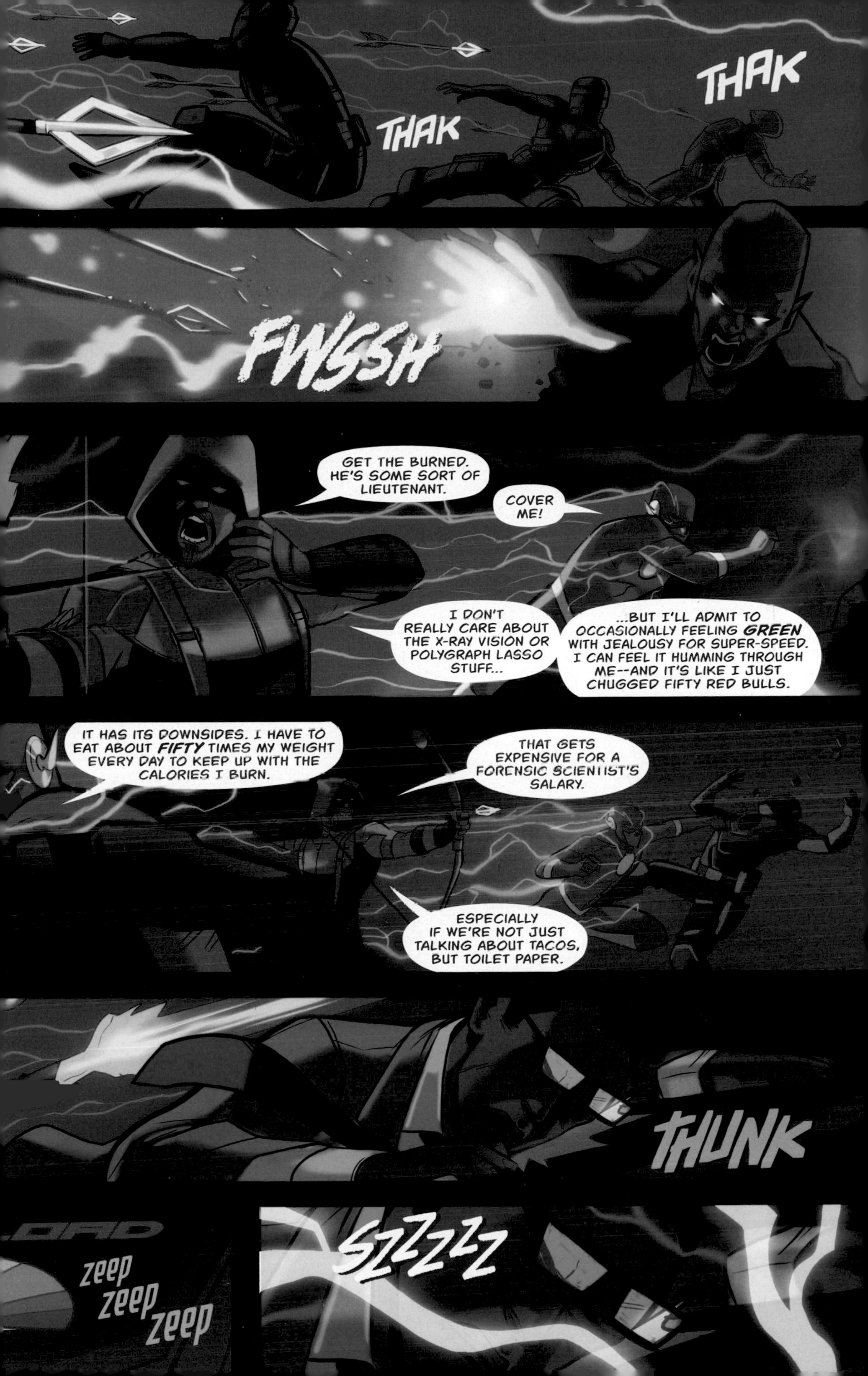
THAK
THAK
FWSSH
GET THE BURNED. HE'S SOME SORT OF LIEUTENANT.
COVER ME!
I DON'T REALLY CARE ABOUT THE X-RAY VISION OR POLYGRAPH LASSO STUFF...
...BUT I'LL ADMIT TO OCCASIONALLY FEELING GREEN WITH JEALOUSY FOR SUPER-SPEED. I CAN FEEL IT HUMMING THROUGH ME--AND IT'S LIKE I JUST CHUGGED FIFTY RED BULLS.
IT HAS ITS DOWNSIDES. I HAVE TO EAT ABOUT FIFTY TIMES MY WEIGHT EVERY DAY TO KEEP UP WITH THE CALORIES I BURN.
THAT GETS EXPENSIVE FOR A FORENSIC SCIENTIST'S SALARY.
ESPECIALLY IF WE'RE NOT JUST TALKING ABOUT TACOS, BUT TOILET PAPER.
THUNK
zeep zeep zeep
SZZZZZ

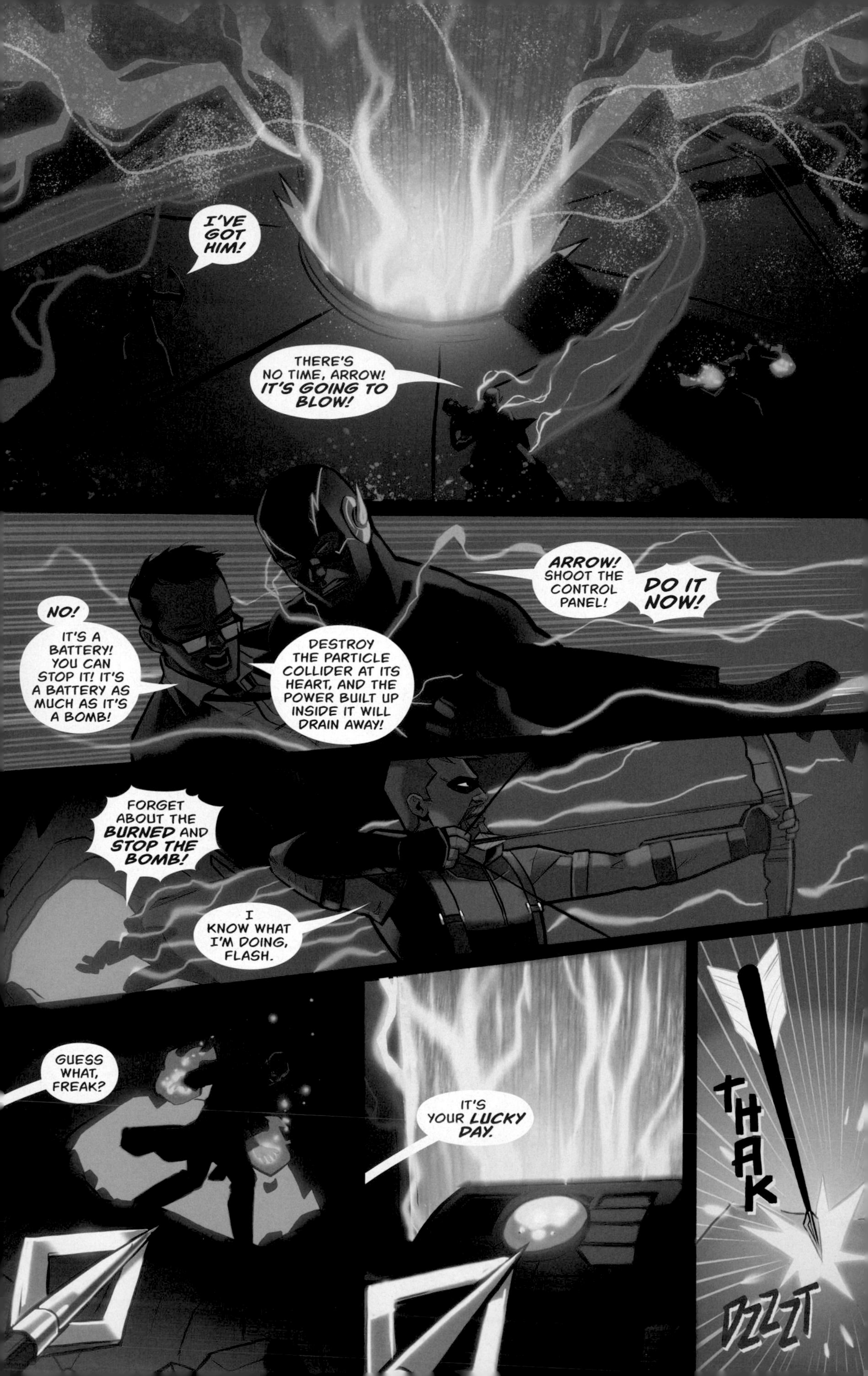
I'VE GOT HIM!
THERE'S NO TIME, ARROW! IT'S GOING TO BLOW!
ARROW! SHOOT THE CONTROL PANEL!
DO IT NOW!
NO!
IT'S A BATTERY! YOU CAN STOP IT! IT'S A BATTERY AS MUCH AS IT'S A BOMB!
DESTROY THE PARTICLE COLLIDER AT ITS HEART, AND THE POWER BUILT UP INSIDE IT WILL DRAIN AWAY!
FORGET ABOUT THE BURNED AND STOP THE BOMB!
I KNOW WHAT I'M DOING, FLASH.
GUESS WHAT, FREAK?
IT'S YOUR LUCKY DAY.
THAK
DZZZT

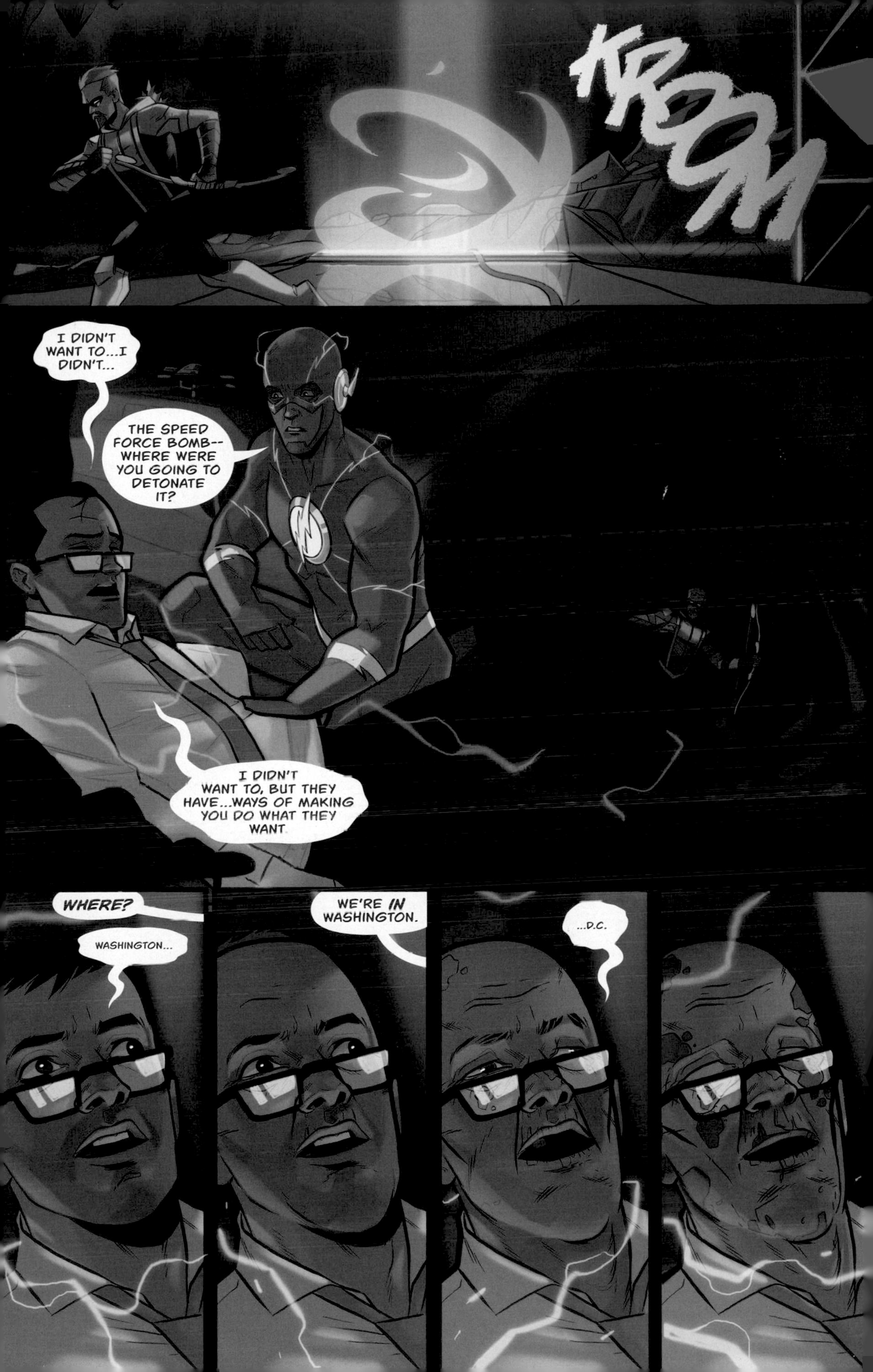
KROOM
I DIDN'T WANT TO...I DIDN'T...
THE SPEED FORCE BOMB-- WHERE WERE YOU GOING TO DETONATE IT?
I DIDN'T WANT TO, BUT THEY HAVE...WAYS OF MAKING YOU DO WHAT THEY WANT.
WHERE?
WASHINGTON...
WE'RE IN WASHINGTON.
...D.C.

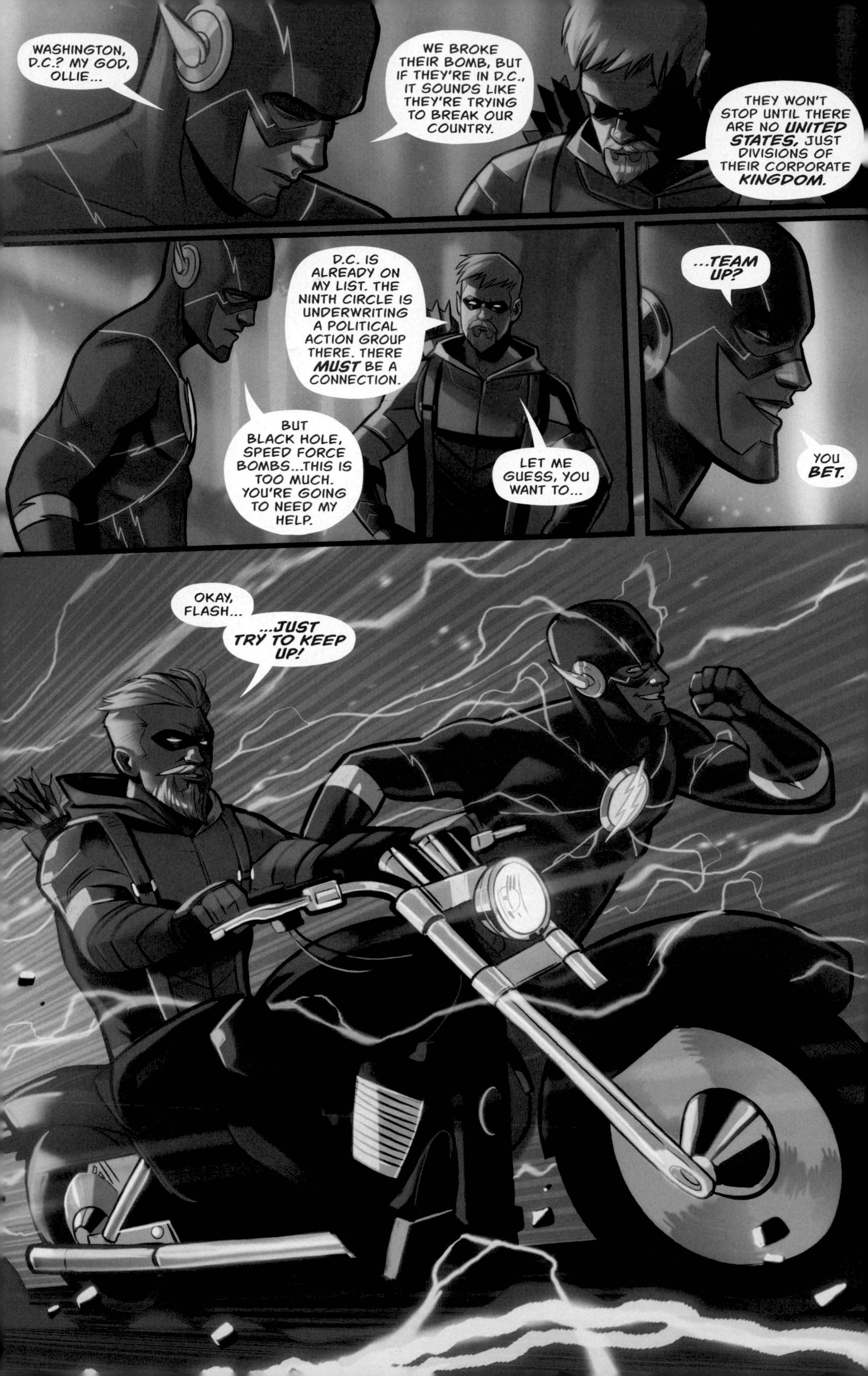
WASHINGTON, D.C.? MY GOD, OLLIE...
WE BROKE THEIR BOMB, BUT IF THEY'RE IN D.C., IT SOUNDS LIKE THEY'RE TRYING TO BREAK OUR COUNTRY.
THEY WON'T STOP UNTIL THERE ARE NO **UNITED STATES,** JUST DIVISIONS OF THEIR CORPORATE **KINGDOM.**
D.C. IS ALREADY ON MY LIST. THE NINTH CIRCLE IS UNDERWRITING A POLITICAL ACTION GROUP THERE. THERE **MUST** BE A CONNECTION.
BUT BLACK HOLE, SPEED FORCE BOMBS...THIS IS TOO MUCH. YOU'RE GOING TO NEED MY HELP.
LET ME GUESS, YOU WANT TO...
**...TEAM UP?**
YOU **BET.**
OKAY, FLASH...
**...JUST TRY TO KEEP UP!**

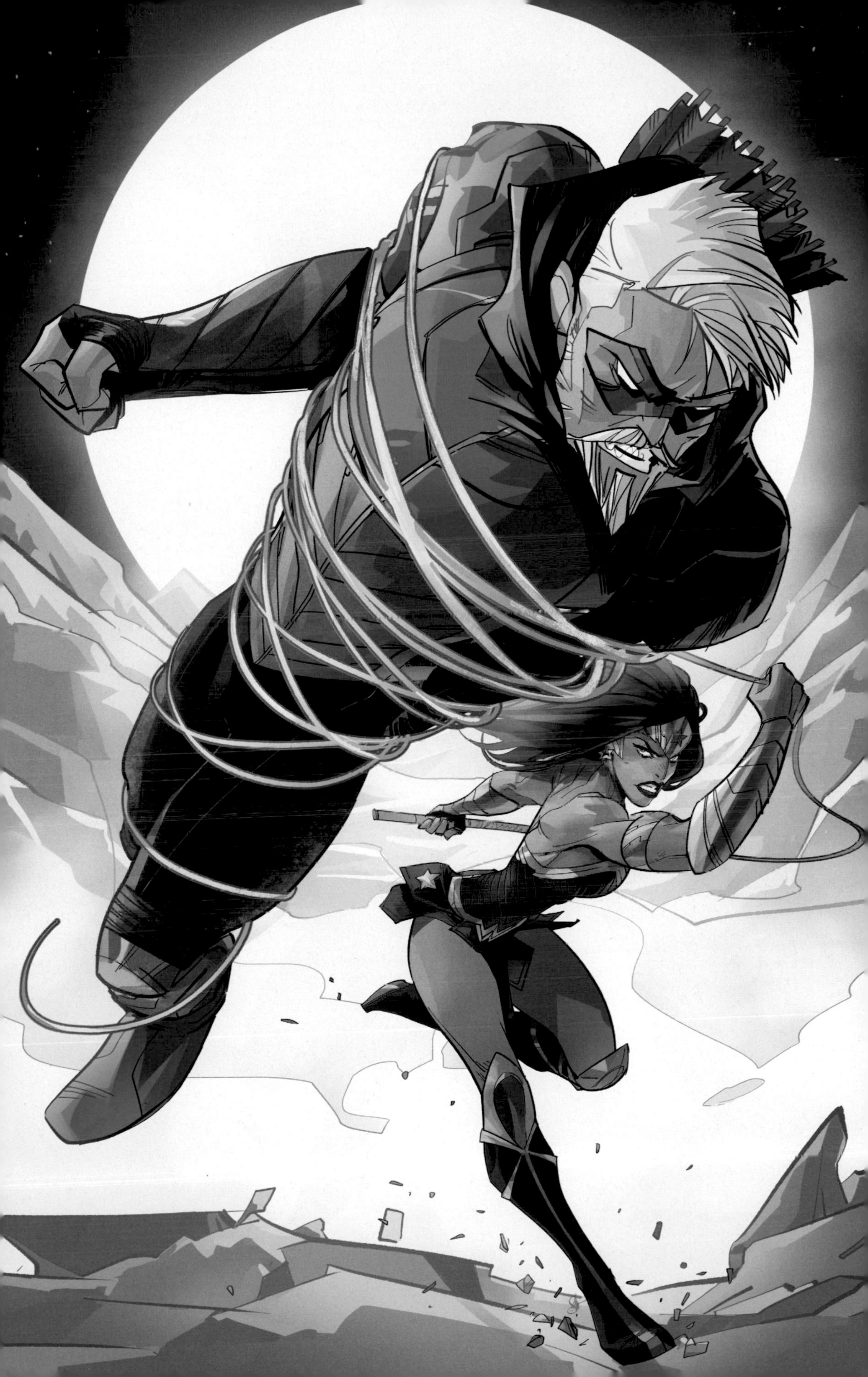

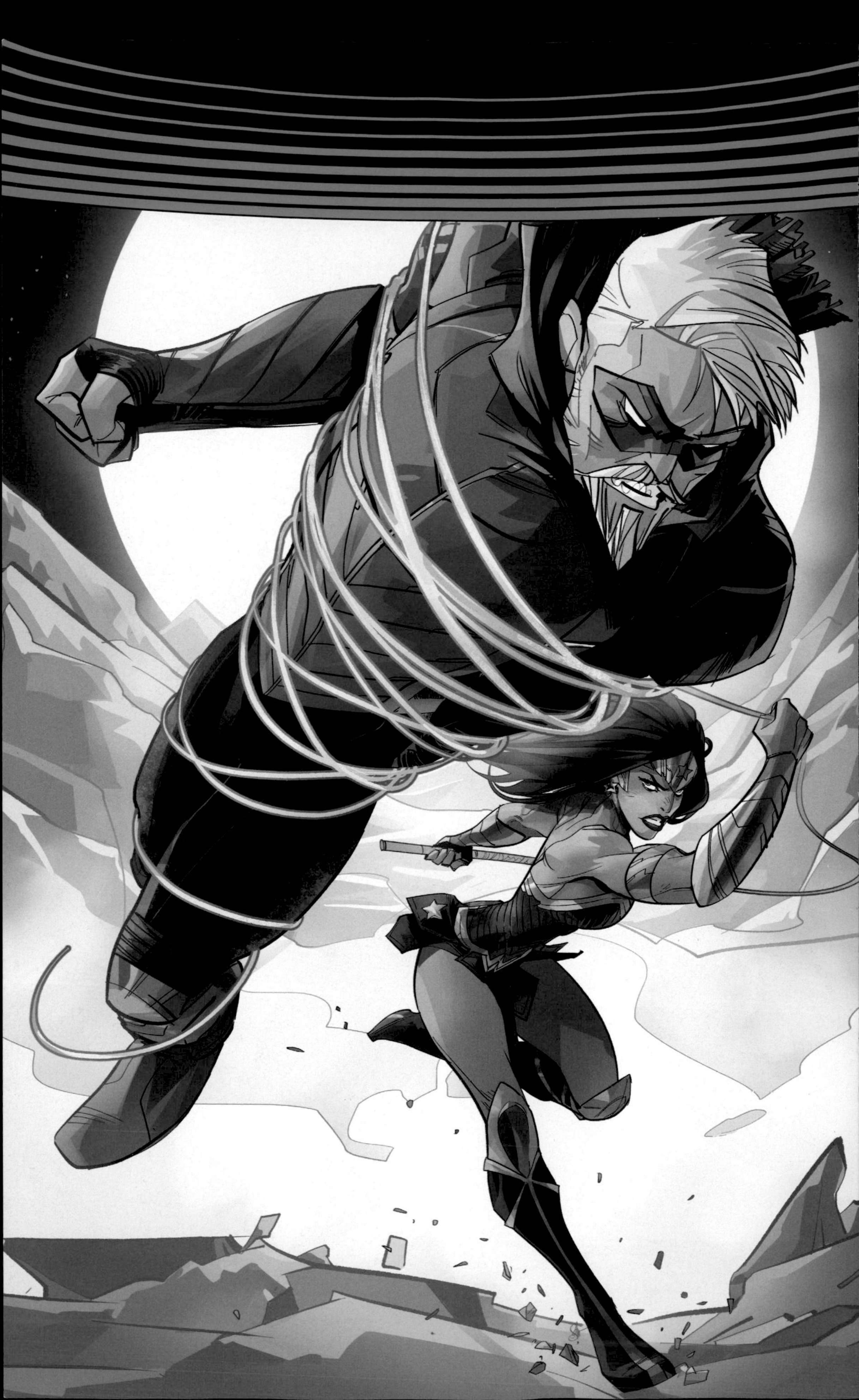

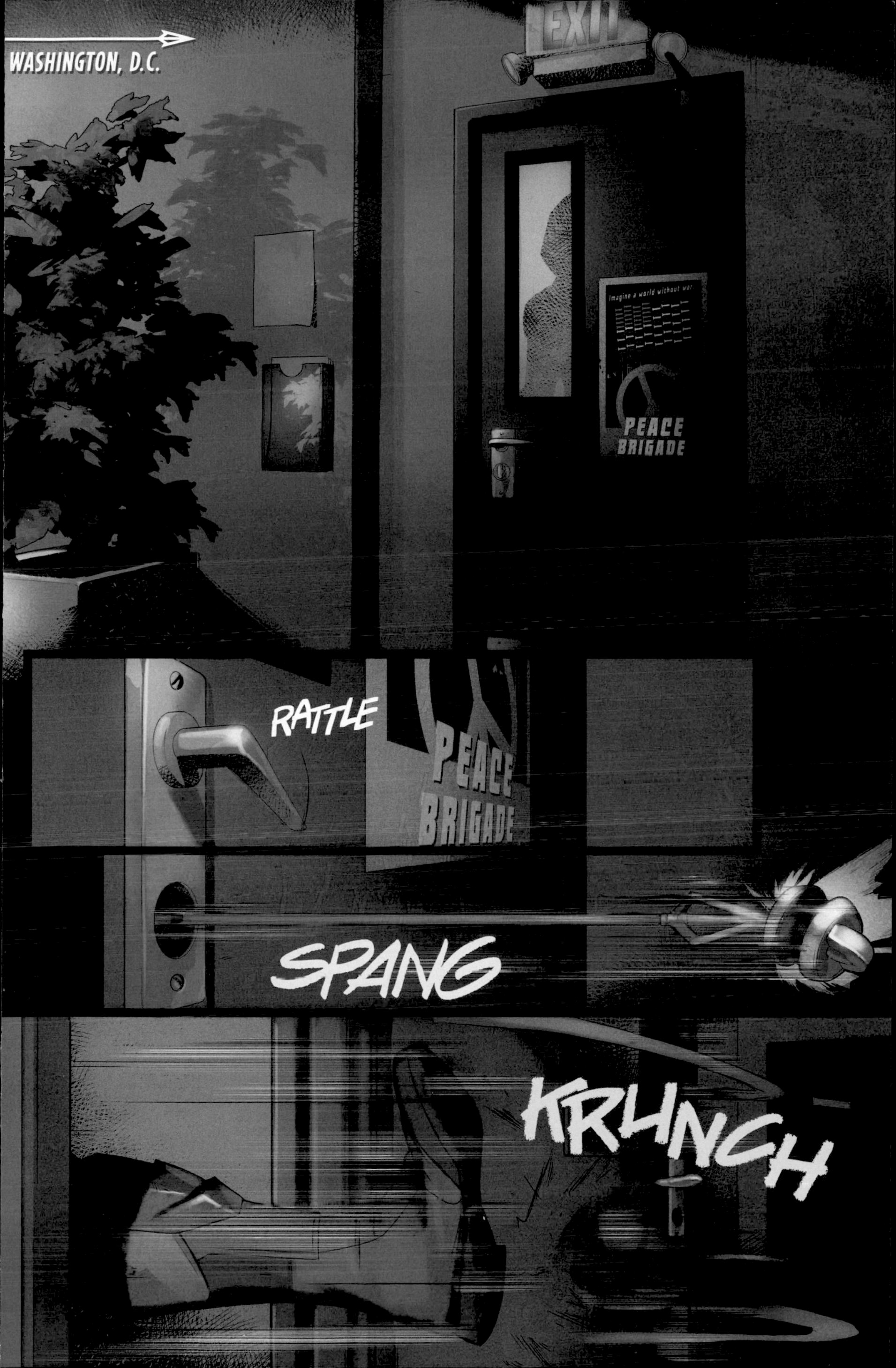
WASHINGTON, D.C.
EXIT
Imagine a world without war.
PEACE BRIGADE
RATTLE
PEACE BRIGADE
SPANG
KRUNCH

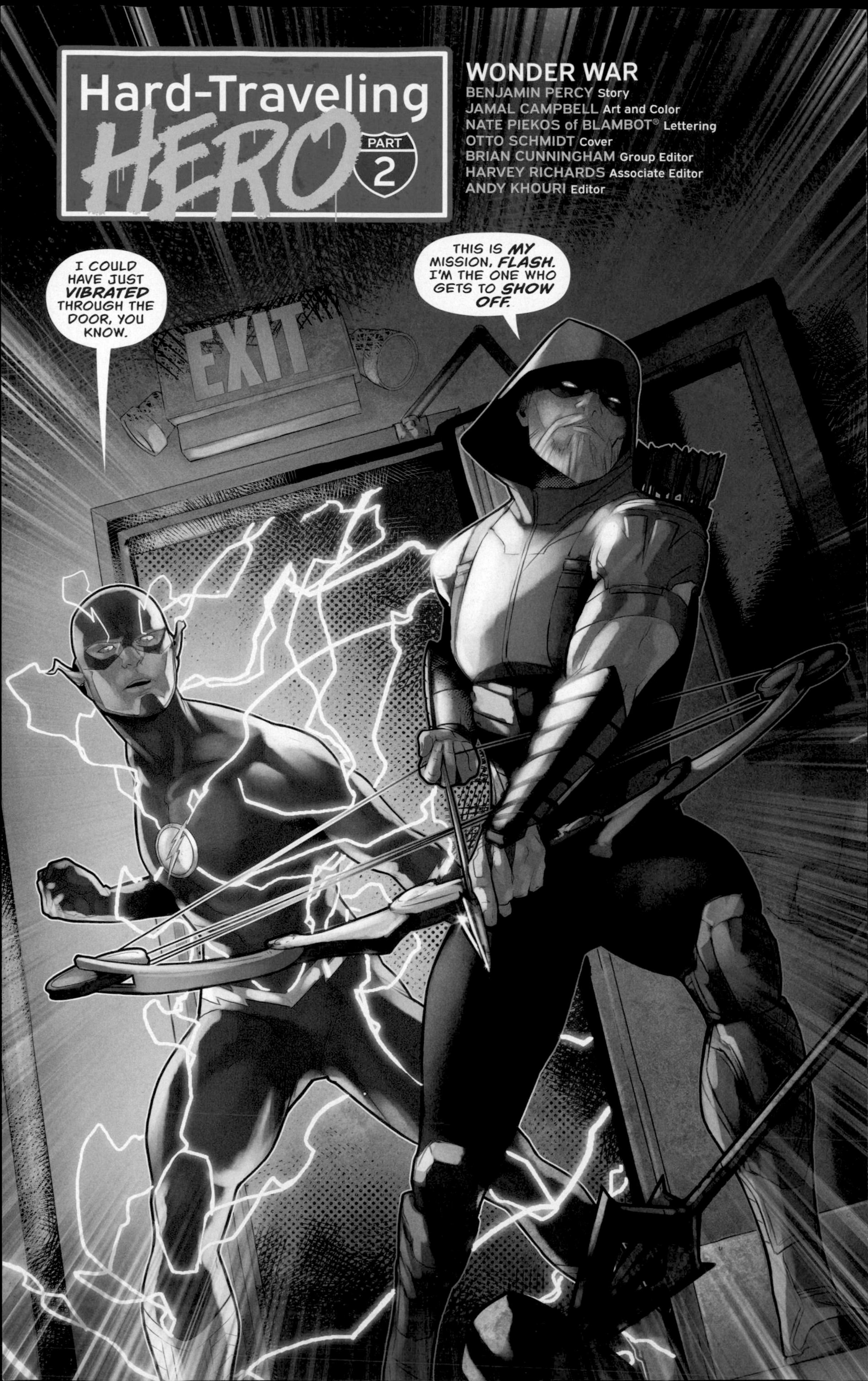
Hard-Traveling
HERO
PART
2
WONDER WAR
BENJAMIN PERCY Story
JAMAL CAMPBELL Art and Color
NATE PIEKOS of BLAMBOT® Lettering
OTTO SCHMIDT Cover
BRIAN CUNNINGHAM Group Editor
HARVEY RICHARDS Associate Editor
ANDY KHOURI Editor
I COULD HAVE JUST VIBRATED THROUGH THE DOOR, YOU KNOW.
THIS IS MY MISSION, FLASH. I'M THE ONE WHO GETS TO SHOW OFF.
EXIT

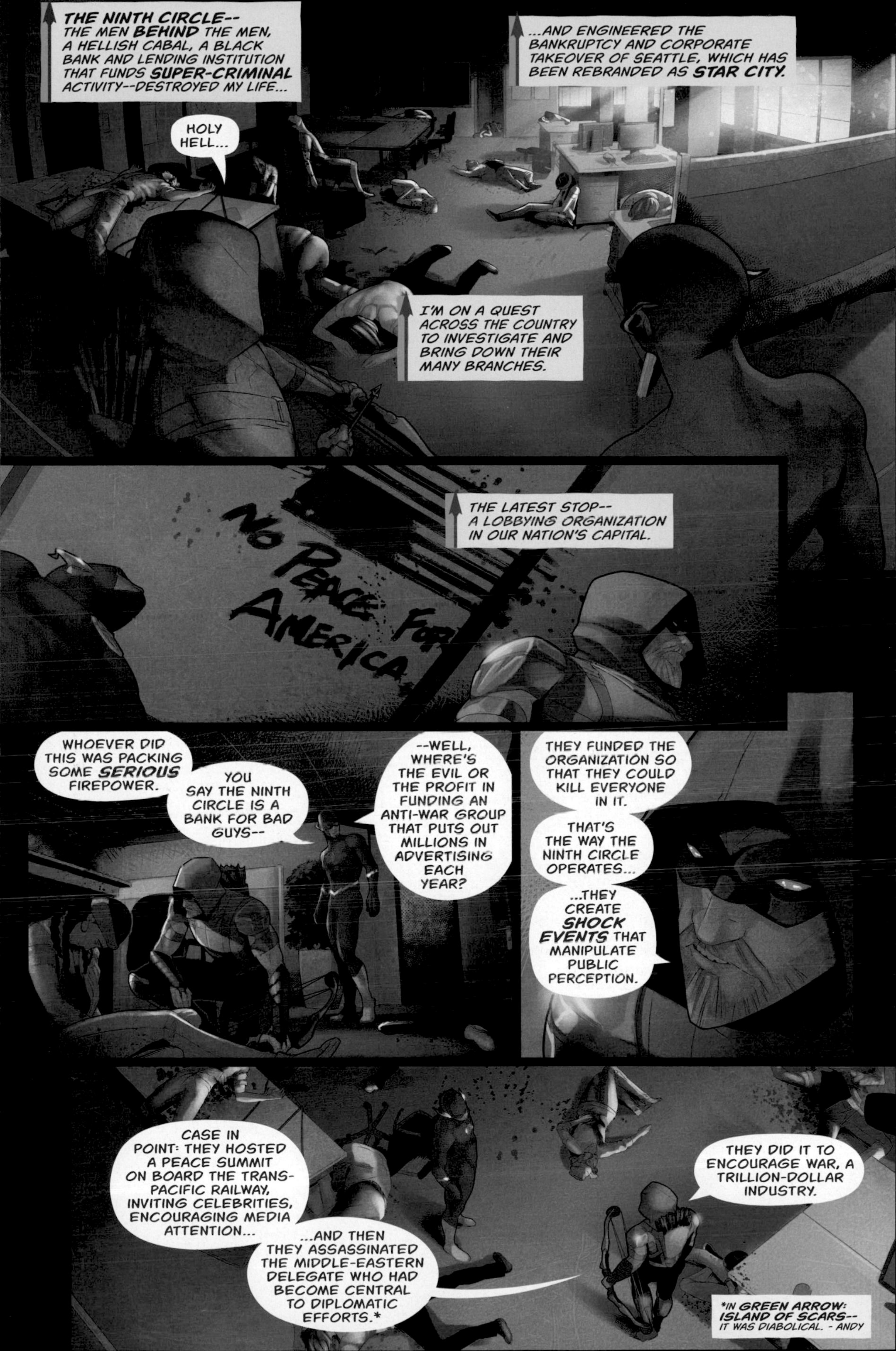

THE NINTH CIRCLE-- THE MEN BEHIND THE MEN, A HELLISH CABAL, A BLACK BANK AND LENDING INSTITUTION THAT FUNDS SUPER-CRIMINAL ACTIVITY--DESTROYED MY LIFE...
...AND ENGINEERED THE BANKRUPTCY AND CORPORATE TAKEOVER OF SEATTLE, WHICH HAS BEEN REBRANDED AS STAR CITY.
HOLY HELL...
I'M ON A QUEST ACROSS THE COUNTRY TO INVESTIGATE AND BRING DOWN THEIR MANY BRANCHES.
THE LATEST STOP-- A LOBBYING ORGANIZATION IN OUR NATION'S CAPITAL.
NO PEACE FOR AMERICA
WHOEVER DID THIS WAS PACKING SOME SERIOUS FIREPOWER.
YOU SAY THE NINTH CIRCLE IS A BANK FOR BAD GUYS--
--WELL, WHERE'S THE EVIL OR THE PROFIT IN FUNDING AN ANTI-WAR GROUP THAT PUTS OUT MILLIONS IN ADVERTISING EACH YEAR?
THEY FUNDED THE ORGANIZATION SO THAT THEY COULD KILL EVERYONE IN IT.
THAT'S THE WAY THE NINTH CIRCLE OPERATES...
...THEY CREATE SHOCK EVENTS THAT MANIPULATE PUBLIC PERCEPTION.
CASE IN POINT: THEY HOSTED A PEACE SUMMIT ON BOARD THE TRANS-PACIFIC RAILWAY, INVITING CELEBRITIES, ENCOURAGING MEDIA ATTENTION...
...AND THEN THEY ASSASSINATED THE MIDDLE-EASTERN DELEGATE WHO HAD BECOME CENTRAL TO DIPLOMATIC EFFORTS.*
THEY DID IT TO ENCOURAGE WAR, A TRILLION-DOLLAR INDUSTRY.
*IN GREEN ARROW: ISLAND OF SCARS-- IT WAS DIABOLICAL. - ANDY

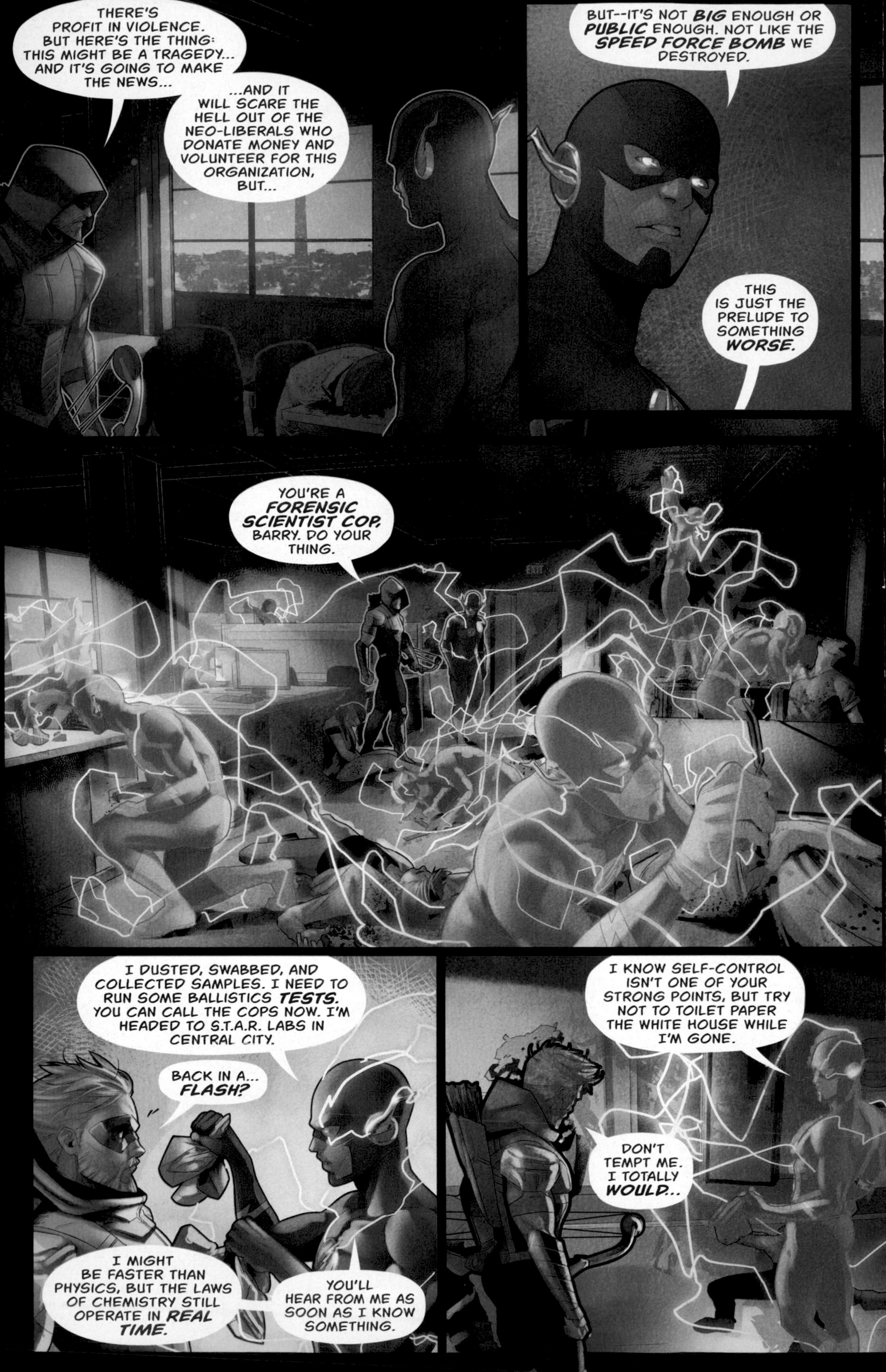

THERE'S PROFIT IN VIOLENCE. BUT HERE'S THE THING: THIS MIGHT BE A TRAGEDY... AND IT'S GOING TO MAKE THE NEWS...
...AND IT WILL SCARE THE HELL OUT OF THE NEO-LIBERALS WHO DONATE MONEY AND VOLUNTEER FOR THIS ORGANIZATION, BUT...
BUT--IT'S NOT BIG ENOUGH OR PUBLIC ENOUGH. NOT LIKE THE SPEED FORCE BOMB WE DESTROYED.
THIS IS JUST THE PRELUDE TO SOMETHING WORSE.
YOU'RE A FORENSIC SCIENTIST COP, BARRY. DO YOUR THING.
EXIT
I DUSTED, SWABBED, AND COLLECTED SAMPLES. I NEED TO RUN SOME BALLISTICS TESTS. YOU CAN CALL THE COPS NOW. I'M HEADED TO S.T.A.R. LABS IN CENTRAL CITY.
BACK IN A... FLASH?
I MIGHT BE FASTER THAN PHYSICS, BUT THE LAWS OF CHEMISTRY STILL OPERATE IN REAL TIME.
YOU'LL HEAR FROM ME AS SOON AS I KNOW SOMETHING.
I KNOW SELF-CONTROL ISN'T ONE OF YOUR STRONG POINTS, BUT TRY NOT TO TOILET PAPER THE WHITE HOUSE WHILE I'M GONE.
DON'T TEMPT ME. I TOTALLY WOULD...

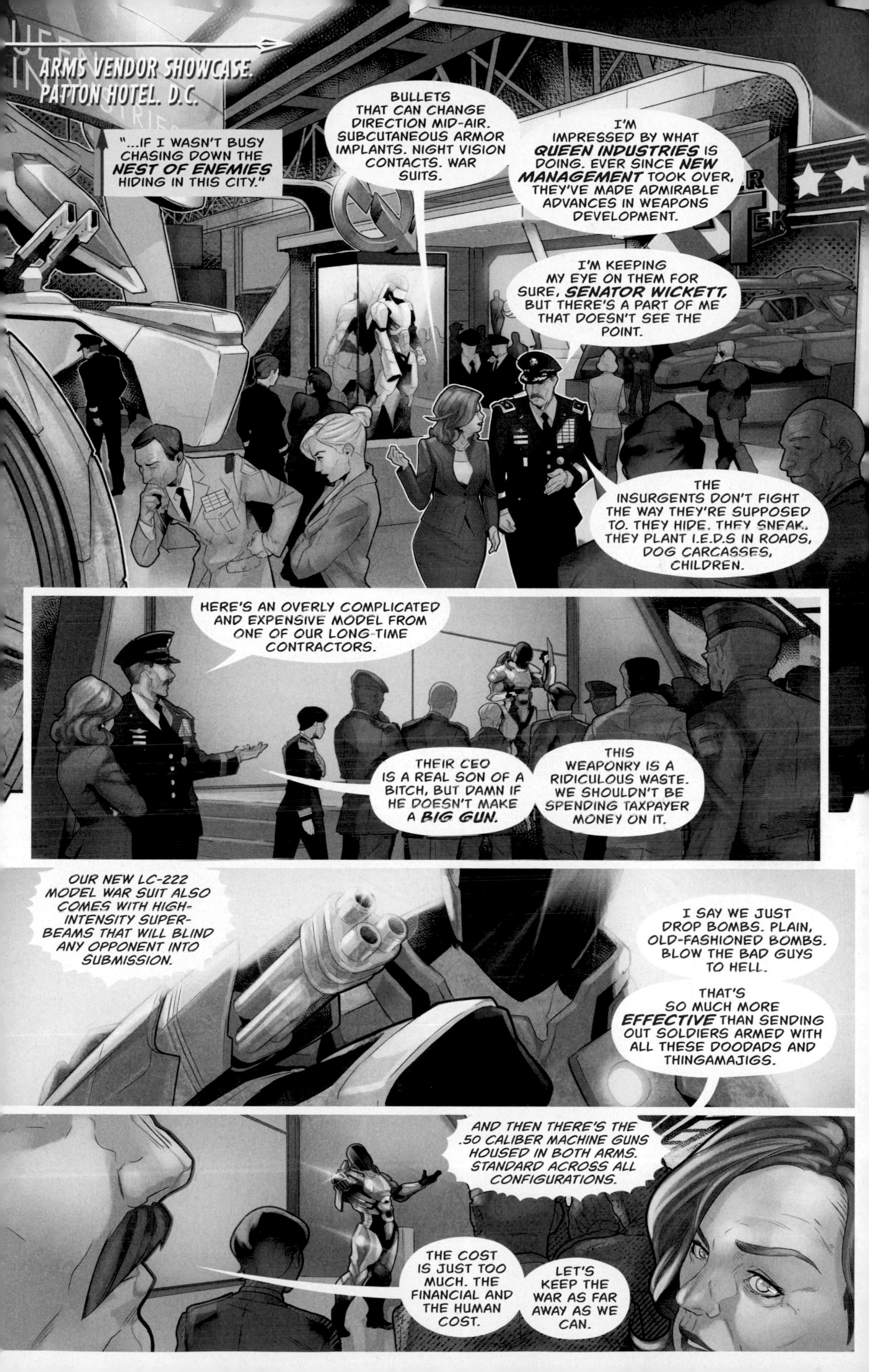
ARMS VENDOR SHOWCASE. PATTON HOTEL. D.C.
"...IF I WASN'T BUSY CHASING DOWN THE NEST OF ENEMIES HIDING IN THIS CITY."
BULLETS THAT CAN CHANGE DIRECTION MID-AIR. SUBCUTANEOUS ARMOR IMPLANTS. NIGHT VISION CONTACTS. WAR SUITS.
I'M IMPRESSED BY WHAT QUEEN INDUSTRIES IS DOING. EVER SINCE NEW MANAGEMENT TOOK OVER, THEY'VE MADE ADMIRABLE ADVANCES IN WEAPONS DEVELOPMENT.
I'M KEEPING MY EYE ON THEM FOR SURE, SENATOR WICKETT, BUT THERE'S A PART OF ME THAT DOESN'T SEE THE POINT.
THE INSURGENTS DON'T FIGHT THE WAY THEY'RE SUPPOSED TO. THEY HIDE. THEY SNEAK. THEY PLANT I.E.D.S IN ROADS, DOG CARCASSES, CHILDREN.
HERE'S AN OVERLY COMPLICATED AND EXPENSIVE MODEL FROM ONE OF OUR LONG-TIME CONTRACTORS.
THEIR CEO IS A REAL SON OF A BITCH, BUT DAMN IF HE DOESN'T MAKE A BIG GUN.
THIS WEAPONRY IS A RIDICULOUS WASTE. WE SHOULDN'T BE SPENDING TAXPAYER MONEY ON IT.
OUR NEW LC-222 MODEL WAR SUIT ALSO COMES WITH HIGH-INTENSITY SUPER-BEAMS THAT WILL BLIND ANY OPPONENT INTO SUBMISSION.
I SAY WE JUST DROP BOMBS. PLAIN, OLD-FASHIONED BOMBS. BLOW THE BAD GUYS TO HELL.
THAT'S SO MUCH MORE EFFECTIVE THAN SENDING OUT SOLDIERS ARMED WITH ALL THESE DOODADS AND THINGAMAJIGS.
AND THEN THERE'S THE .50 CALIBER MACHINE GUNS HOUSED IN BOTH ARMS. STANDARD ACROSS ALL CONFIGURATIONS.
THE COST IS JUST TOO MUCH. THE FINANCIAL AND THE HUMAN COST.
LET'S KEEP THE WAR AS FAR AWAY AS WE CAN.

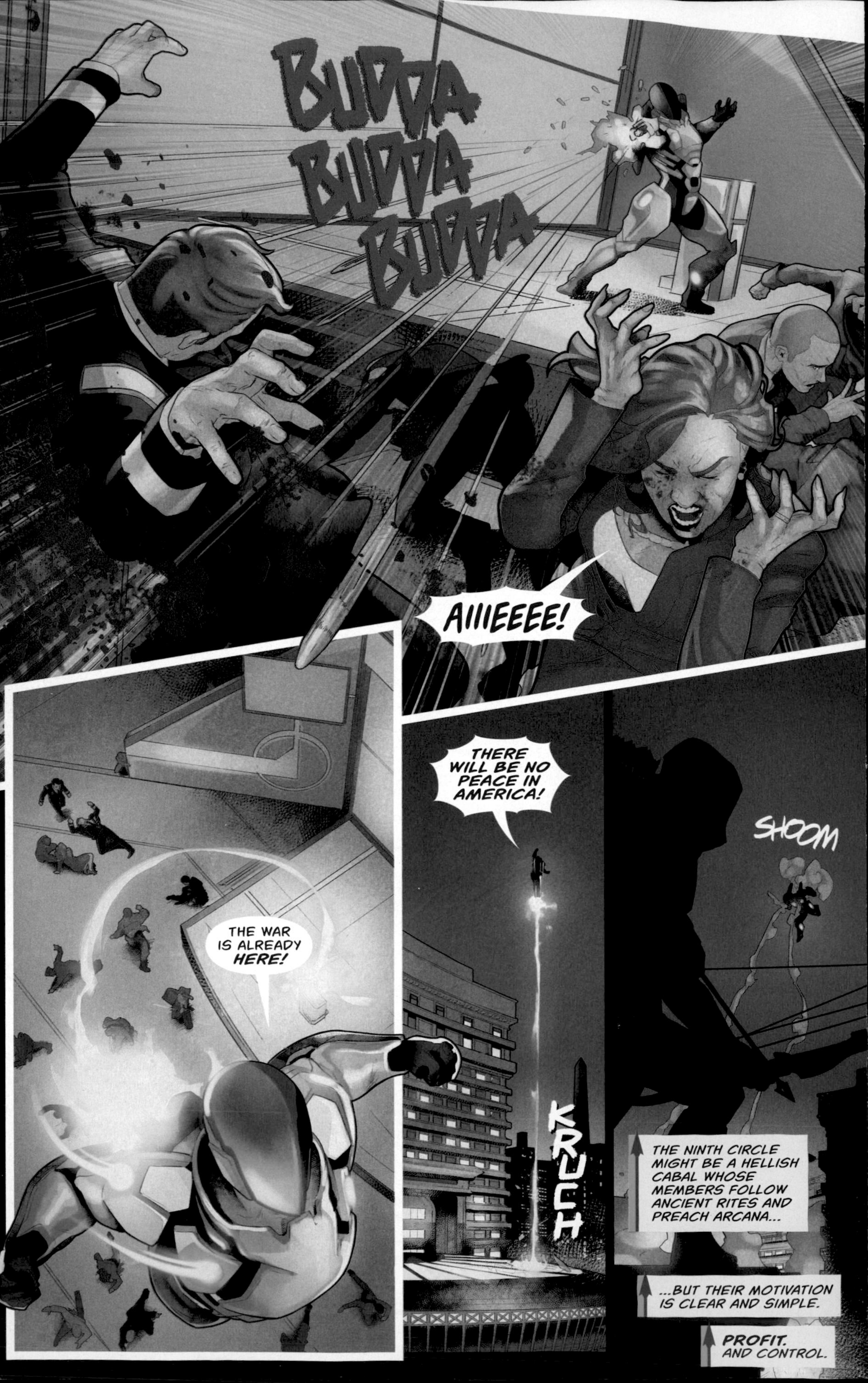
BUDDA BUDDA BUDDA
AIIIEEEE!
THE WAR IS ALREADY HERE!
THERE WILL BE NO PEACE IN AMERICA!
KRUCH
SHOOM
THE NINTH CIRCLE MIGHT BE A HELLISH CABAL WHOSE MEMBERS FOLLOW ANCIENT RITES AND PREACH ARCANA...
...BUT THEIR MOTIVATION IS CLEAR AND SIMPLE.
PROFIT. AND CONTROL.

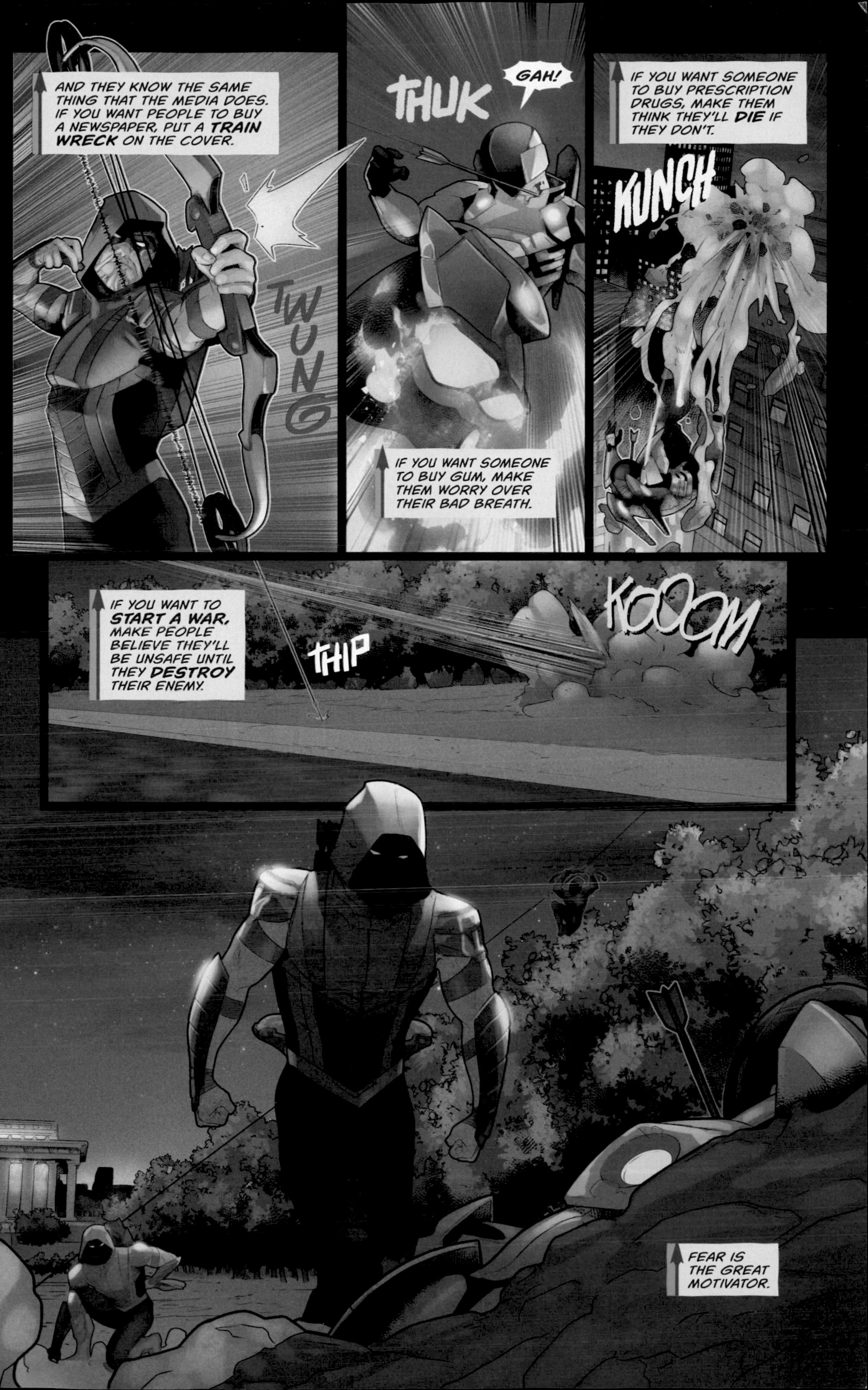
AND THEY KNOW THE SAME THING THAT THE MEDIA DOES. IF YOU WANT PEOPLE TO BUY A NEWSPAPER, PUT A TRAIN WRECK ON THE COVER.
TWUNG
THUK
GAH!
IF YOU WANT SOMEONE TO BUY GUM, MAKE THEM WORRY OVER THEIR BAD BREATH.
IF YOU WANT SOMEONE TO BUY PRESCRIPTION DRUGS, MAKE THEM THINK THEY'LL DIE IF THEY DON'T.
KUNCH
IF YOU WANT TO START A WAR, MAKE PEOPLE BELIEVE THEY'LL BE UNSAFE UNTIL THEY DESTROY THEIR ENEMY.
THIP
KOOOM
FEAR IS THE GREAT MOTIVATOR.

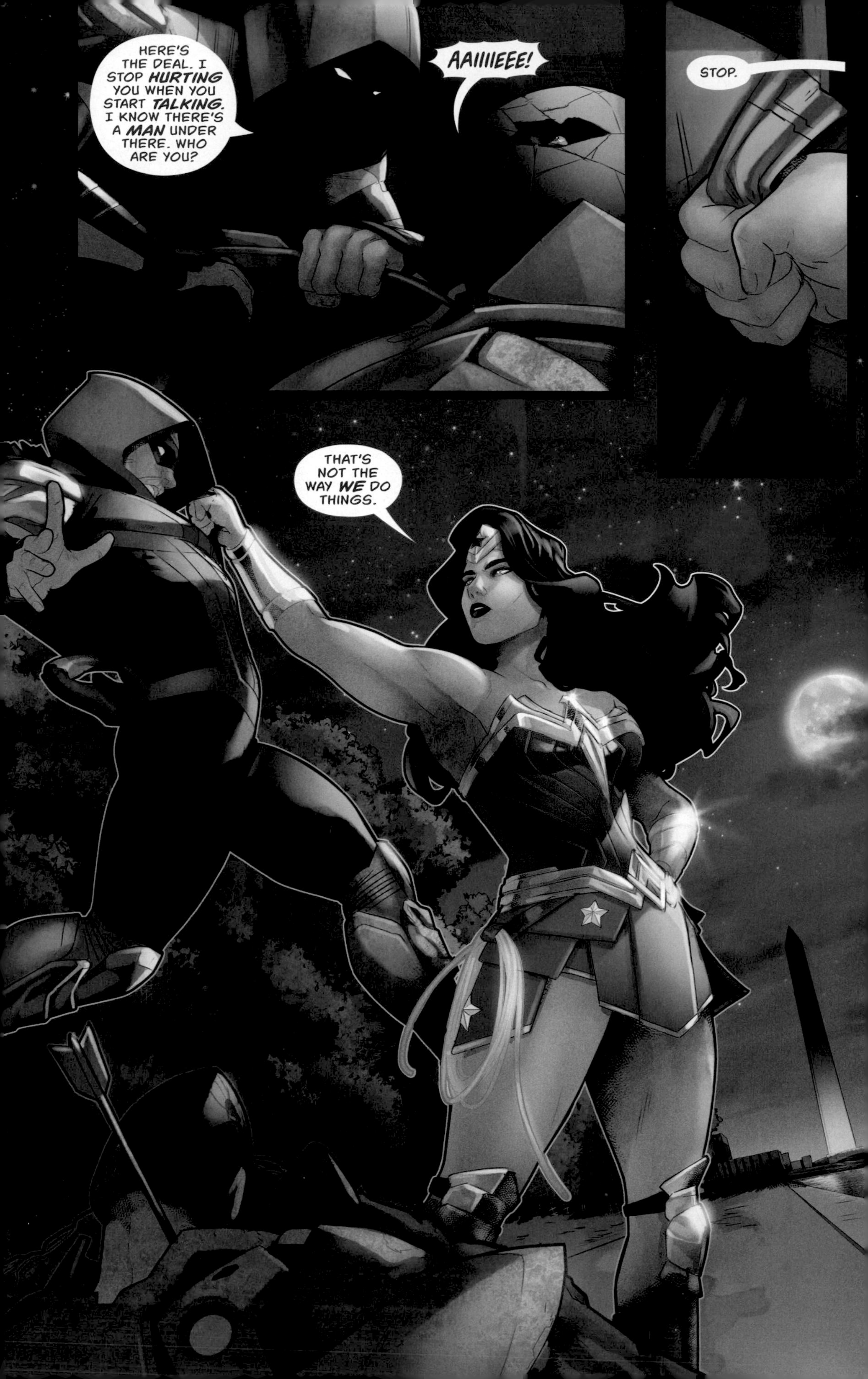
HERE'S THE DEAL. I STOP HURTING YOU WHEN YOU START TALKING. I KNOW THERE'S A MAN UNDER THERE. WHO ARE YOU?
AAIIIIEEE!
STOP.
THAT'S NOT THE WAY WE DO THINGS.

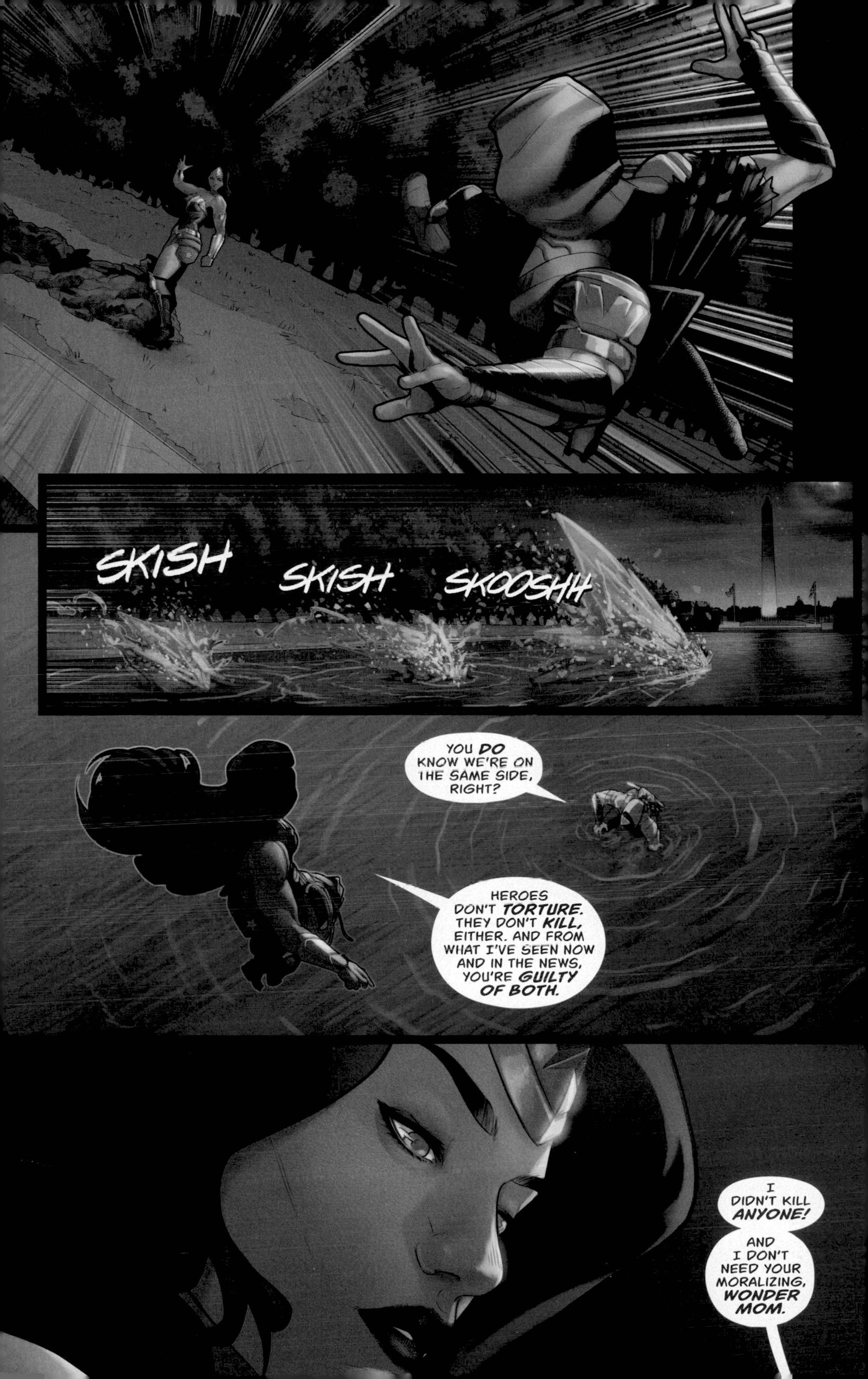
SKISH
SKISH
SKOOSHH
YOU DO KNOW WE'RE ON THE SAME SIDE, RIGHT?
HEROES DON'T TORTURE. THEY DON'T KILL, EITHER. AND FROM WHAT I'VE SEEN NOW AND IN THE NEWS, YOU'RE GUILTY OF BOTH.
I DIDN'T KILL ANYONE!
AND I DON'T NEED YOUR MORALIZING, WONDER MOM.

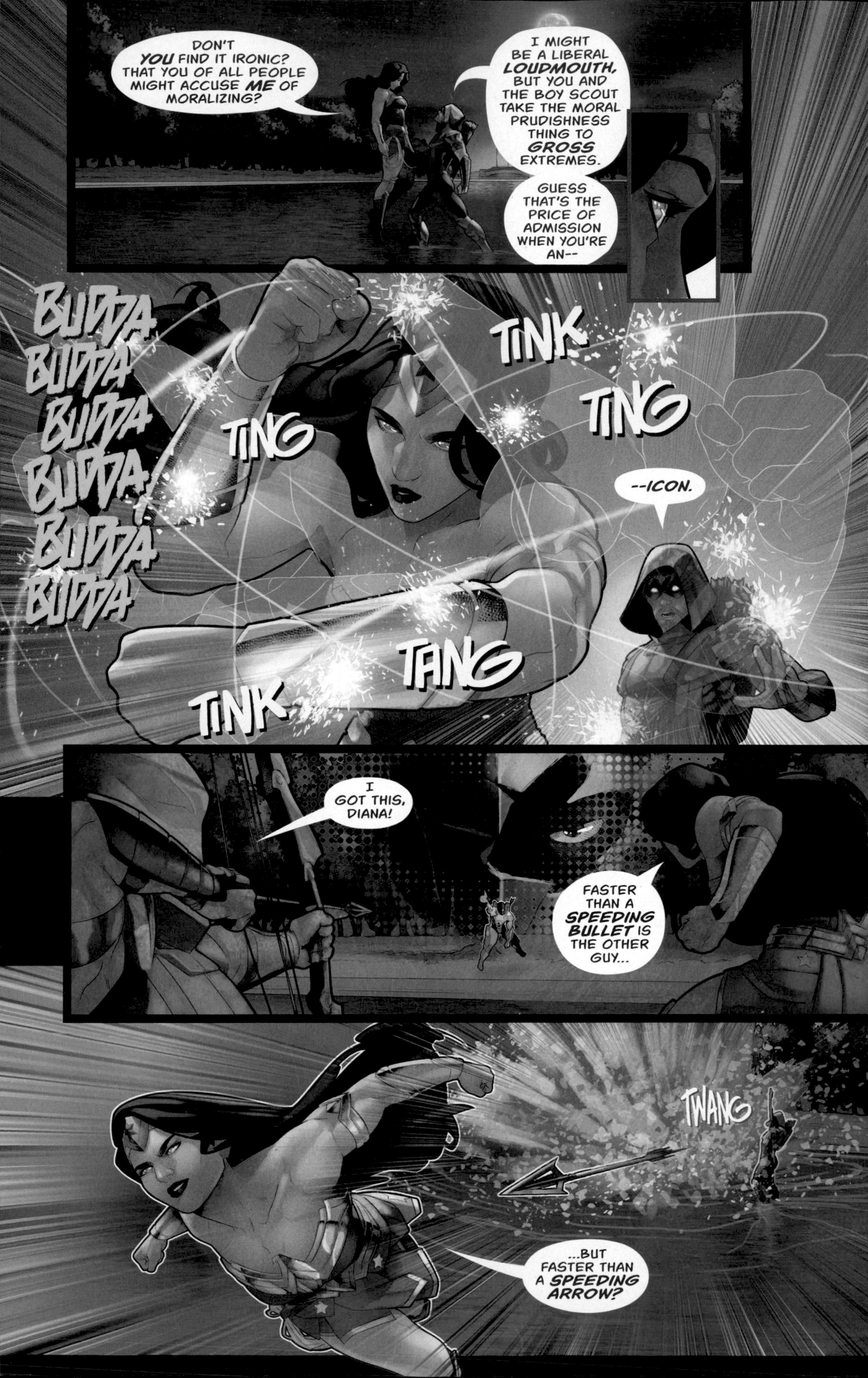
DON'T YOU FIND IT IRONIC? THAT YOU OF ALL PEOPLE MIGHT ACCUSE ME OF MORALIZING?
I MIGHT BE A LIBERAL LOUDMOUTH, BUT YOU AND THE BOY SCOUT TAKE THE MORAL PRUDISHNESS THING TO GROSS EXTREMES.
GUESS THAT'S THE PRICE OF ADMISSION WHEN YOU'RE AN--
BUDDA BUDDA BUDDA BUDDA BUDDA BUDDA
TINK
TING
TING
--ICON.
TANG
TINK
I GOT THIS, DIANA!
FASTER THAN A SPEEDING BULLET IS THE OTHER GUY...
TWANG
...BUT FASTER THAN A SPEEDING ARROW?

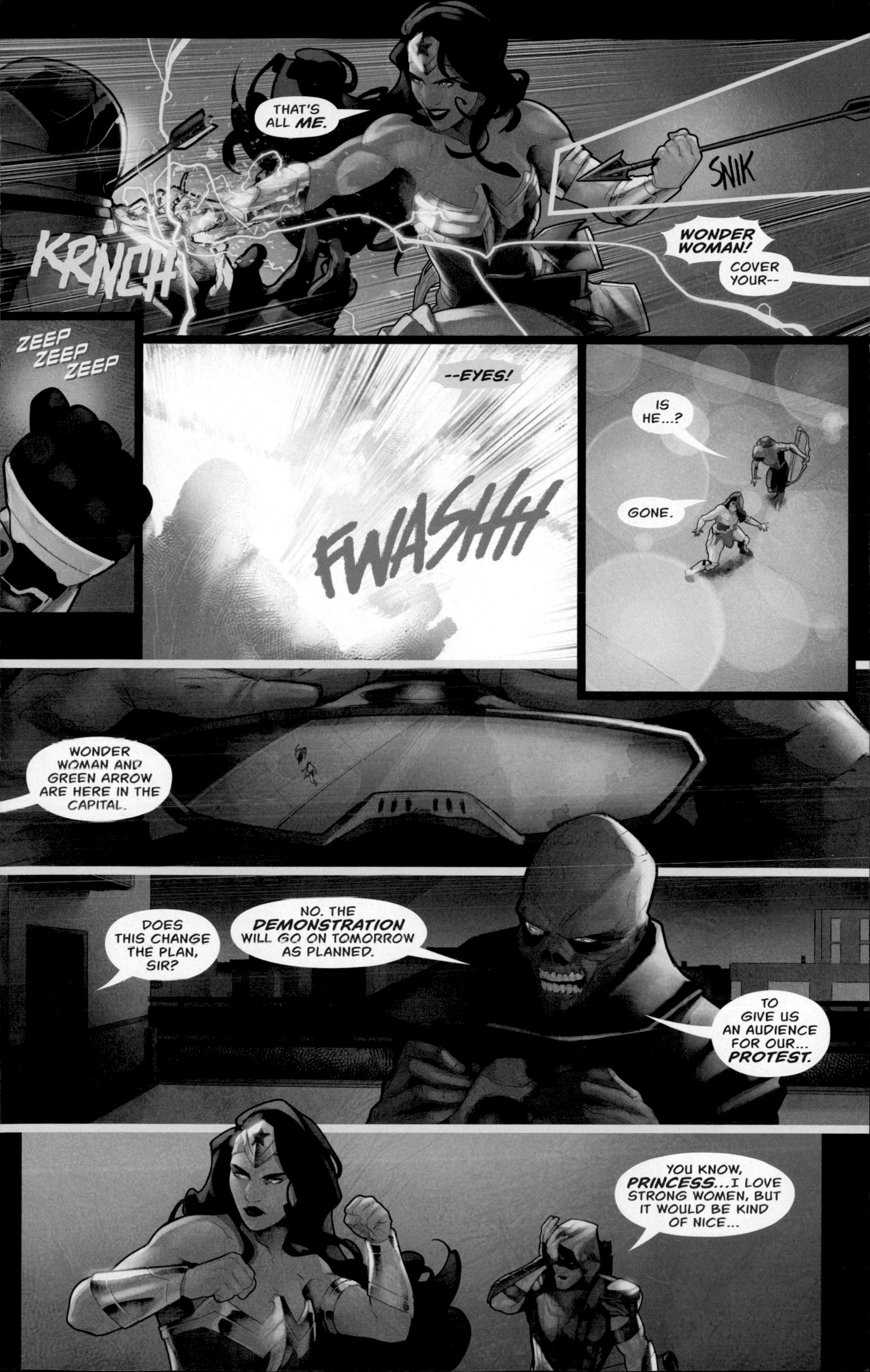
THAT'S ALL ME.
SNIK
KRNCH
WONDER WOMAN!
COVER YOUR--
ZEEP ZEEP ZEEP
--EYES!
FWASHH
IS HE...?
GONE.
WONDER WOMAN AND GREEN ARROW ARE HERE IN THE CAPITAL.
DOES THIS CHANGE THE PLAN, SIR?
NO. THE DEMONSTRATION WILL GO ON TOMORROW AS PLANNED.
TO GIVE US AN AUDIENCE FOR OUR... PROTEST.
YOU KNOW, PRINCESS...I LOVE STRONG WOMEN, BUT IT WOULD BE KIND OF NICE...

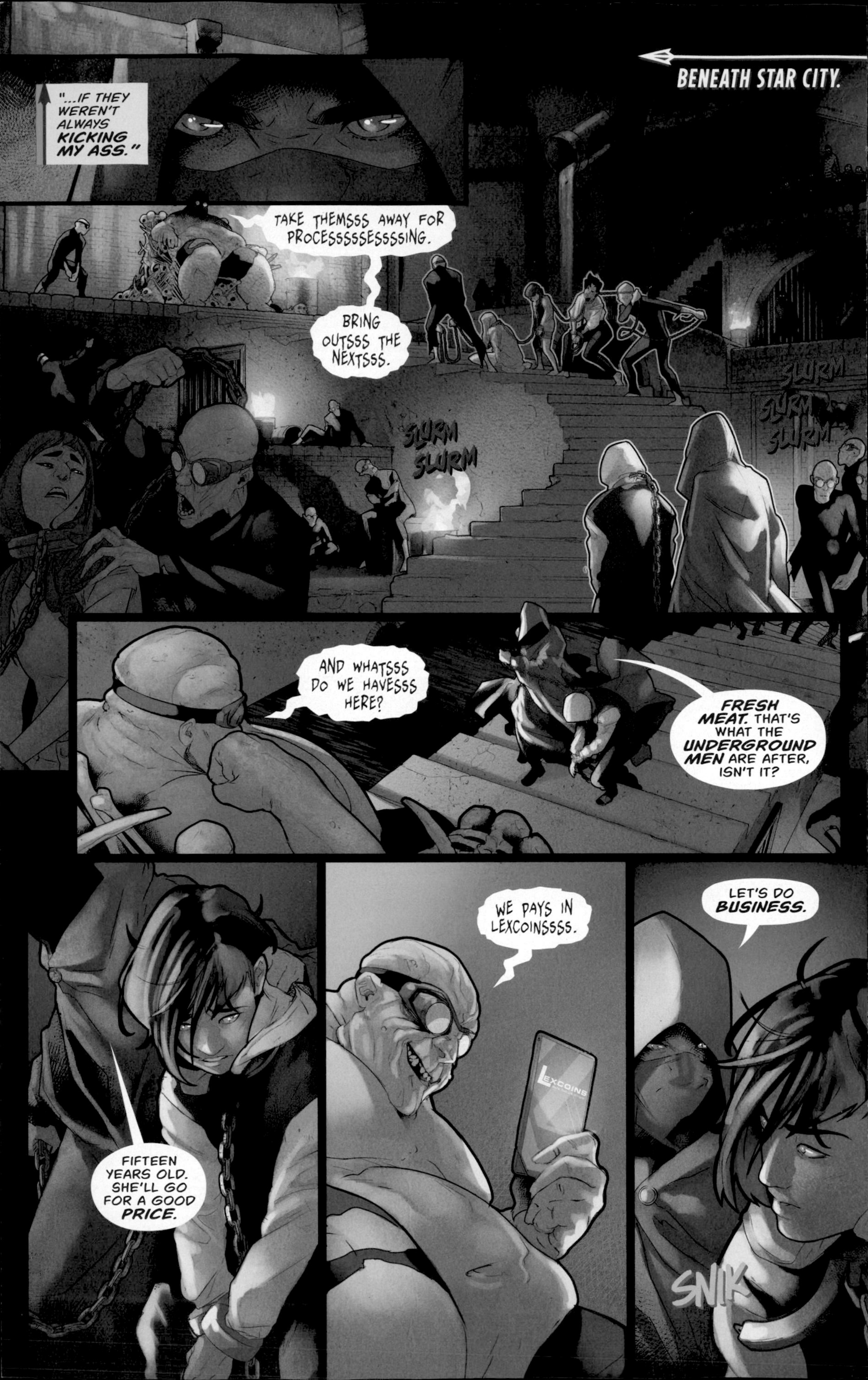
BENEATH STAR CITY.
"...IF THEY WEREN'T ALWAYS KICKING MY ASS."
TAKE THEMSSS AWAY FOR PROCESSSSSSESSSSING.
BRING OUTSSS THE NEXTSSS.
SLURM SLURM
SLURM SLURM SLURM
AND WHATSSS DO WE HAVESSS HERE?
FRESH MEAT. THAT'S WHAT THE UNDERGROUND MEN ARE AFTER, ISN'T IT?
FIFTEEN YEARS OLD. SHE'LL GO FOR A GOOD PRICE.
WE PAYS IN LEXCOINSSSS.
LEXCOINS
LET'S DO BUSINESS.
SNIK

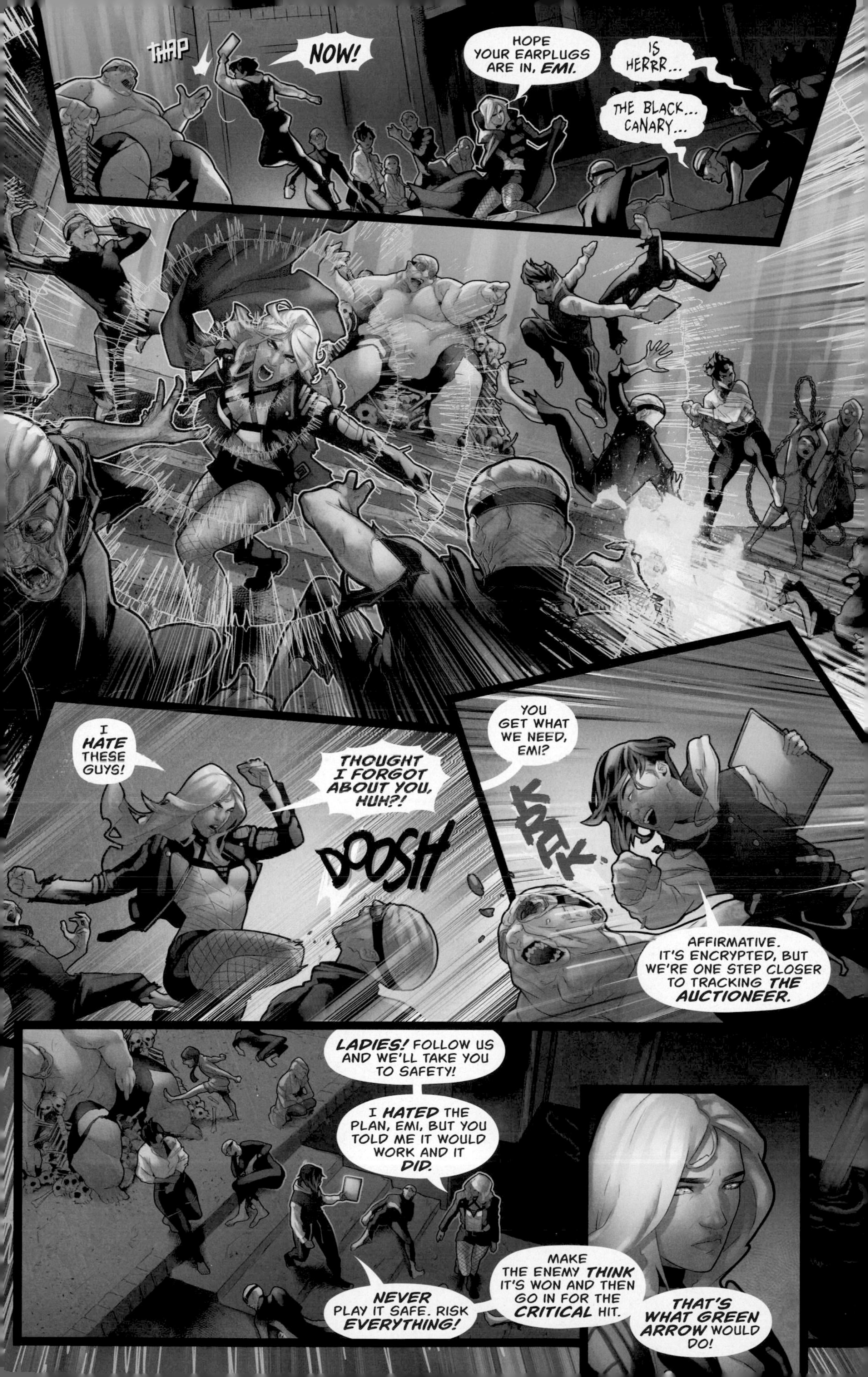

THAP
NOW!
HOPE YOUR EARPLUGS ARE IN, EMI.
IS HERRR...
THE BLACK... CANARY...
I HATE THESE GUYS!
THOUGHT I FORGOT ABOUT YOU, HUH?!
DOOSH
YOU GET WHAT WE NEED, EMI?
KRAK
AFFIRMATIVE. IT'S ENCRYPTED, BUT WE'RE ONE STEP CLOSER TO TRACKING THE AUCTIONEER.
LADIES! FOLLOW US AND WE'LL TAKE YOU TO SAFETY!
I HATED THE PLAN, EMI, BUT YOU TOLD ME IT WOULD WORK AND IT DID.
NEVER PLAY IT SAFE. RISK EVERYTHING!
MAKE THE ENEMY THINK IT'S WON AND THEN GO IN FOR THE CRITICAL HIT.
THAT'S WHAT GREEN ARROW WOULD DO!

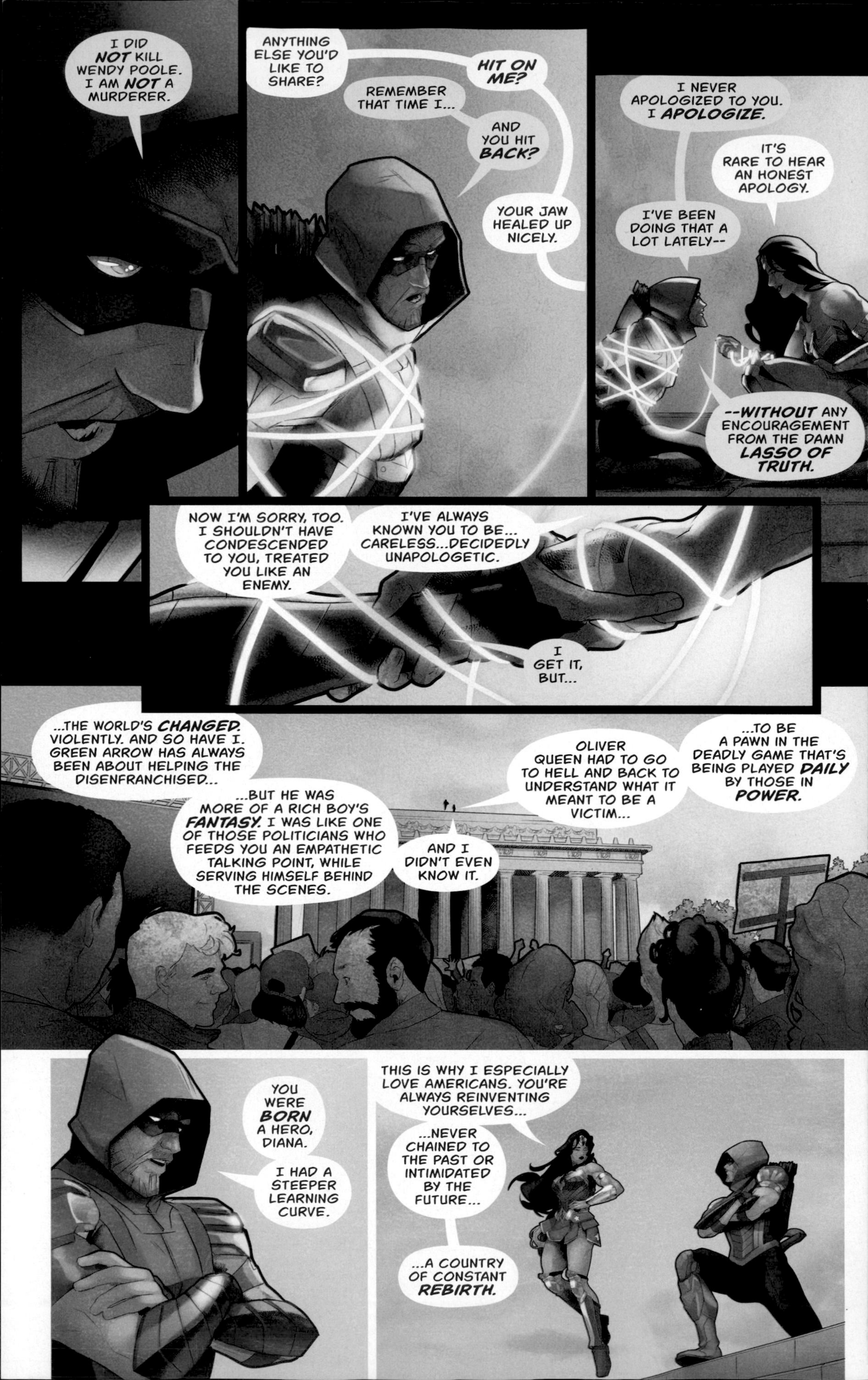
I DID NOT KILL WENDY POOLE. I AM NOT A MURDERER.
ANYTHING ELSE YOU'D LIKE TO SHARE?
HIT ON ME?
REMEMBER THAT TIME I...
AND YOU HIT BACK?
YOUR JAW HEALED UP NICELY.
I NEVER APOLOGIZED TO YOU. I APOLOGIZE.
IT'S RARE TO HEAR AN HONEST APOLOGY.
I'VE BEEN DOING THAT A LOT LATELY--
--WITHOUT ANY ENCOURAGEMENT FROM THE DAMN LASSO OF TRUTH.
NOW I'M SORRY, TOO. I SHOULDN'T HAVE CONDESCENDED TO YOU, TREATED YOU LIKE AN ENEMY.
I'VE ALWAYS KNOWN YOU TO BE... CARELESS...DECIDEDLY UNAPOLOGETIC.
I GET IT, BUT...
...THE WORLD'S CHANGED. VIOLENTLY. AND SO HAVE I. GREEN ARROW HAS ALWAYS BEEN ABOUT HELPING THE DISENFRANCHISED...
...BUT HE WAS MORE OF A RICH BOY'S FANTASY. I WAS LIKE ONE OF THOSE POLITICIANS WHO FEEDS YOU AN EMPATHETIC TALKING POINT, WHILE SERVING HIMSELF BEHIND THE SCENES.
AND I DIDN'T EVEN KNOW IT.
OLIVER QUEEN HAD TO GO TO HELL AND BACK TO UNDERSTAND WHAT IT MEANT TO BE A VICTIM...
...TO BE A PAWN IN THE DEADLY GAME THAT'S BEING PLAYED DAILY BY THOSE IN POWER.
YOU WERE BORN A HERO, DIANA.
I HAD A STEEPER LEARNING CURVE.
THIS IS WHY I ESPECIALLY LOVE AMERICANS. YOU'RE ALWAYS REINVENTING YOURSELVES...
...NEVER CHAINED TO THE PAST OR INTIMIDATED BY THE FUTURE...
...A COUNTRY OF CONSTANT REBIRTH.

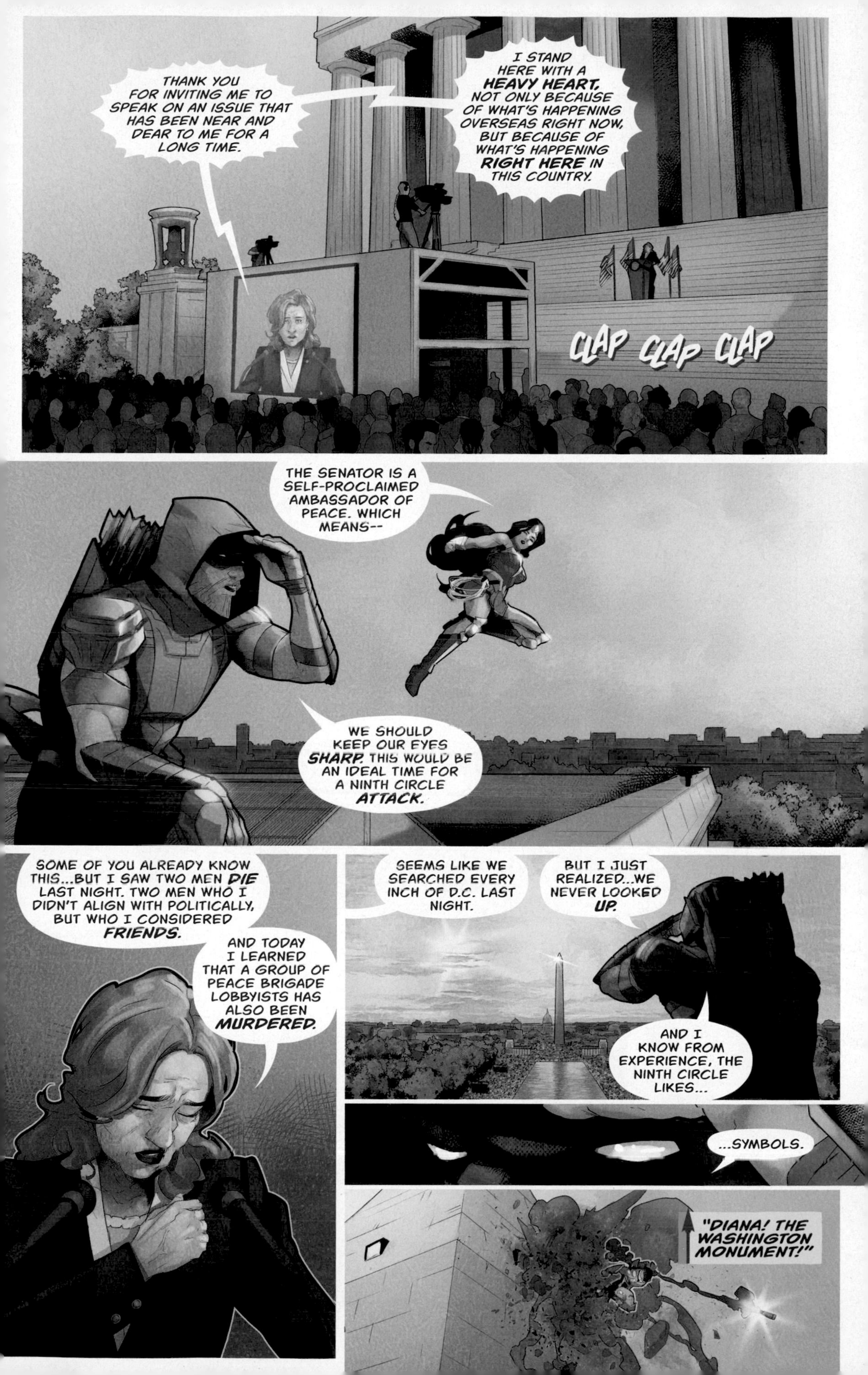
THANK YOU FOR INVITING ME TO SPEAK ON AN ISSUE THAT HAS BEEN NEAR AND DEAR TO ME FOR A LONG TIME.
I STAND HERE WITH A HEAVY HEART, NOT ONLY BECAUSE OF WHAT'S HAPPENING OVERSEAS RIGHT NOW, BUT BECAUSE OF WHAT'S HAPPENING RIGHT HERE IN THIS COUNTRY.
CLAP CLAP CLAP
THE SENATOR IS A SELF-PROCLAIMED AMBASSADOR OF PEACE. WHICH MEANS--
WE SHOULD KEEP OUR EYES SHARP. THIS WOULD BE AN IDEAL TIME FOR A NINTH CIRCLE ATTACK.
SOME OF YOU ALREADY KNOW THIS...BUT I SAW TWO MEN DIE LAST NIGHT. TWO MEN WHO I DIDN'T ALIGN WITH POLITICALLY, BUT WHO I CONSIDERED FRIENDS.
AND TODAY I LEARNED THAT A GROUP OF PEACE BRIGADE LOBBYISTS HAS ALSO BEEN MURDERED.
SEEMS LIKE WE SEARCHED EVERY INCH OF D.C. LAST NIGHT.
BUT I JUST REALIZED...WE NEVER LOOKED UP.
AND I KNOW FROM EXPERIENCE, THE NINTH CIRCLE LIKES...
...SYMBOLS.
"DIANA! THE WASHINGTON MONUMENT!"

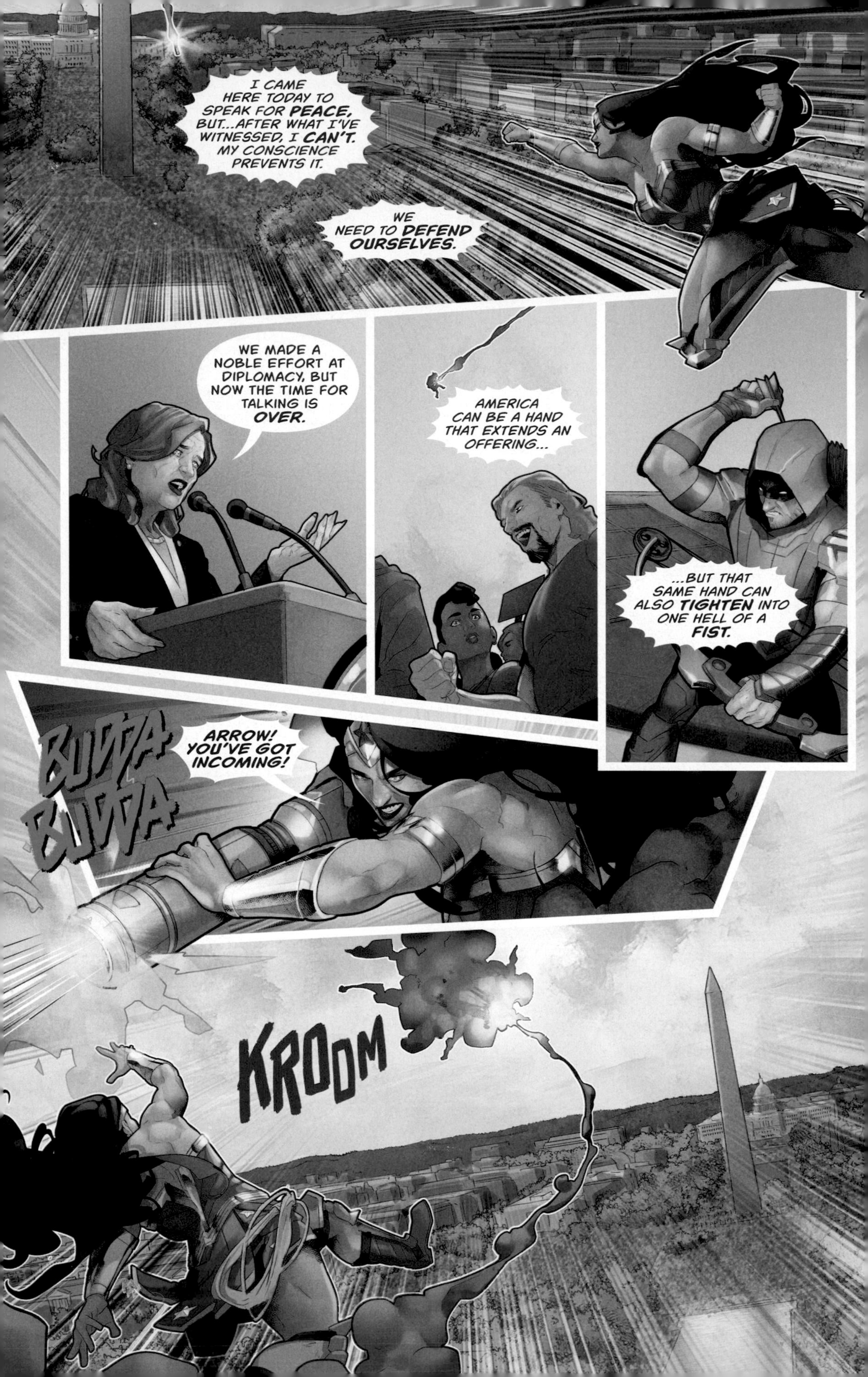
I CAME HERE TODAY TO SPEAK FOR PEACE, BUT...AFTER WHAT I'VE WITNESSED, I CAN'T. MY CONSCIENCE PREVENTS IT.
WE NEED TO DEFEND OURSELVES.
WE MADE A NOBLE EFFORT AT DIPLOMACY, BUT NOW THE TIME FOR TALKING IS OVER.
AMERICA CAN BE A HAND THAT EXTENDS AN OFFERING...
...BUT THAT SAME HAND CAN ALSO TIGHTEN INTO ONE HELL OF A FIST.
BUDDA BUDDA
ARROW! YOU'VE GOT INCOMING!
KROOM

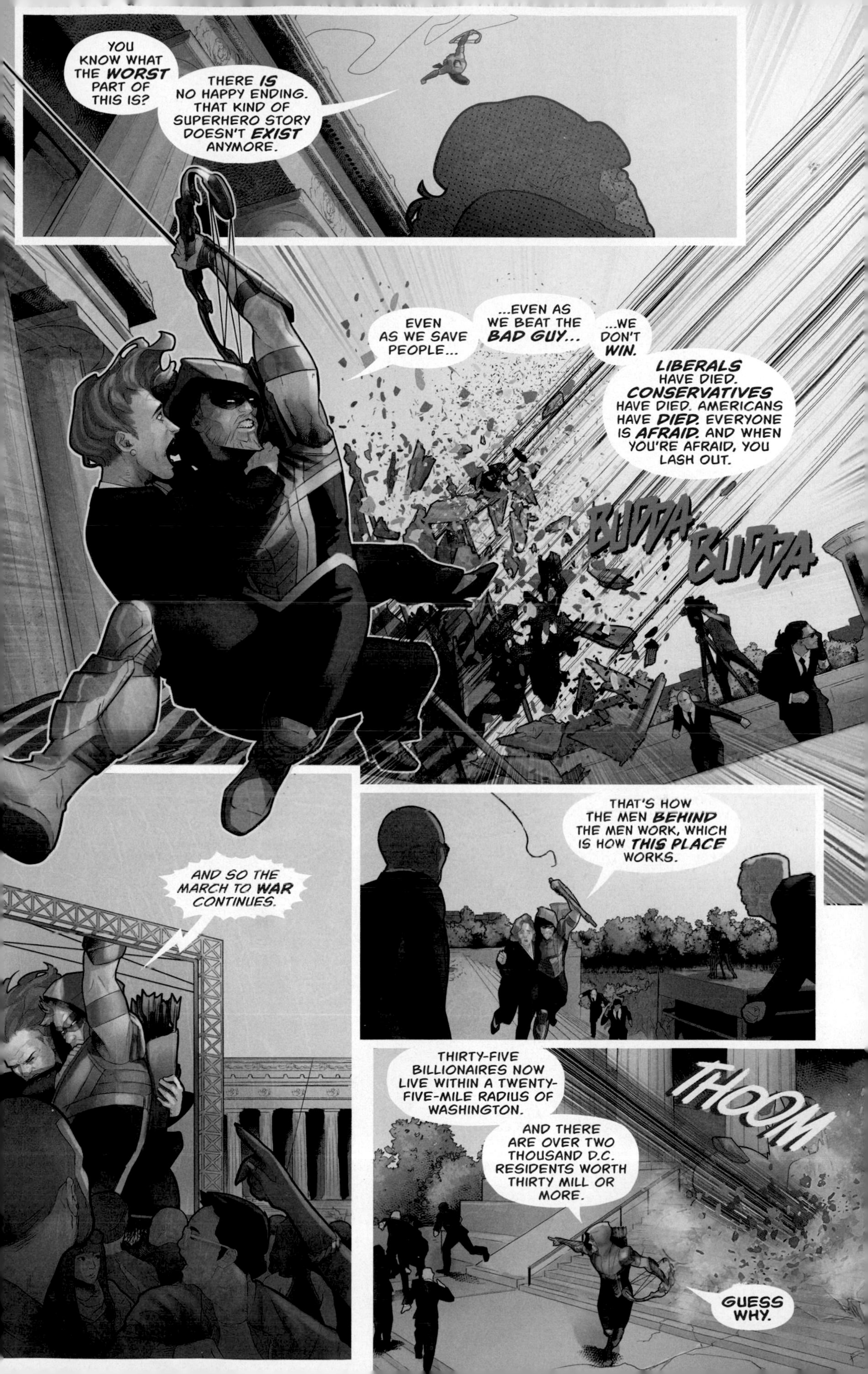
YOU KNOW WHAT THE WORST PART OF THIS IS?
THERE IS NO HAPPY ENDING. THAT KIND OF SUPERHERO STORY DOESN'T EXIST ANYMORE.
EVEN AS WE SAVE PEOPLE...
...EVEN AS WE BEAT THE BAD GUY...
...WE DON'T WIN.
LIBERALS HAVE DIED. CONSERVATIVES HAVE DIED. AMERICANS HAVE DIED. EVERYONE IS AFRAID. AND WHEN YOU'RE AFRAID, YOU LASH OUT.
BUDDA BUDDA
AND SO THE MARCH TO WAR CONTINUES.
THAT'S HOW THE MEN BEHIND THE MEN WORK, WHICH IS HOW THIS PLACE WORKS.
THIRTY-FIVE BILLIONAIRES NOW LIVE WITHIN A TWENTY-FIVE-MILE RADIUS OF WASHINGTON.
AND THERE ARE OVER TWO THOUSAND D.C. RESIDENTS WORTH THIRTY MILL OR MORE.
THOOM
GUESS WHY.

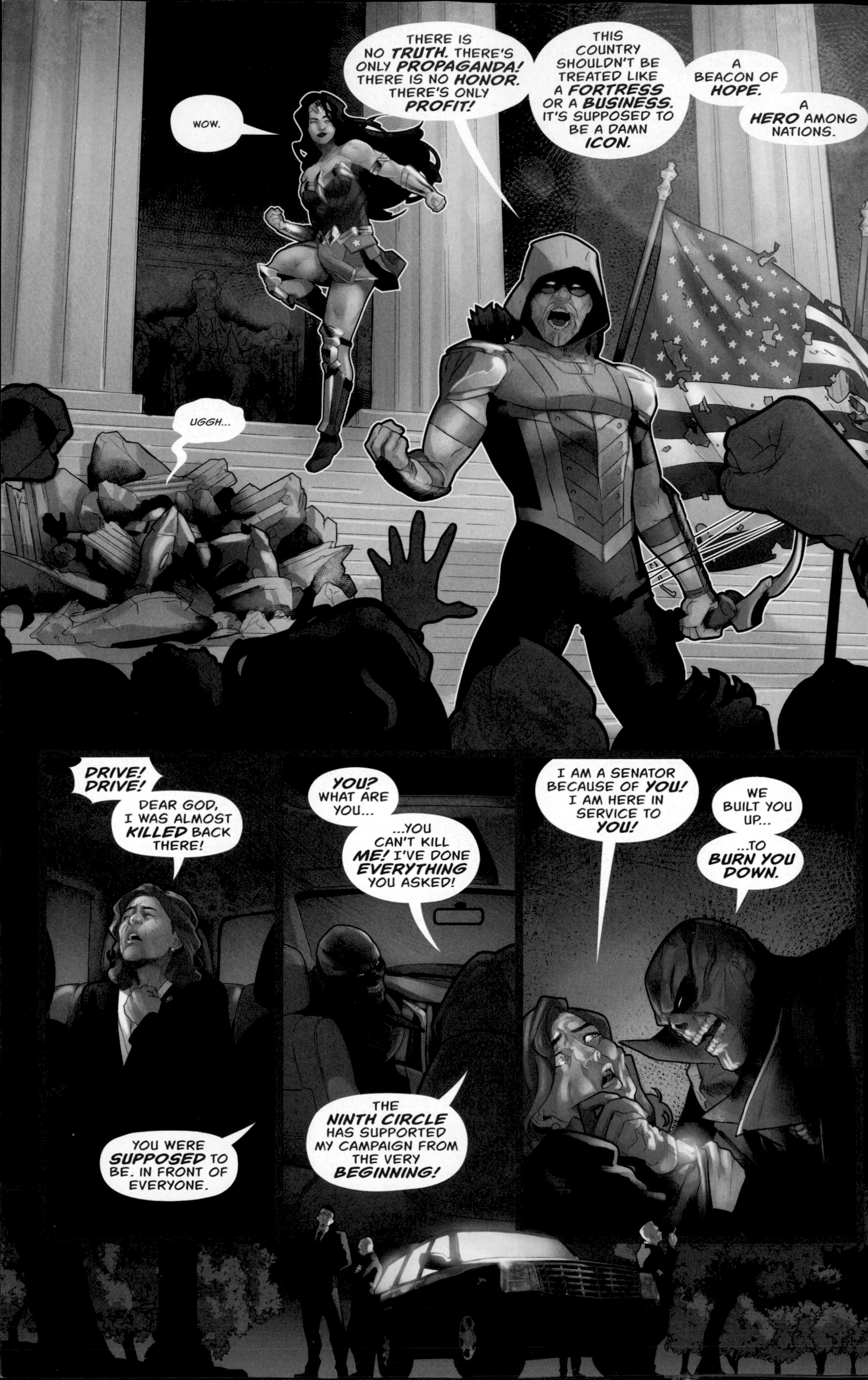
WOW.
THERE IS NO TRUTH. THERE'S ONLY PROPAGANDA! THERE IS NO HONOR. THERE'S ONLY PROFIT!
THIS COUNTRY SHOULDN'T BE TREATED LIKE A FORTRESS OR A BUSINESS. IT'S SUPPOSED TO BE A DAMN ICON.
A BEACON OF HOPE.
A HERO AMONG NATIONS.
UGGH...
DRIVE! DRIVE!
DEAR GOD, I WAS ALMOST KILLED BACK THERE!
YOU WERE SUPPOSED TO BE. IN FRONT OF EVERYONE.
YOU? WHAT ARE YOU...
...YOU CAN'T KILL ME! I'VE DONE EVERYTHING YOU ASKED!
THE NINTH CIRCLE HAS SUPPORTED MY CAMPAIGN FROM THE VERY BEGINNING!
I AM A SENATOR BECAUSE OF YOU! I AM HERE IN SERVICE TO YOU!
WE BUILT YOU UP...
...TO BURN YOU DOWN.

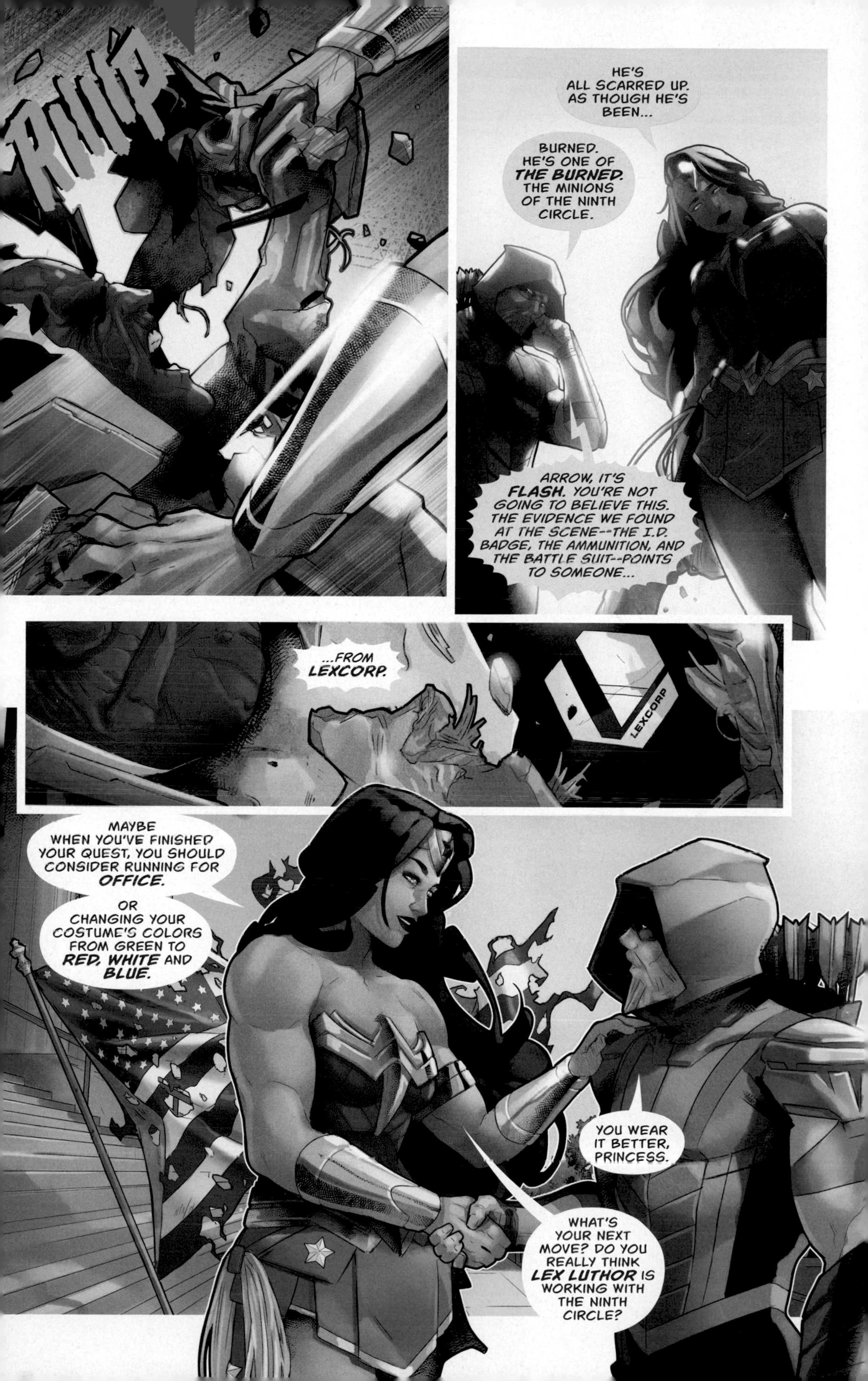
RIIIIP
HE'S ALL SCARRED UP. AS THOUGH HE'S BEEN...
BURNED. HE'S ONE OF THE BURNED. THE MINIONS OF THE NINTH CIRCLE.
ARROW, IT'S FLASH. YOU'RE NOT GOING TO BELIEVE THIS. THE EVIDENCE WE FOUND AT THE SCENE--THE I.D. BADGE, THE AMMUNITION, AND THE BATTLE SUIT--POINTS TO SOMEONE...
...FROM LEXCORP.
LEXCORP
MAYBE WHEN YOU'VE FINISHED YOUR QUEST, YOU SHOULD CONSIDER RUNNING FOR OFFICE.
OR CHANGING YOUR COSTUME'S COLORS FROM GREEN TO RED, WHITE AND BLUE.
YOU WEAR IT BETTER, PRINCESS.
WHAT'S YOUR NEXT MOVE? DO YOU REALLY THINK LEX LUTHOR IS WORKING WITH THE NINTH CIRCLE?

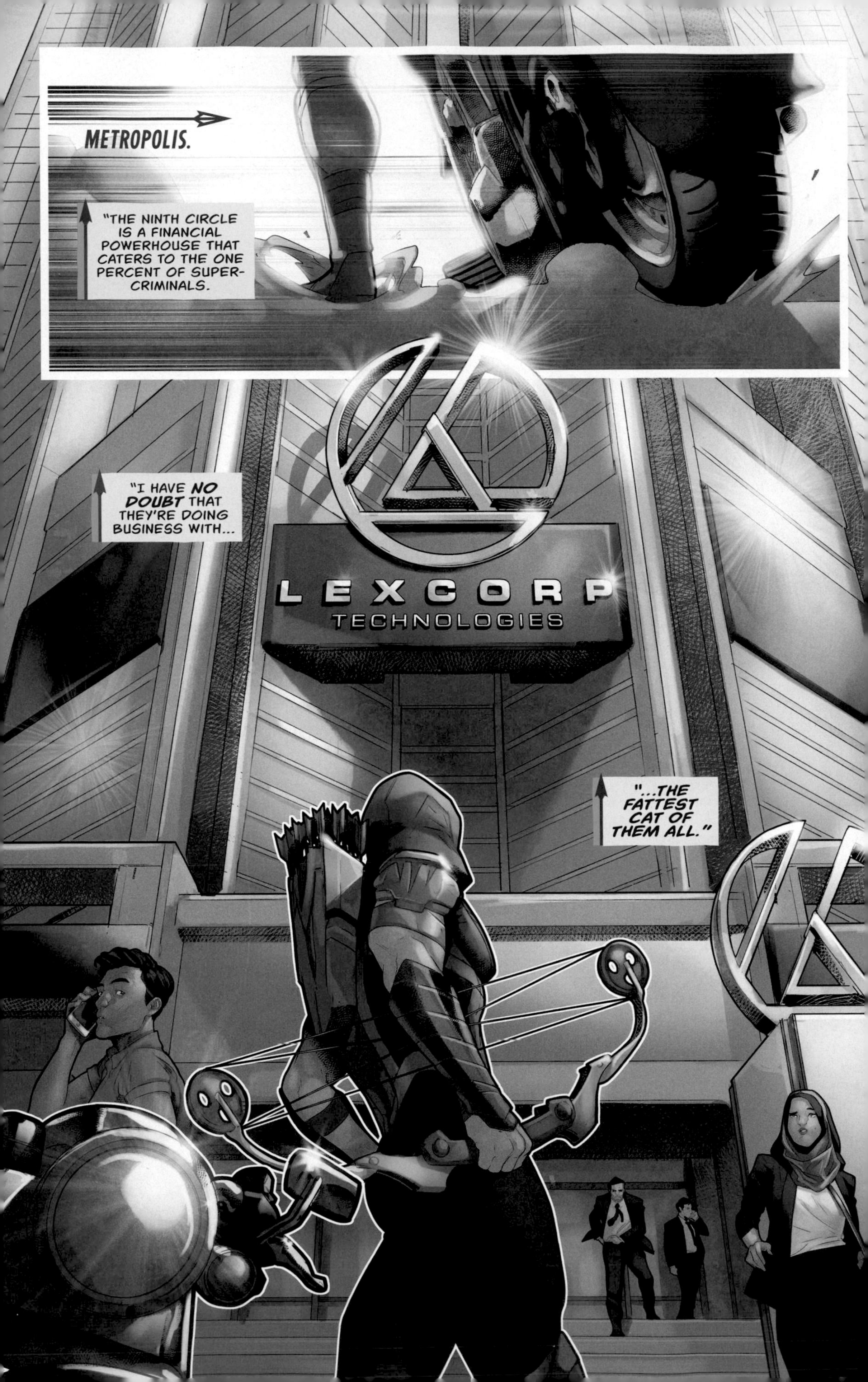
METROPOLIS.
"THE NINTH CIRCLE IS A FINANCIAL POWERHOUSE THAT CATERS TO THE ONE PERCENT OF SUPER-CRIMINALS.
"I HAVE NO DOUBT THAT THEY'RE DOING BUSINESS WITH...
LEXCORP
TECHNOLOGIES
"...THE FATTEST CAT OF THEM ALL."

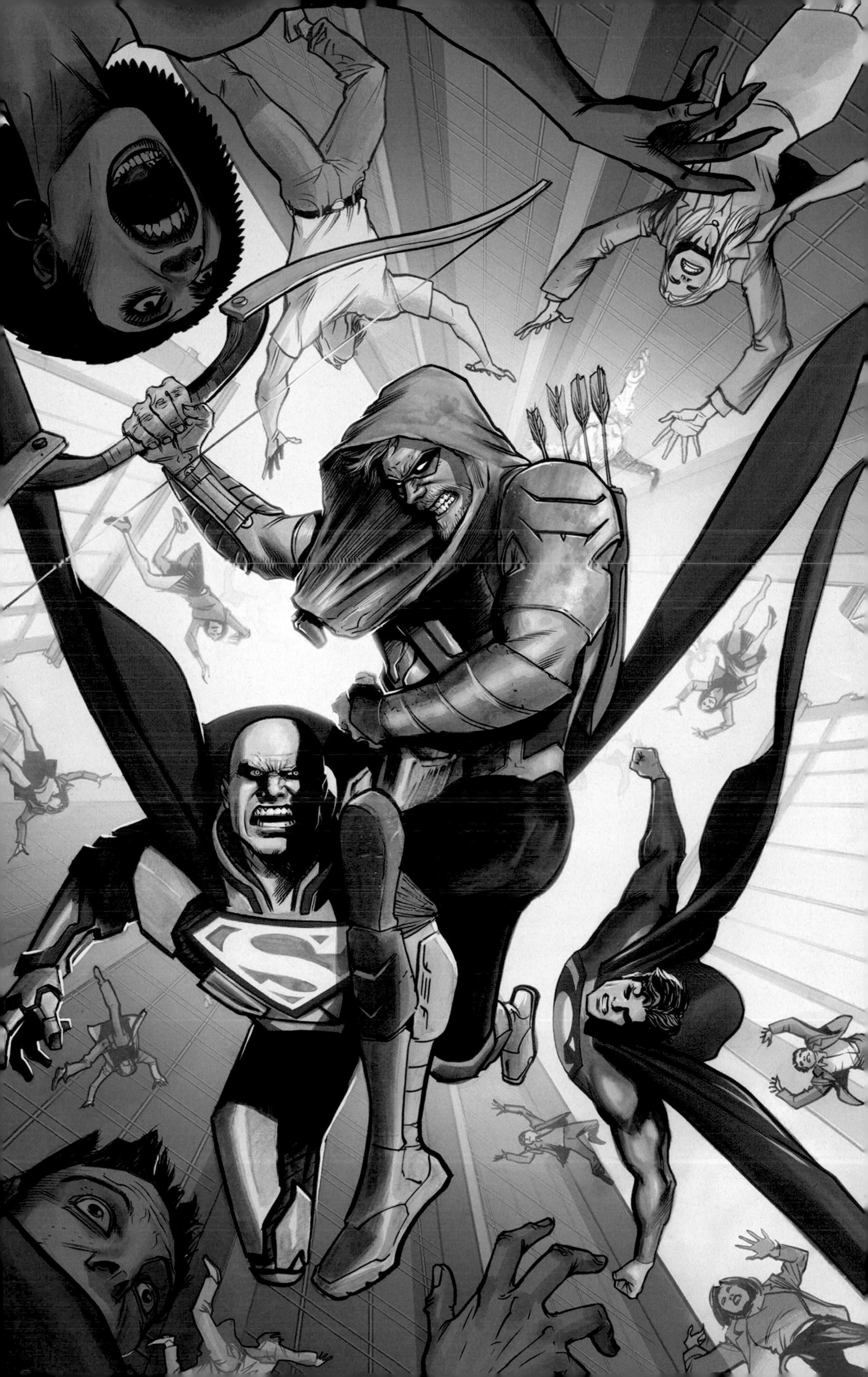

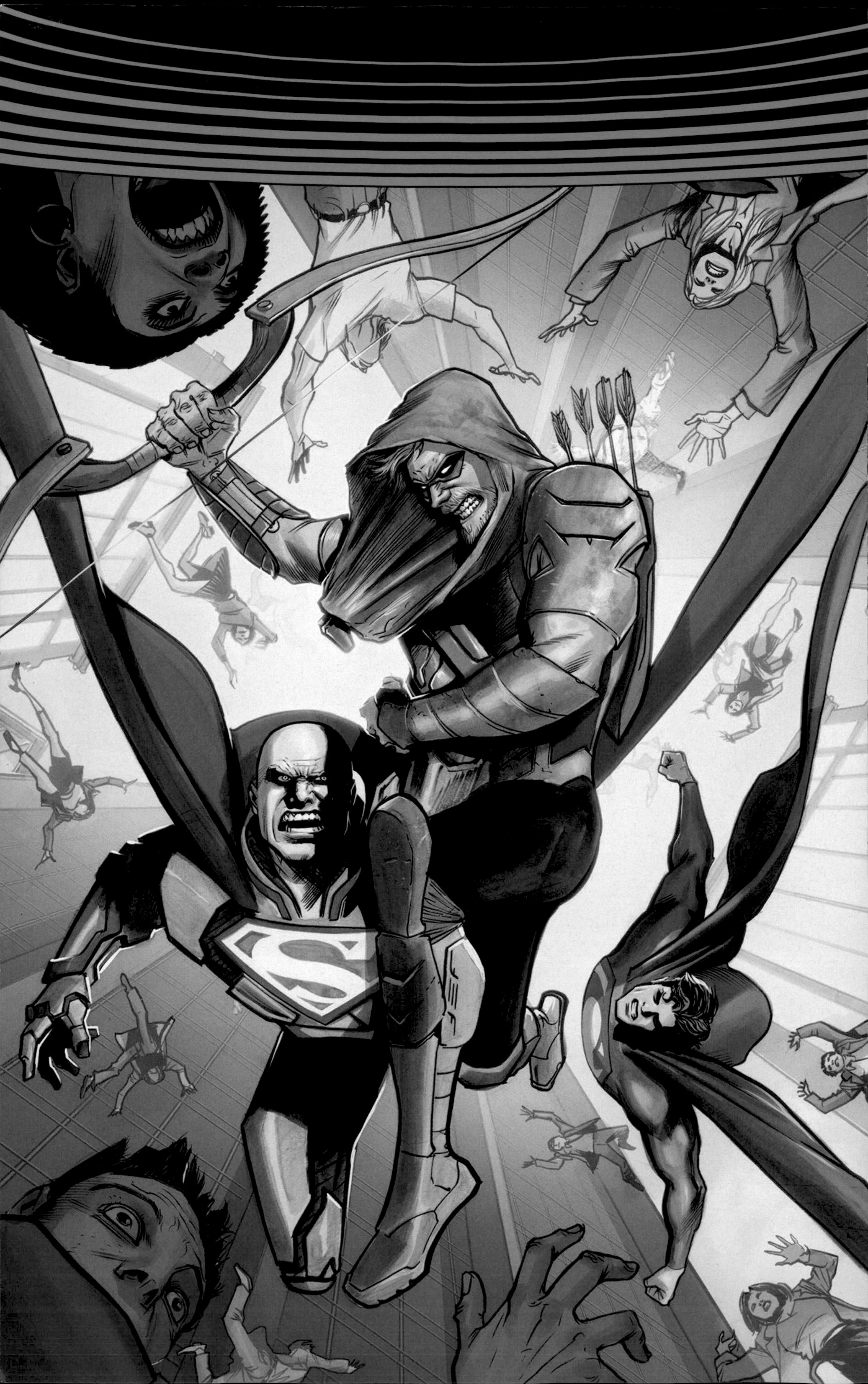

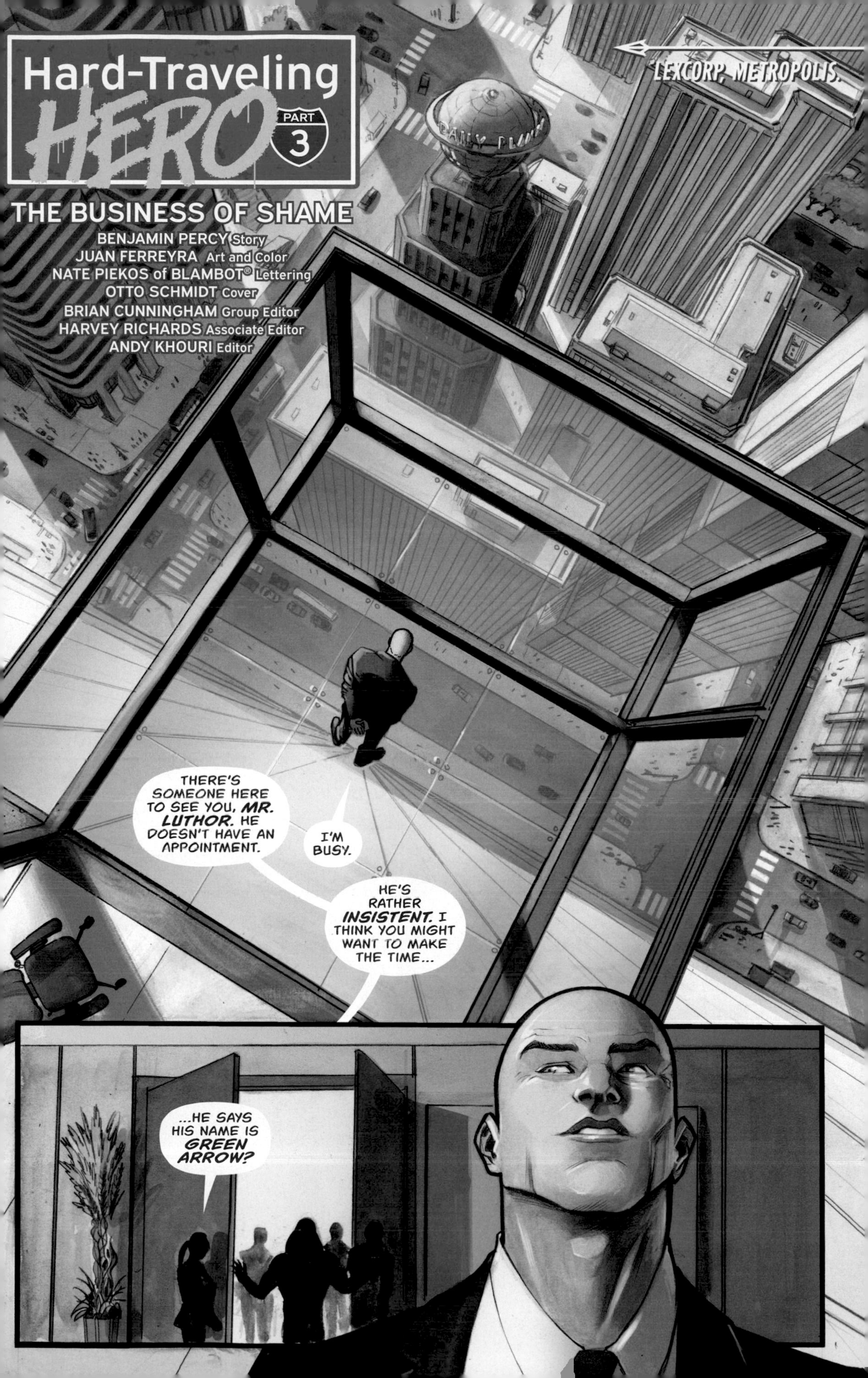
Hard-Traveling
HERO
PART 3
THE BUSINESS OF SHAME
BENJAMIN PERCY Story
JUAN FERREYRA Art and Color
NATE PIEKOS of BLAMBOT® Lettering
OTTO SCHMIDT Cover
BRIAN CUNNINGHAM Group Editor
HARVEY RICHARDS Associate Editor
ANDY KHOURI Editor
LEXCORP, METROPOLIS.
THERE'S SOMEONE HERE TO SEE YOU, MR. LUTHOR. HE DOESN'T HAVE AN APPOINTMENT.
I'M BUSY.
HE'S RATHER INSISTENT. I THINK YOU MIGHT WANT TO MAKE THE TIME...
...HE SAYS HIS NAME IS GREEN ARROW?

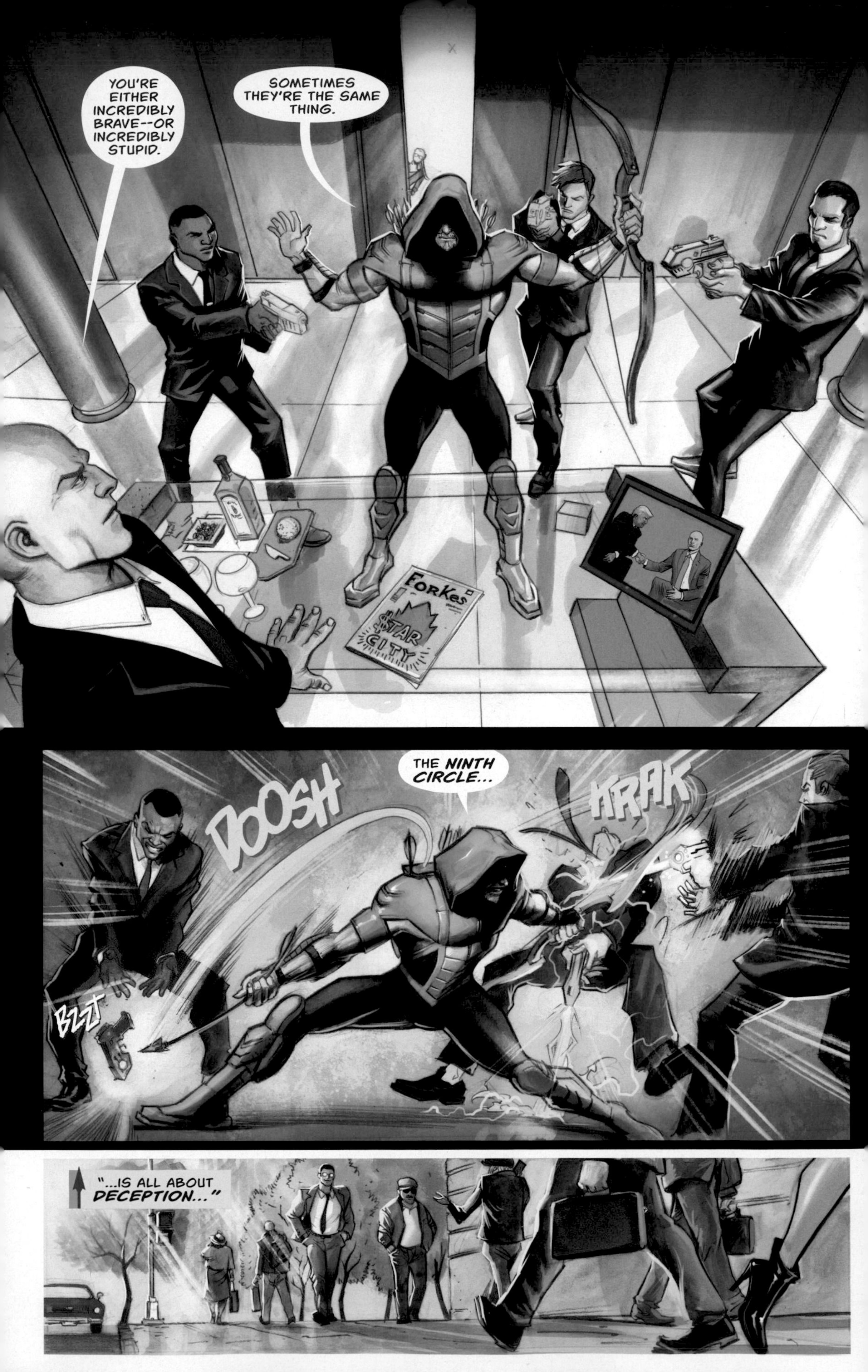
YOU'RE EITHER INCREDIBLY BRAVE--OR INCREDIBLY STUPID.
SOMETIMES THEY'RE THE SAME THING.
ForKes
$STAR CITY
DOOSH
THE *NINTH CIRCLE*...
KRAK
BZZT
"...IS ALL ABOUT *DECEPTION*..."

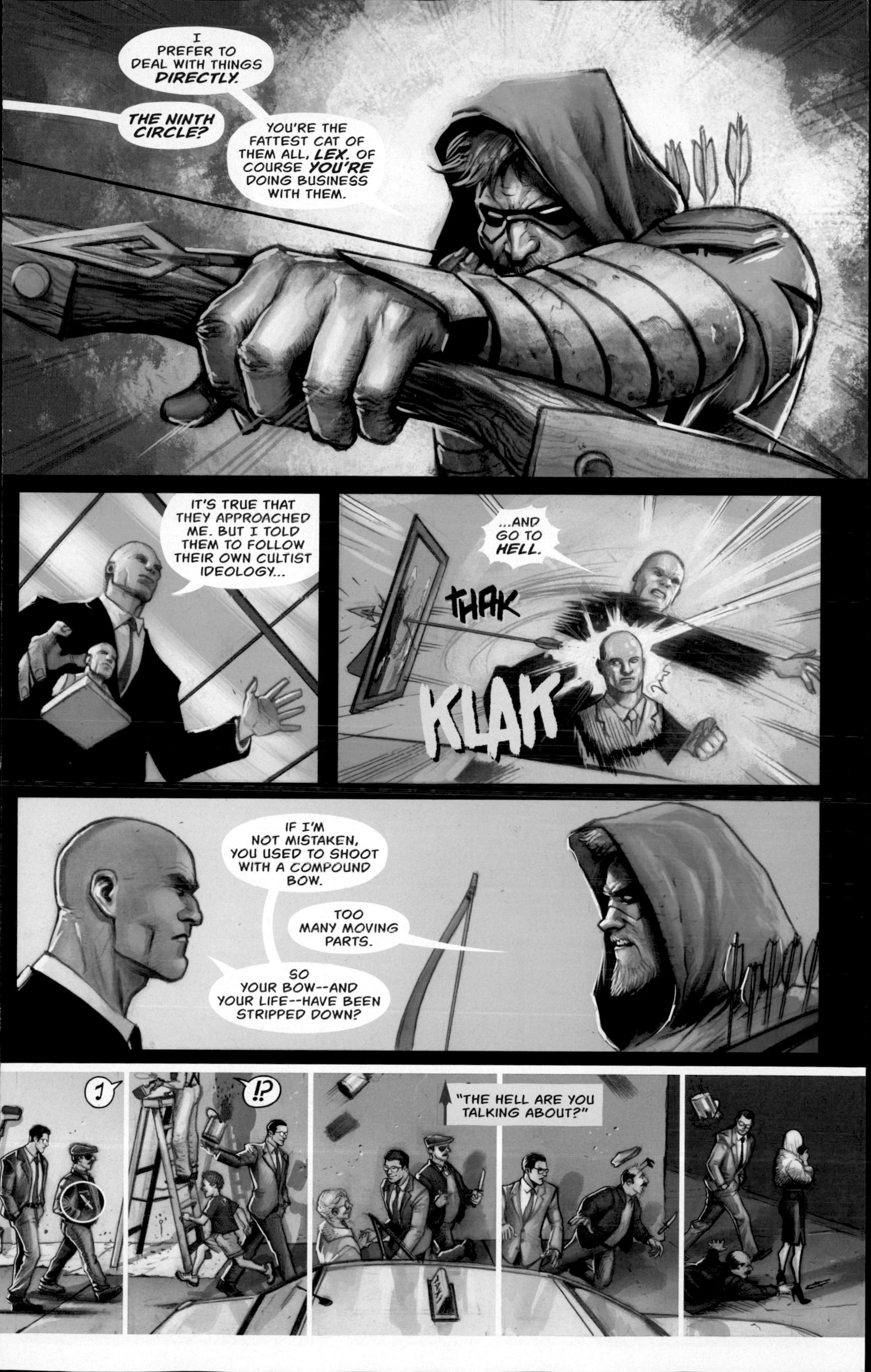

I PREFER TO DEAL WITH THINGS DIRECTLY.
THE NINTH CIRCLE?
YOU'RE THE FATTEST CAT OF THEM ALL, LEX. OF COURSE YOU'RE DOING BUSINESS WITH THEM.
IT'S TRUE THAT THEY APPROACHED ME. BUT I TOLD THEM TO FOLLOW THEIR OWN CULTIST IDEOLOGY...
...AND GO TO HELL.
THAK
KLAK
IF I'M NOT MISTAKEN, YOU USED TO SHOOT WITH A COMPOUND BOW.
TOO MANY MOVING PARTS.
SO YOUR BOW--AND YOUR LIFE--HAVE BEEN STRIPPED DOWN?
!?
"THE HELL ARE YOU TALKING ABOUT?"

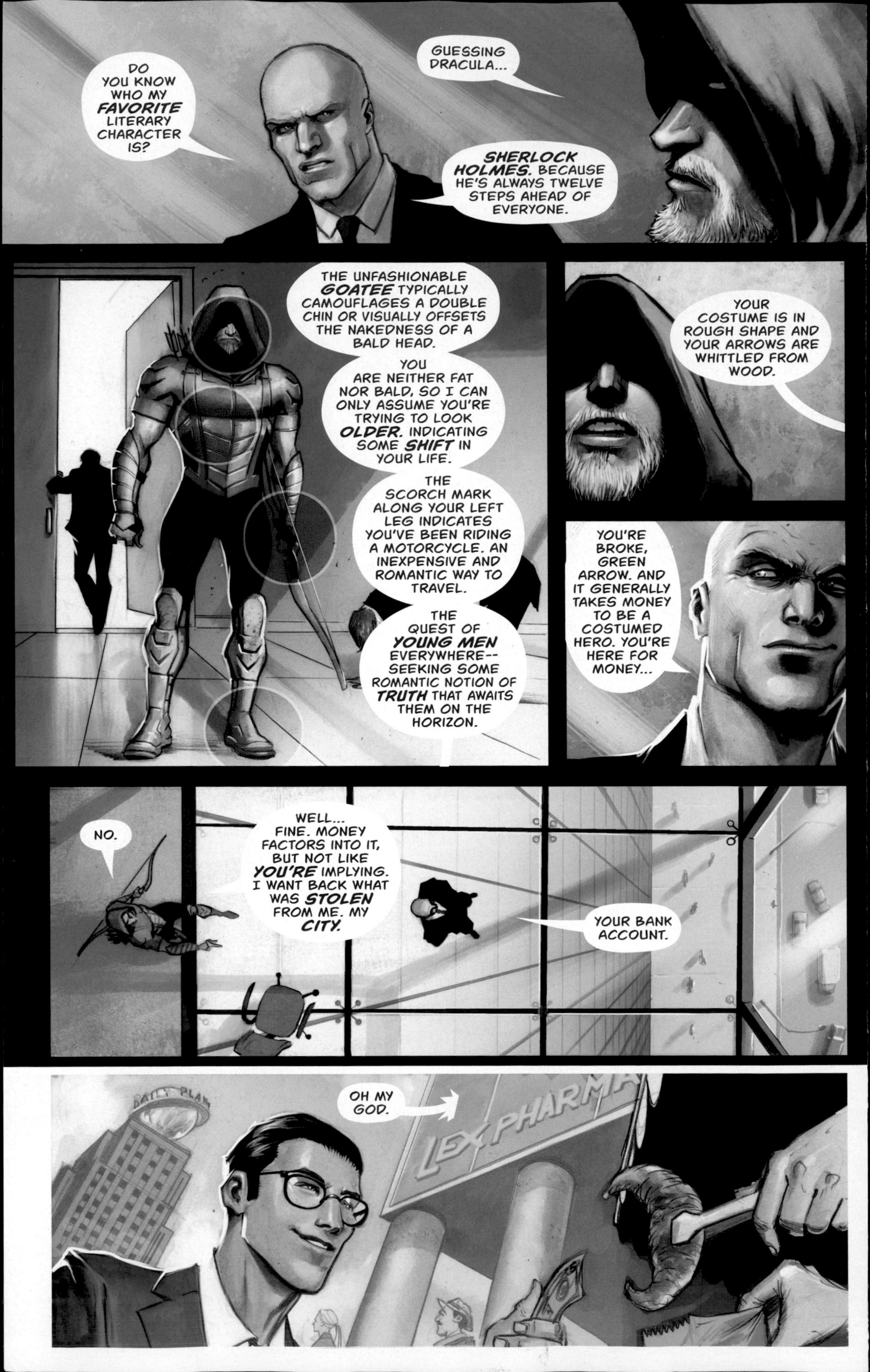
DO YOU KNOW WHO MY FAVORITE LITERARY CHARACTER IS?
GUESSING DRACULA...
SHERLOCK HOLMES. BECAUSE HE'S ALWAYS TWELVE STEPS AHEAD OF EVERYONE.
THE UNFASHIONABLE GOATEE TYPICALLY CAMOUFLAGES A DOUBLE CHIN OR VISUALLY OFFSETS THE NAKEDNESS OF A BALD HEAD.
YOU ARE NEITHER FAT NOR BALD, SO I CAN ONLY ASSUME YOU'RE TRYING TO LOOK OLDER. INDICATING SOME SHIFT IN YOUR LIFE.
THE SCORCH MARK ALONG YOUR LEFT LEG INDICATES YOU'VE BEEN RIDING A MOTORCYCLE. AN INEXPENSIVE AND ROMANTIC WAY TO TRAVEL.
THE QUEST OF YOUNG MEN EVERYWHERE--SEEKING SOME ROMANTIC NOTION OF TRUTH THAT AWAITS THEM ON THE HORIZON.
YOUR COSTUME IS IN ROUGH SHAPE AND YOUR ARROWS ARE WHITTLED FROM WOOD.
YOU'RE BROKE, GREEN ARROW. AND IT GENERALLY TAKES MONEY TO BE A COSTUMED HERO. YOU'RE HERE FOR MONEY...
NO.
WELL... FINE. MONEY FACTORS INTO IT, BUT NOT LIKE YOU'RE IMPLYING. I WANT BACK WHAT WAS STOLEN FROM ME. MY CITY.
YOUR BANK ACCOUNT.
OH MY GOD.
LEX PHARMA

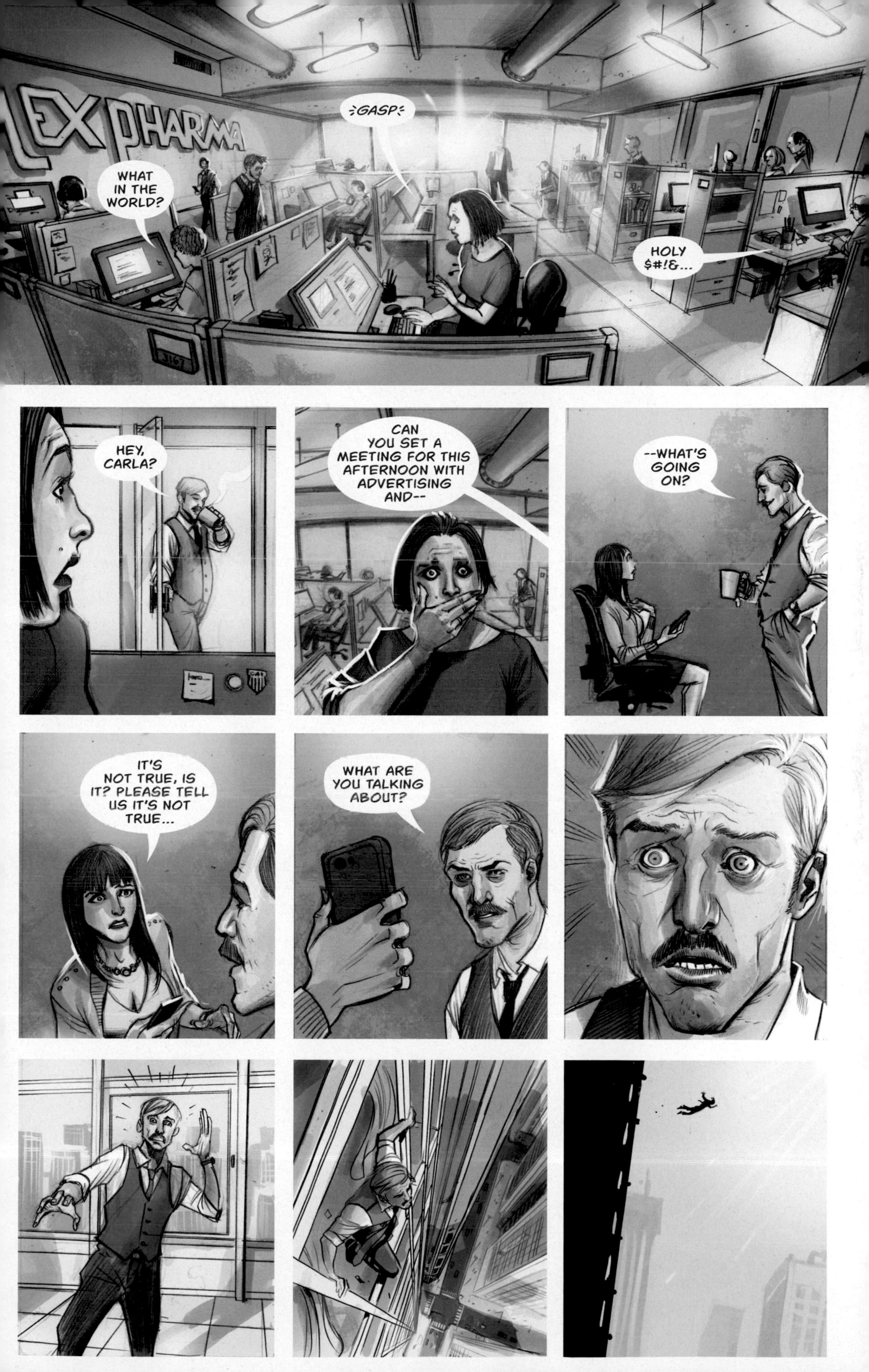
EX PHARMA
WHAT IN THE WORLD?
GASP
HOLY $#!&...
HEY, CARLA?
CAN YOU SET A MEETING FOR THIS AFTERNOON WITH ADVERTISING AND--
--WHAT'S GOING ON?
IT'S NOT TRUE, IS IT? PLEASE TELL US IT'S NOT TRUE...
WHAT ARE YOU TALKING ABOUT?

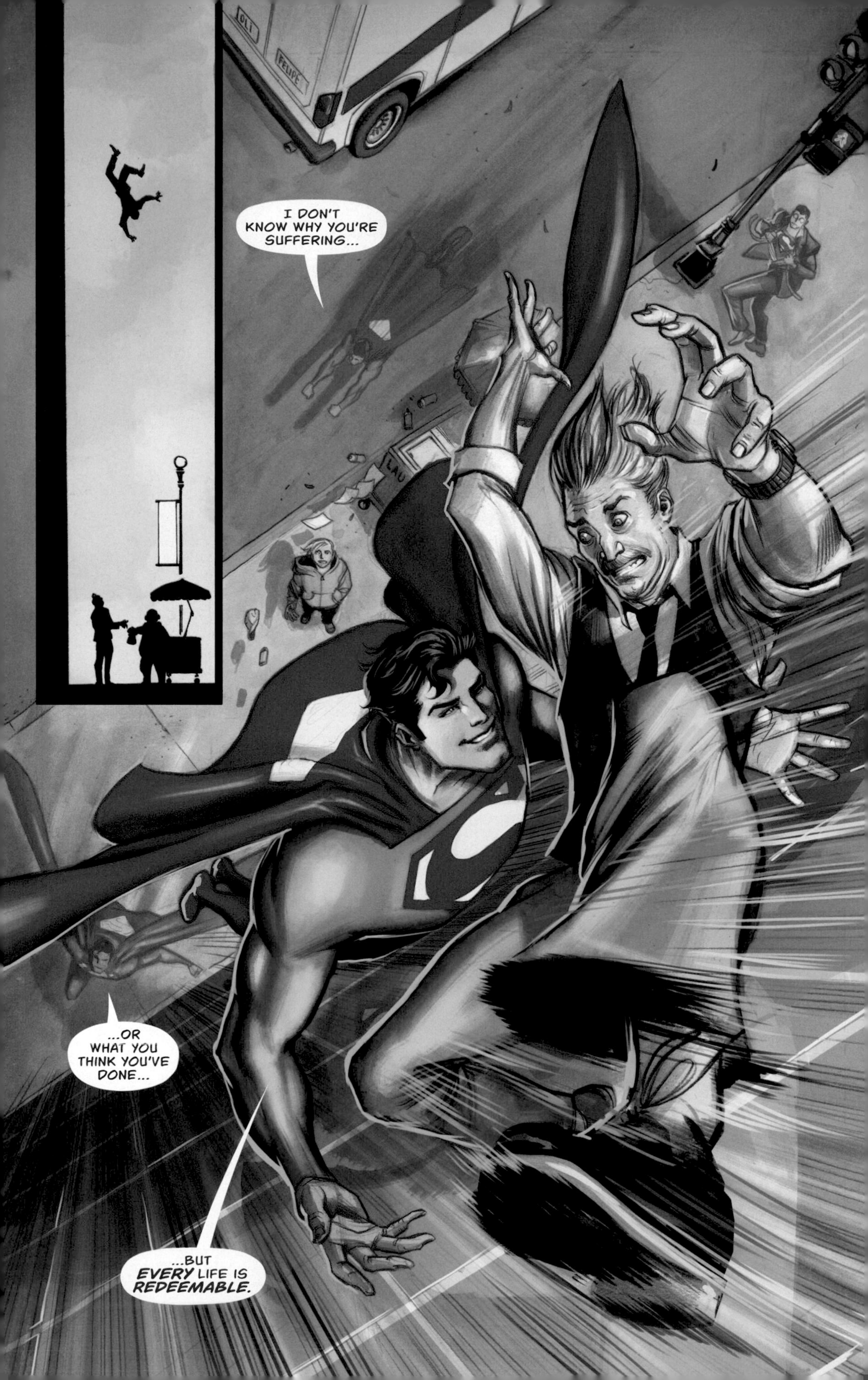
I DON'T KNOW WHY YOU'RE SUFFERING...
...OR WHAT YOU THINK YOU'VE DONE...
...BUT *EVERY* LIFE IS *REDEEMABLE.*

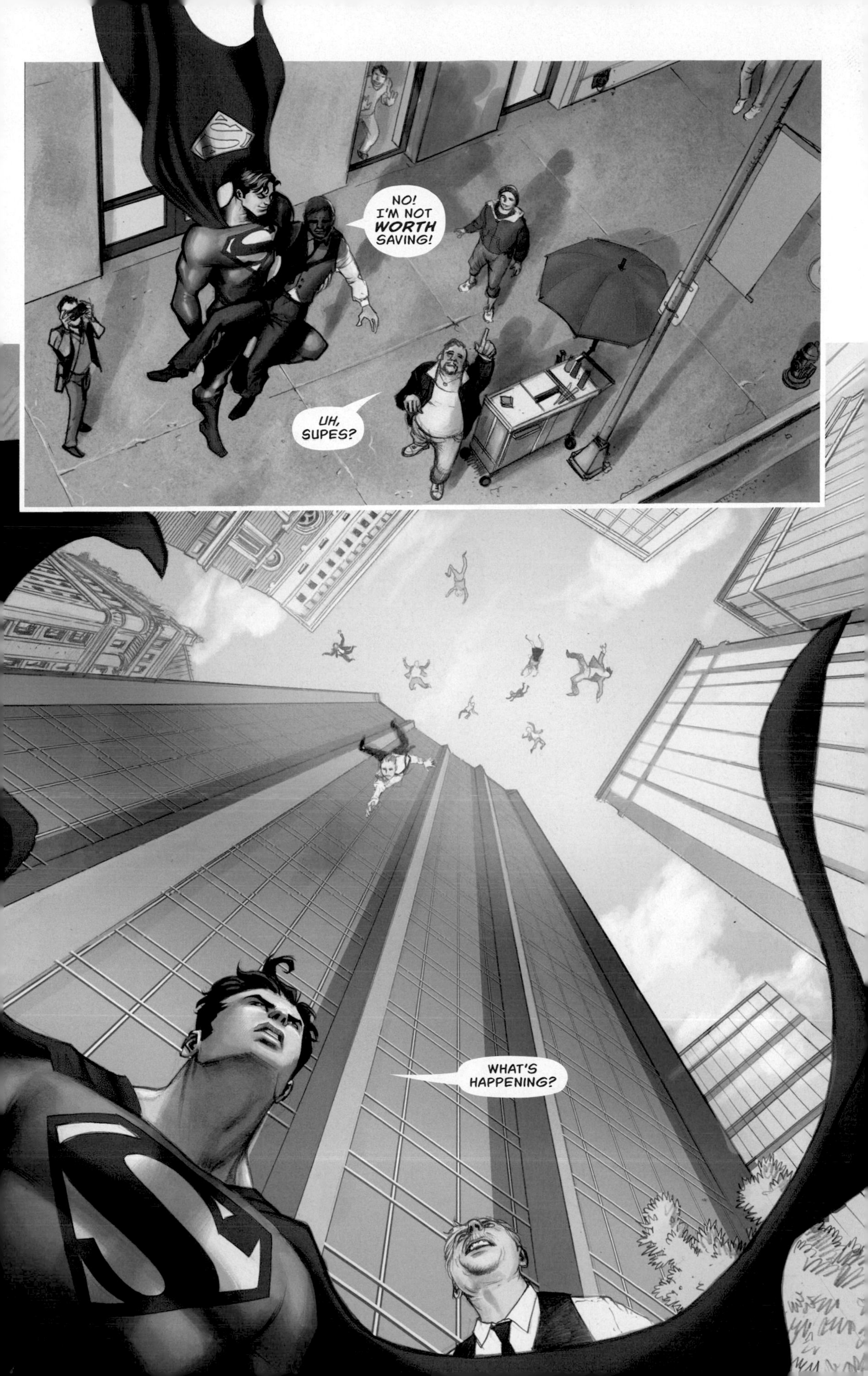
NO! I'M NOT WORTH SAVING!
UH, SUPES?
WHAT'S HAPPENING?

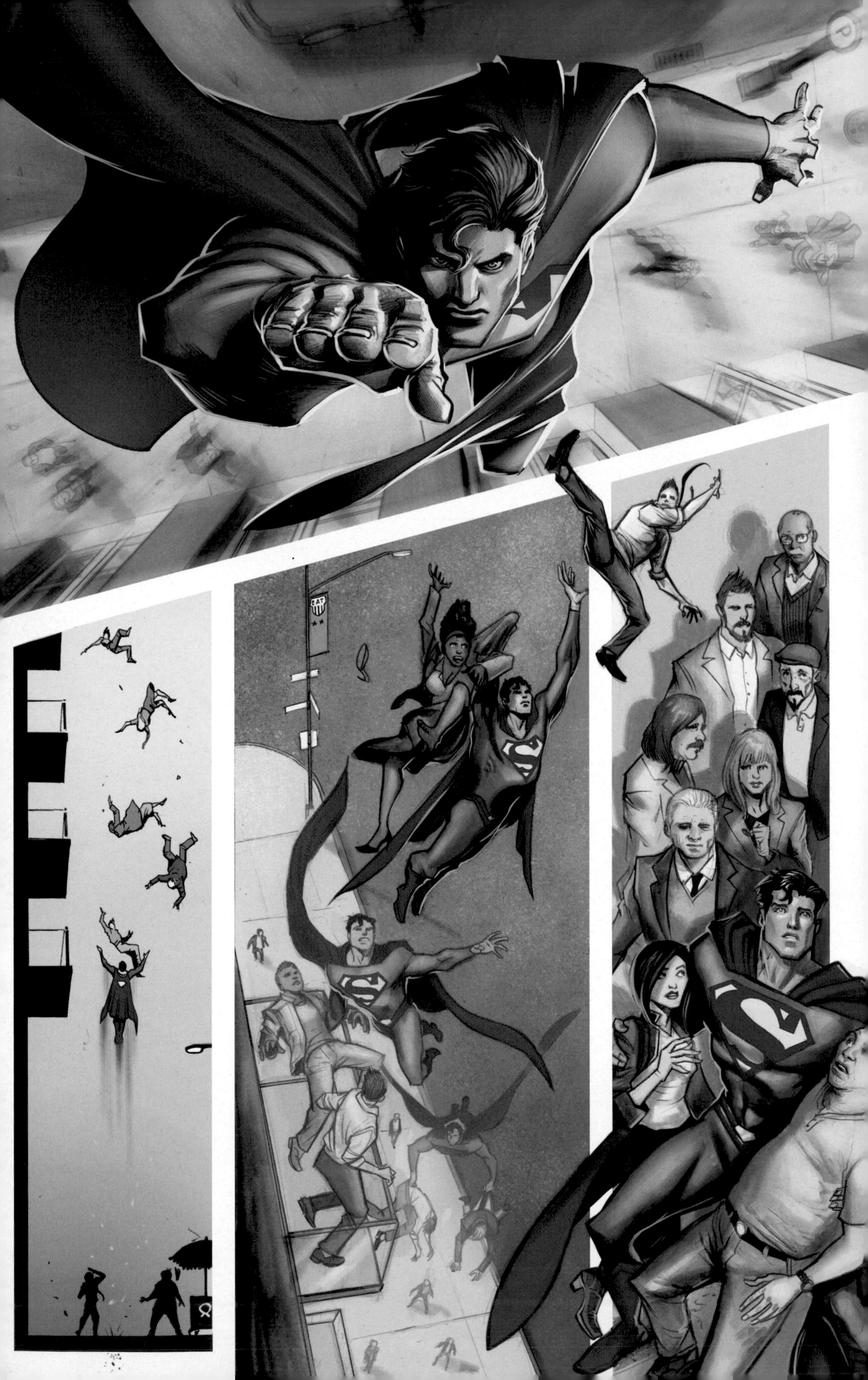

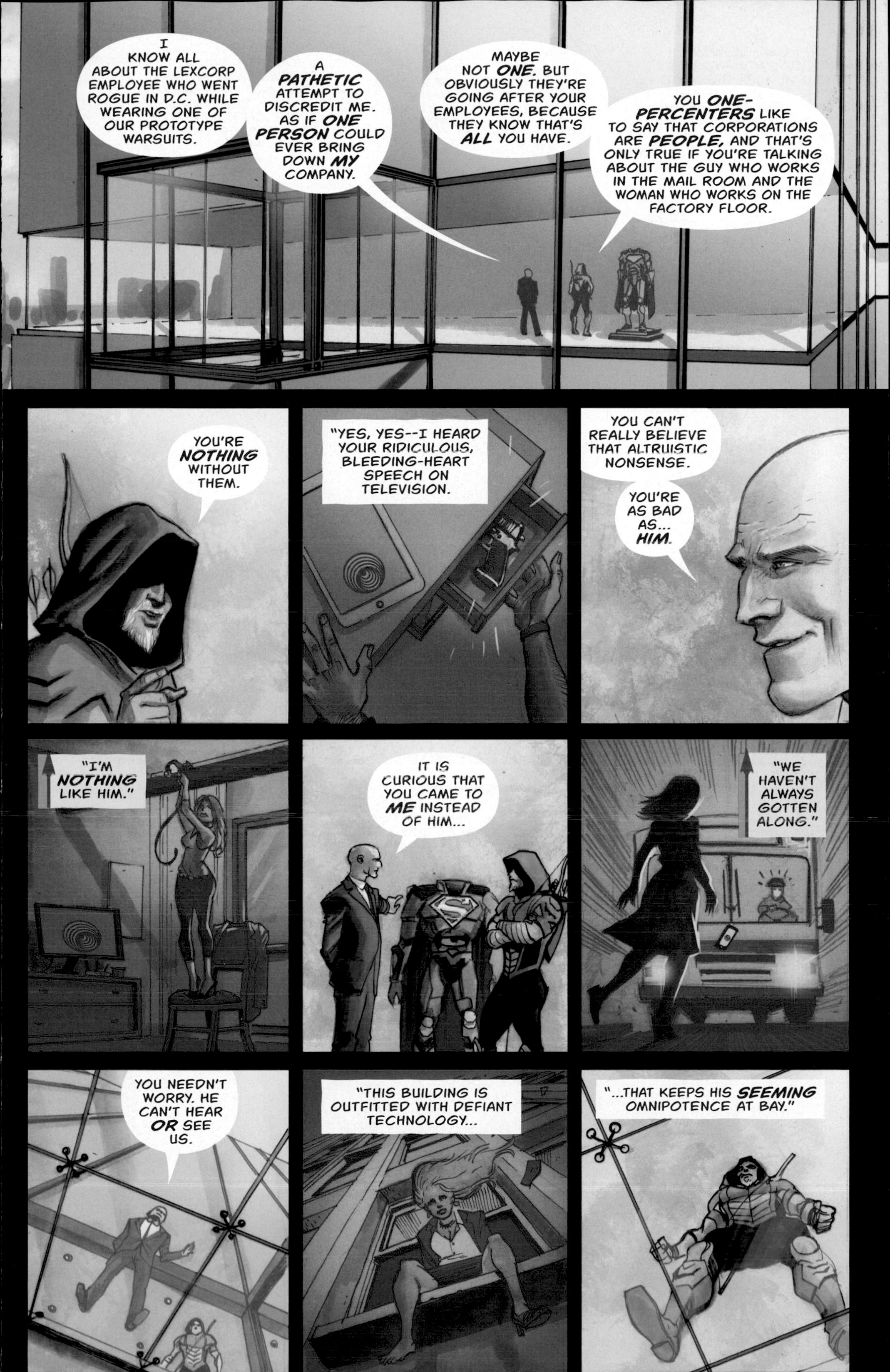
I KNOW ALL ABOUT THE LEXCORP EMPLOYEE WHO WENT ROGUE IN D.C. WHILE WEARING ONE OF OUR PROTOTYPE WARSUITS.
A PATHETIC ATTEMPT TO DISCREDIT ME. AS IF ONE PERSON COULD EVER BRING DOWN MY COMPANY.
MAYBE NOT ONE. BUT OBVIOUSLY THEY'RE GOING AFTER YOUR EMPLOYEES, BECAUSE THEY KNOW THAT'S ALL YOU HAVE.
YOU ONE-PERCENTERS LIKE TO SAY THAT CORPORATIONS ARE PEOPLE, AND THAT'S ONLY TRUE IF YOU'RE TALKING ABOUT THE GUY WHO WORKS IN THE MAIL ROOM AND THE WOMAN WHO WORKS ON THE FACTORY FLOOR.
YOU'RE NOTHING WITHOUT THEM.
"YES, YES--I HEARD YOUR RIDICULOUS, BLEEDING-HEART SPEECH ON TELEVISION.
YOU CAN'T REALLY BELIEVE THAT ALTRUISTIC NONSENSE.
YOU'RE AS BAD AS... HIM.
"I'M NOTHING LIKE HIM."
IT IS CURIOUS THAT YOU CAME TO ME INSTEAD OF HIM...
"WE HAVEN'T ALWAYS GOTTEN ALONG."
YOU NEEDN'T WORRY. HE CAN'T HEAR OR SEE US.
"THIS BUILDING IS OUTFITTED WITH DEFIANT TECHNOLOGY...
"...THAT KEEPS HIS SEEMING OMNIPOTENCE AT BAY."

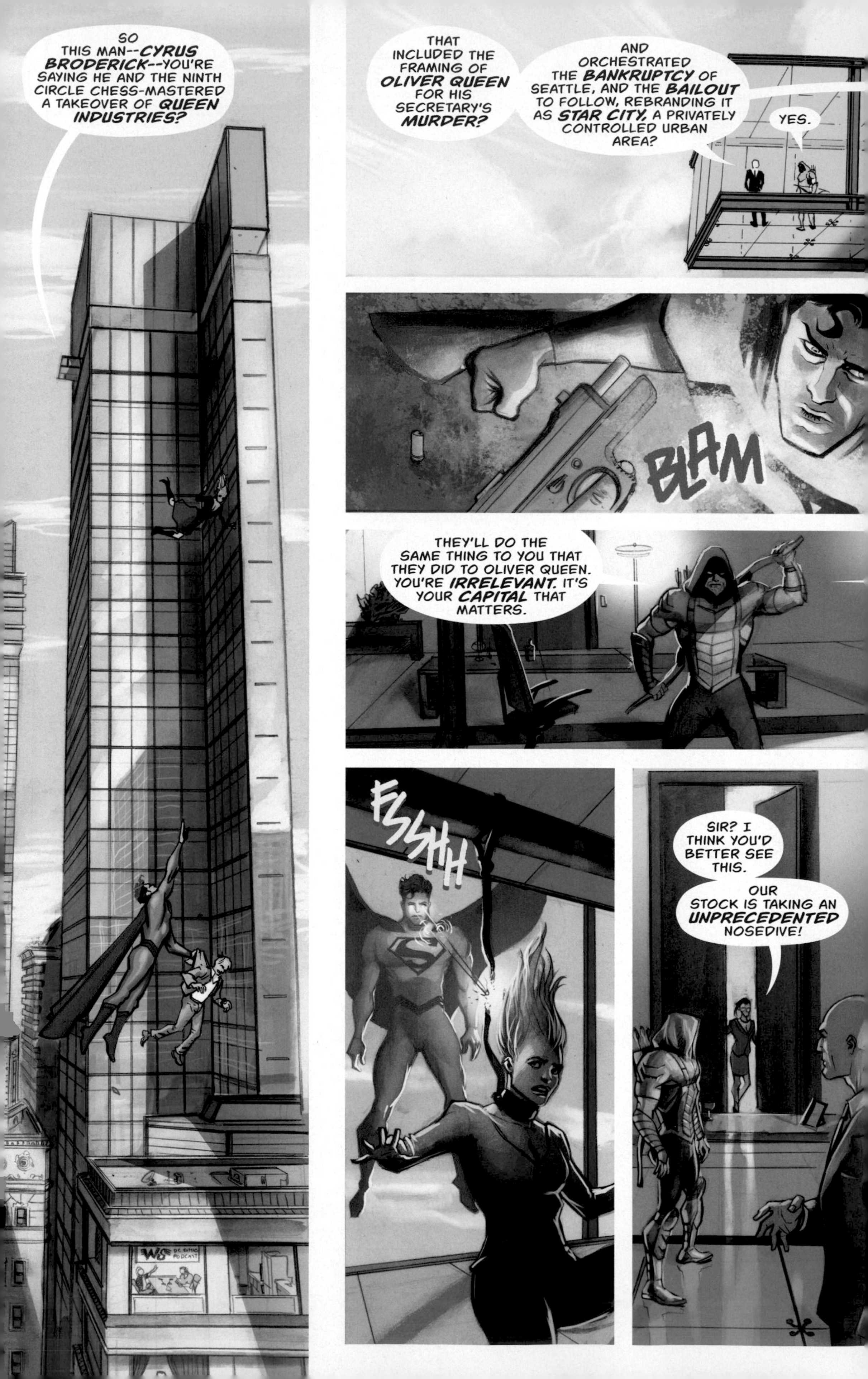
SO THIS MAN--CYRUS BRODERICK--YOU'RE SAYING HE AND THE NINTH CIRCLE CHESS-MASTERED A TAKEOVER OF QUEEN INDUSTRIES?
THAT INCLUDED THE FRAMING OF OLIVER QUEEN FOR HIS SECRETARY'S MURDER?
AND ORCHESTRATED THE BANKRUPTCY OF SEATTLE, AND THE BAILOUT TO FOLLOW, REBRANDING IT AS STAR CITY, A PRIVATELY CONTROLLED URBAN AREA?
YES.
BLAM
THEY'LL DO THE SAME THING TO YOU THAT THEY DID TO OLIVER QUEEN. YOU'RE IRRELEVANT. IT'S YOUR CAPITAL THAT MATTERS.
FSSHH
SIR? I THINK YOU'D BETTER SEE THIS.
OUR STOCK IS TAKING AN UNPRECEDENTED NOSEDIVE!

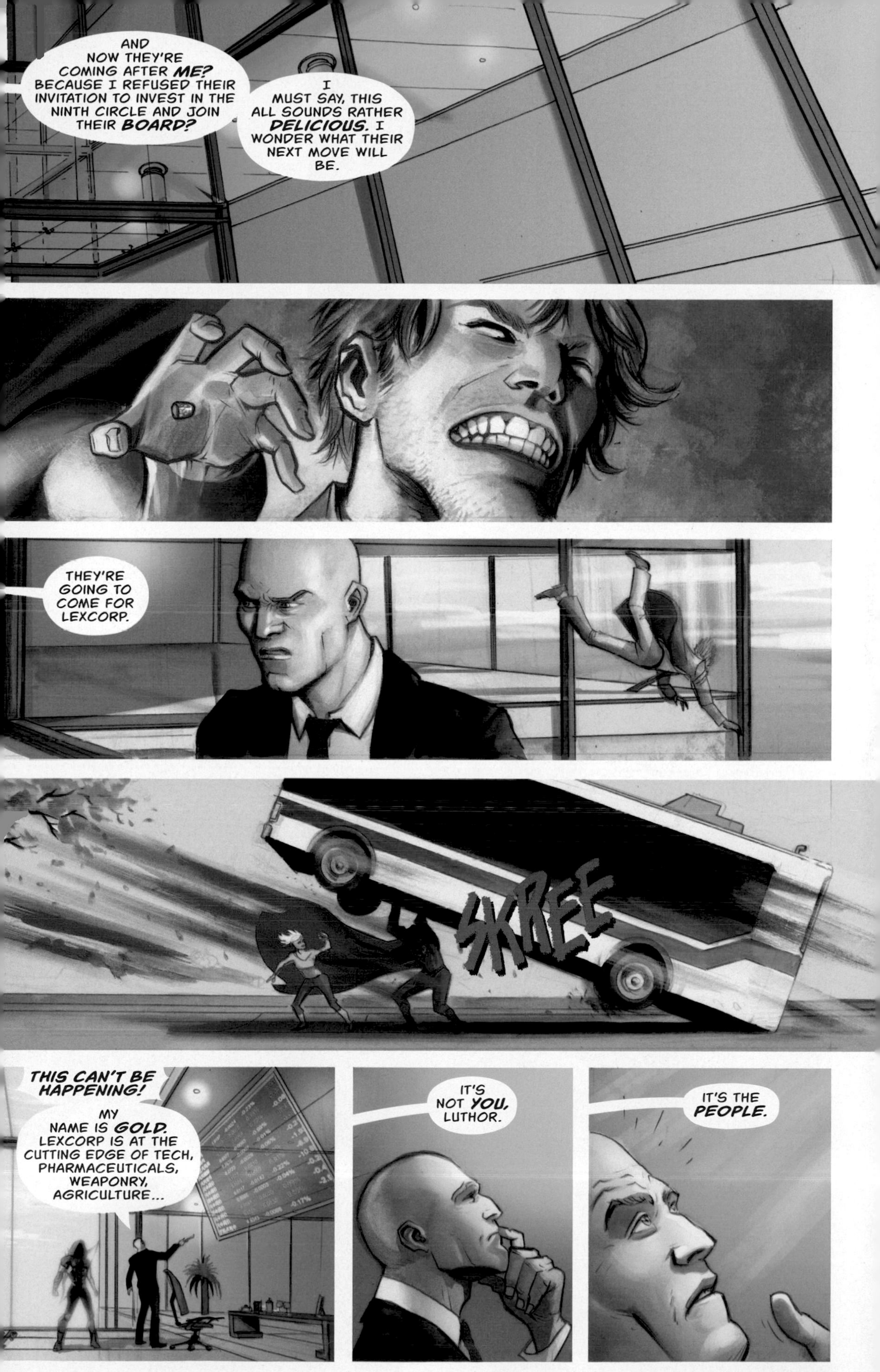
AND NOW THEY'RE COMING AFTER ME? BECAUSE I REFUSED THEIR INVITATION TO INVEST IN THE NINTH CIRCLE AND JOIN THEIR BOARD?
I MUST SAY, THIS ALL SOUNDS RATHER DELICIOUS. I WONDER WHAT THEIR NEXT MOVE WILL BE.
THEY'RE GOING TO COME FOR LEXCORP.
SKREE
THIS CAN'T BE HAPPENING!
MY NAME IS GOLD. LEXCORP IS AT THE CUTTING EDGE OF TECH, PHARMACEUTICALS, WEAPONRY, AGRICULTURE...
IT'S NOT YOU, LUTHOR.
IT'S THE PEOPLE.

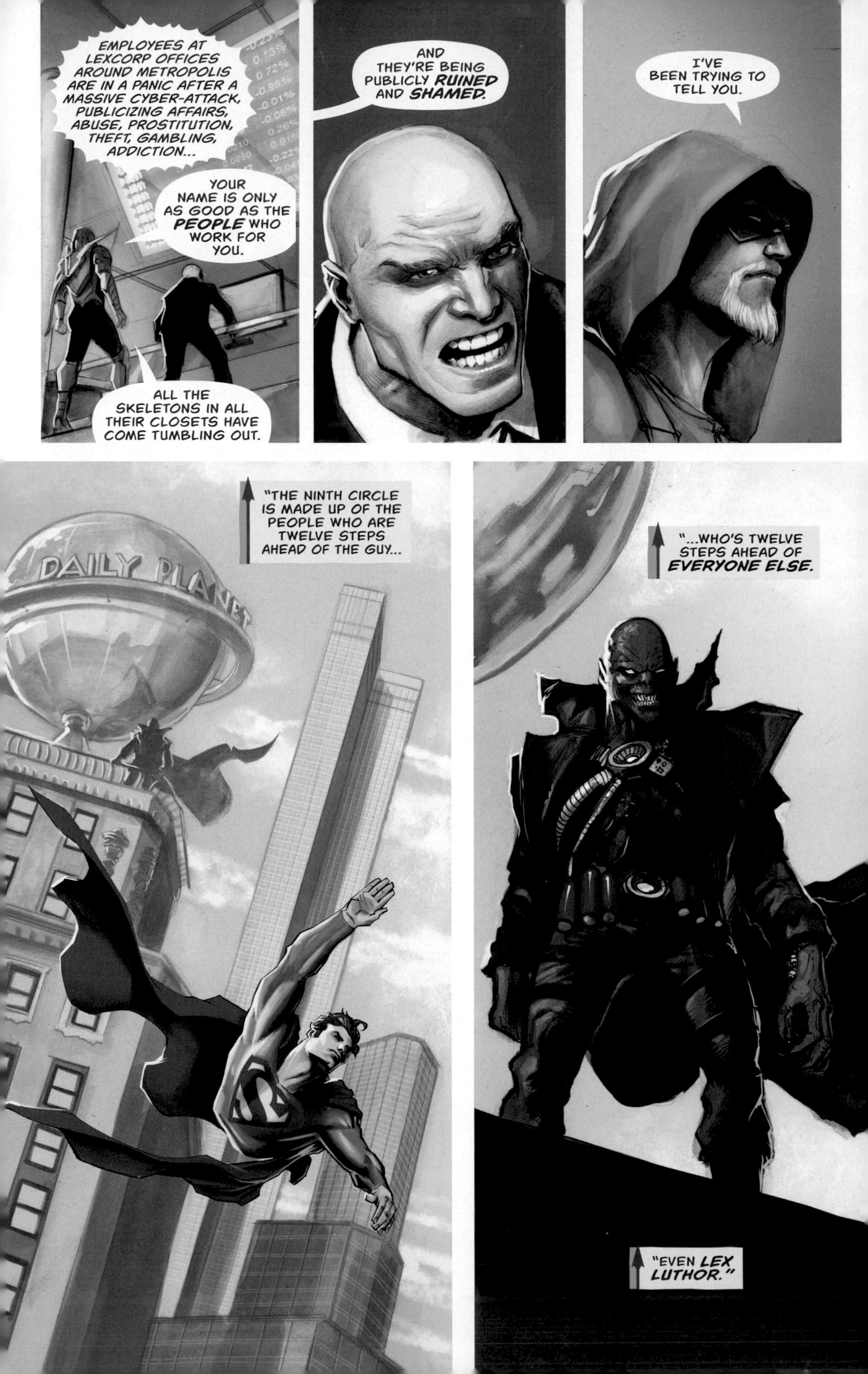
EMPLOYEES AT LEXCORP OFFICES AROUND METROPOLIS ARE IN A PANIC AFTER A MASSIVE CYBER-ATTACK, PUBLICIZING AFFAIRS, ABUSE, PROSTITUTION, THEFT, GAMBLING, ADDICTION...
YOUR NAME IS ONLY AS GOOD AS THE PEOPLE WHO WORK FOR YOU.
ALL THE SKELETONS IN ALL THEIR CLOSETS HAVE COME TUMBLING OUT.
AND THEY'RE BEING PUBLICLY RUINED AND SHAMED.
I'VE BEEN TRYING TO TELL YOU.
DAILY PLANET
"THE NINTH CIRCLE IS MADE UP OF THE PEOPLE WHO ARE TWELVE STEPS AHEAD OF THE GUY...
"...WHO'S TWELVE STEPS AHEAD OF EVERYONE ELSE.
"EVEN LEX LUTHOR."

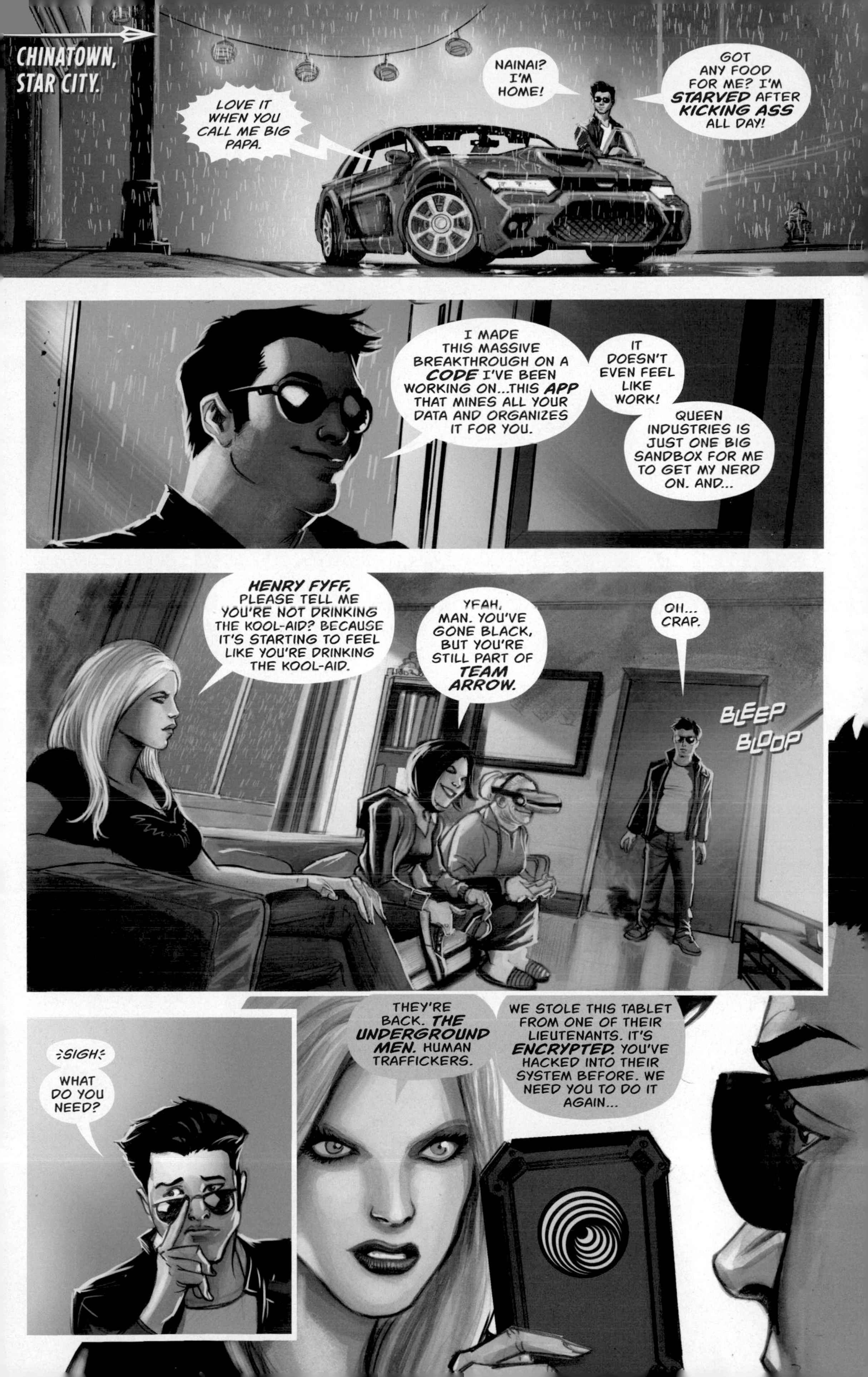
CHINATOWN, STAR CITY.
LOVE IT WHEN YOU CALL ME BIG PAPA.
NAINAI? I'M HOME!
GOT ANY FOOD FOR ME? I'M STARVED AFTER KICKING ASS ALL DAY!
I MADE THIS MASSIVE BREAKTHROUGH ON A CODE I'VE BEEN WORKING ON...THIS APP THAT MINES ALL YOUR DATA AND ORGANIZES IT FOR YOU.
IT DOESN'T EVEN FEEL LIKE WORK!
QUEEN INDUSTRIES IS JUST ONE BIG SANDBOX FOR ME TO GET MY NERD ON. AND...
HENRY FYFF, PLEASE TELL ME YOU'RE NOT DRINKING THE KOOL-AID? BECAUSE IT'S STARTING TO FEEL LIKE YOU'RE DRINKING THE KOOL-AID.
YEAH, MAN. YOU'VE GONE BLACK, BUT YOU'RE STILL PART OF TEAM ARROW.
OH... CRAP.
BLEEP BLOOP
SIGH
WHAT DO YOU NEED?
THEY'RE BACK. THE UNDERGROUND MEN. HUMAN TRAFFICKERS.
WE STOLE THIS TABLET FROM ONE OF THEIR LIEUTENANTS. IT'S ENCRYPTED. YOU'VE HACKED INTO THEIR SYSTEM BEFORE. WE NEED YOU TO DO IT AGAIN...

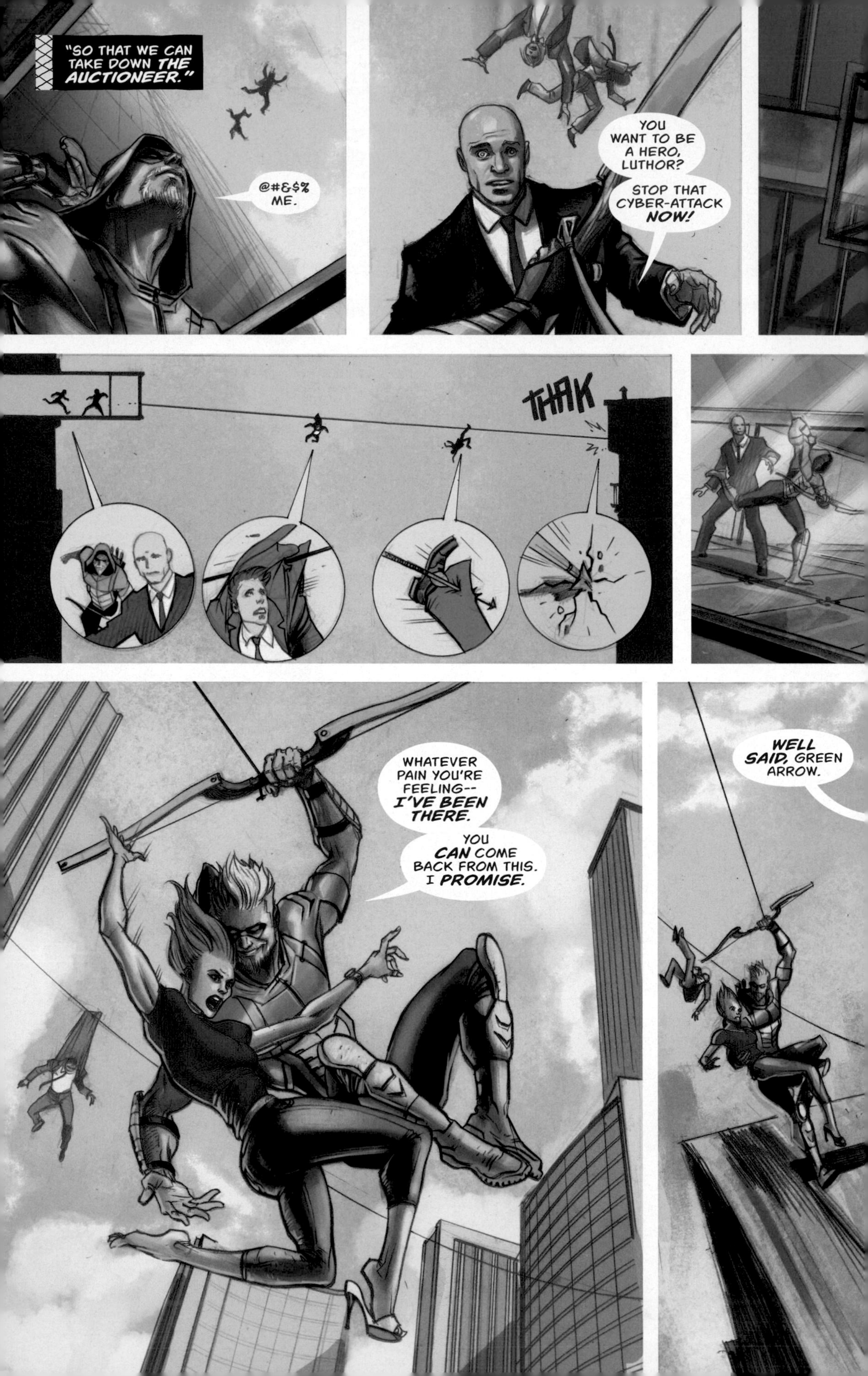

"SO THAT WE CAN TAKE DOWN THE AUCTIONEER."
@#&$% ME.
YOU WANT TO BE A HERO, LUTHOR?
STOP THAT CYBER-ATTACK NOW!
THAK
WHATEVER PAIN YOU'RE FEELING-- I'VE BEEN THERE.
YOU CAN COME BACK FROM THIS. I PROMISE.
WELL SAID, GREEN ARROW.

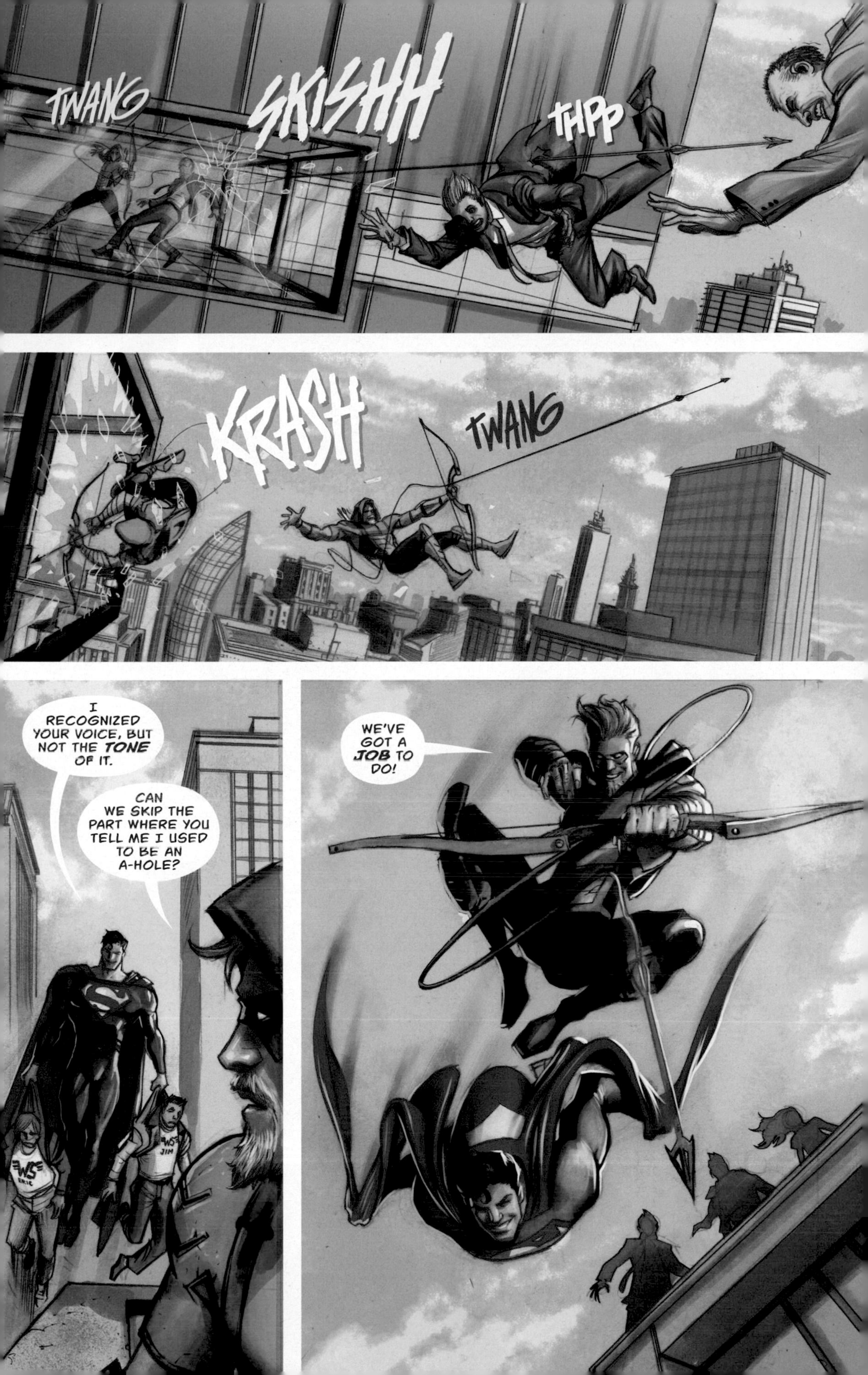
TWANG
SKISHH
THPP
KRASH
TWANG
I RECOGNIZED YOUR VOICE, BUT NOT THE *TONE* OF IT.
CAN WE SKIP THE PART WHERE YOU TELL ME I USED TO BE AN A-HOLE?
WE'VE GOT A *JOB* TO DO!

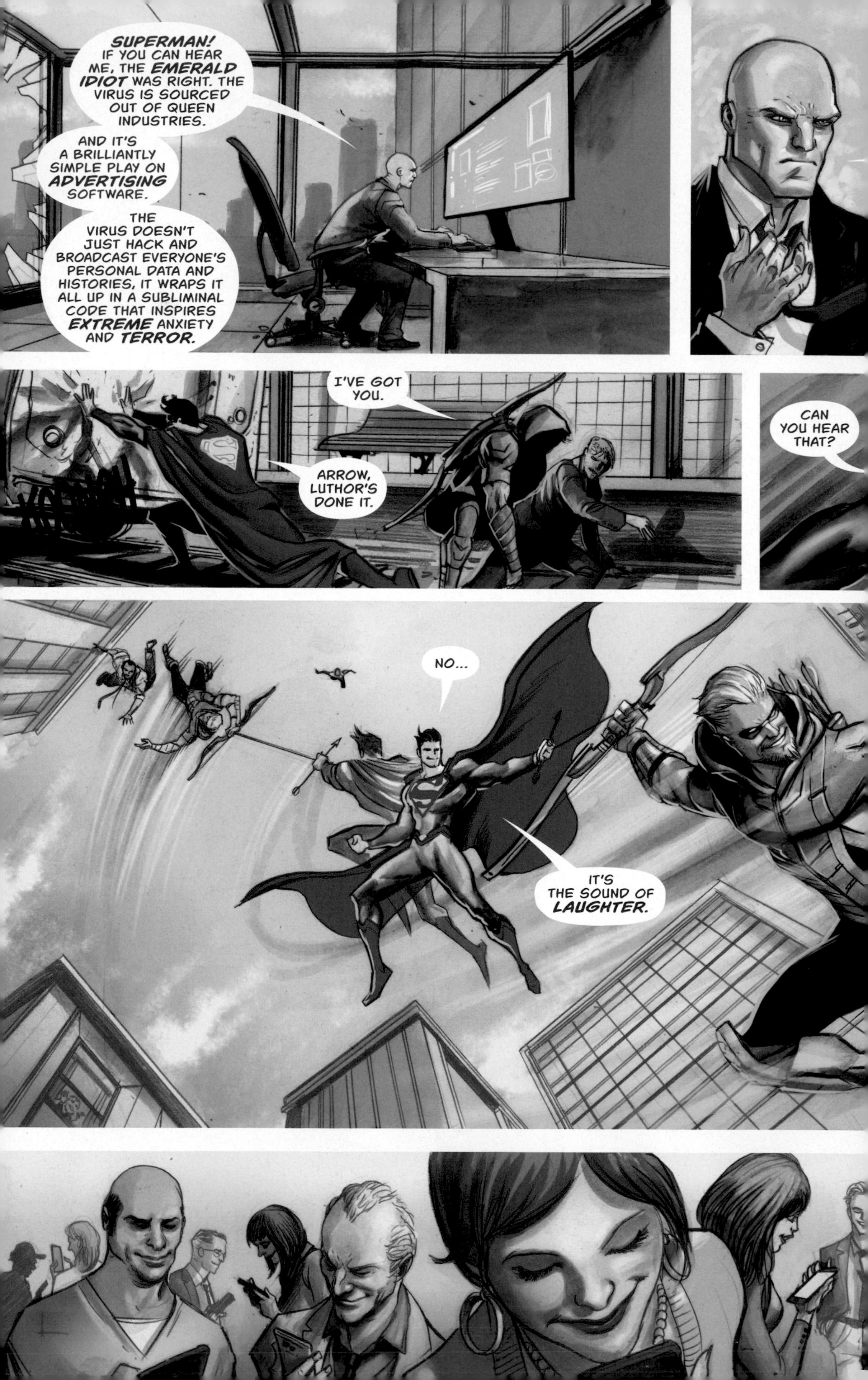

SUPERMAN! IF YOU CAN HEAR ME, THE EMERALD IDIOT WAS RIGHT. THE VIRUS IS SOURCED OUT OF QUEEN INDUSTRIES.
AND IT'S A BRILLIANTLY SIMPLE PLAY ON ADVERTISING SOFTWARE.
THE VIRUS DOESN'T JUST HACK AND BROADCAST EVERYONE'S PERSONAL DATA AND HISTORIES, IT WRAPS IT ALL UP IN A SUBLIMINAL CODE THAT INSPIRES EXTREME ANXIETY AND TERROR.
I'VE GOT YOU.
ARROW, LUTHOR'S DONE IT.
CAN YOU HEAR THAT?
NO...
IT'S THE SOUND OF LAUGHTER.

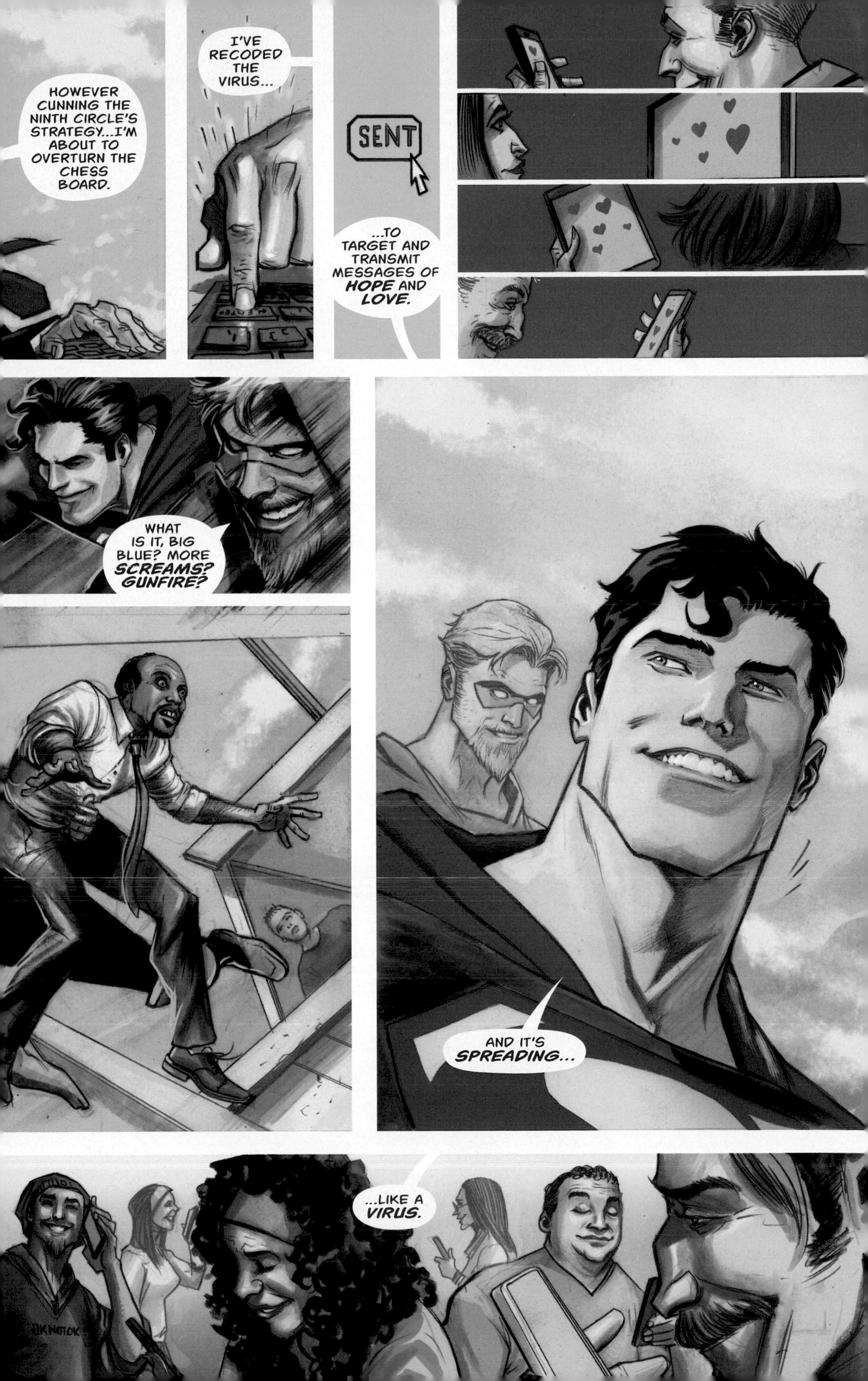
HOWEVER CUNNING THE NINTH CIRCLE'S STRATEGY...I'M ABOUT TO OVERTURN THE CHESS BOARD.
I'VE RECODED THE VIRUS...
SENT
...TO TARGET AND TRANSMIT MESSAGES OF HOPE AND LOVE.
WHAT IS IT, BIG BLUE? MORE SCREAMS? GUNFIRE?
AND IT'S SPREADING...
...LIKE A VIRUS.

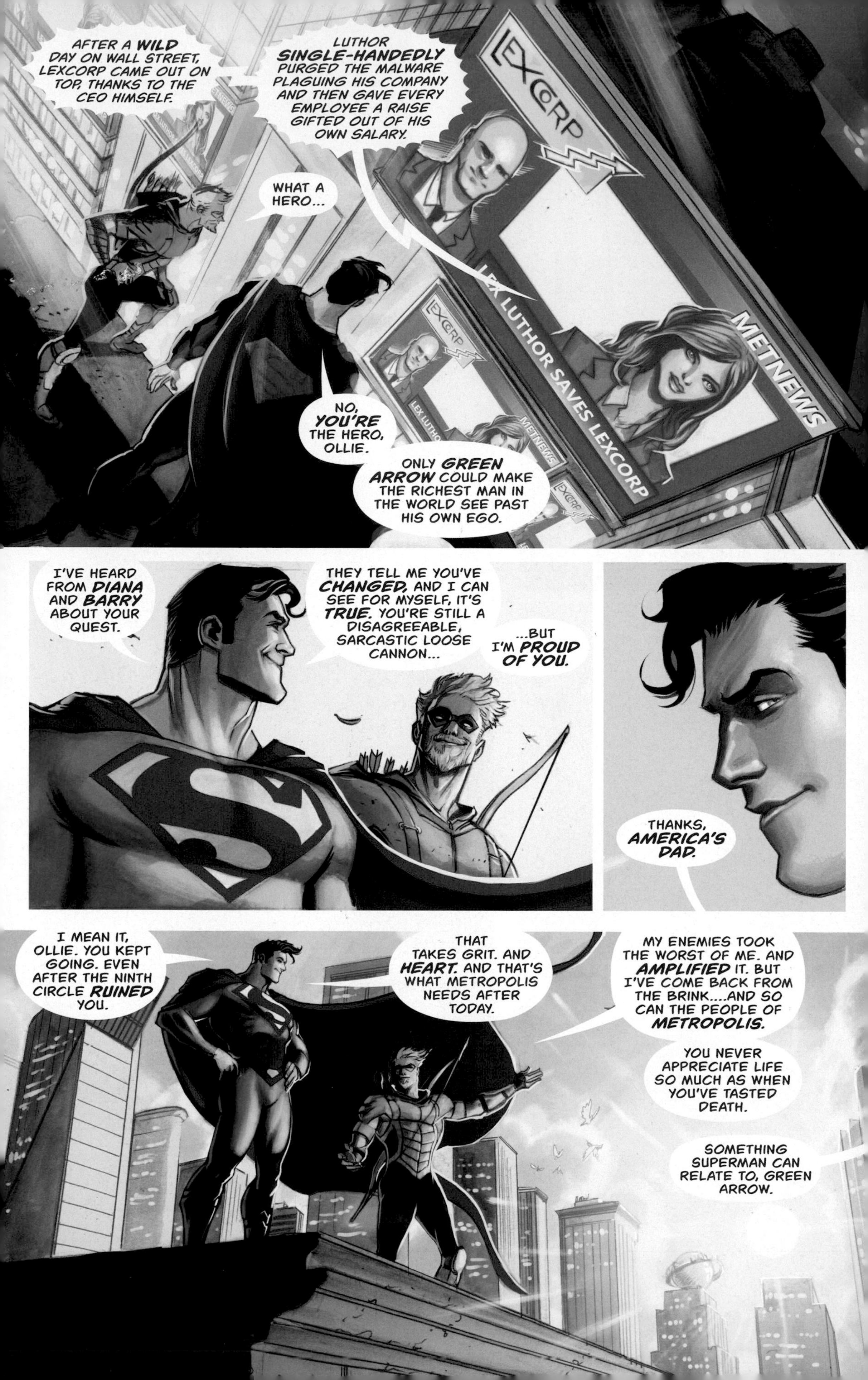
AFTER A WILD DAY ON WALL STREET, LEXCORP CAME OUT ON TOP, THANKS TO THE CEO HIMSELF.
LUTHOR SINGLE-HANDEDLY PURGED THE MALWARE PLAGUING HIS COMPANY AND THEN GAVE EVERY EMPLOYEE A RAISE GIFTED OUT OF HIS OWN SALARY.
LEXCORP
LEX LUTHOR SAVES LEXCORP
METNEWS
WHAT A HERO...
NO, YOU'RE THE HERO, OLLIE.
ONLY GREEN ARROW COULD MAKE THE RICHEST MAN IN THE WORLD SEE PAST HIS OWN EGO.
I'VE HEARD FROM DIANA AND BARRY ABOUT YOUR QUEST.
THEY TELL ME YOU'VE CHANGED, AND I CAN SEE FOR MYSELF, IT'S TRUE. YOU'RE STILL A DISAGREEABLE, SARCASTIC LOOSE CANNON...
...BUT I'M PROUD OF YOU.
THANKS, AMERICA'S DAD.
I MEAN IT, OLLIE. YOU KEPT GOING. EVEN AFTER THE NINTH CIRCLE RUINED YOU.
THAT TAKES GRIT. AND HEART. AND THAT'S WHAT METROPOLIS NEEDS AFTER TODAY.
MY ENEMIES TOOK THE WORST OF ME. AND AMPLIFIED IT. BUT I'VE COME BACK FROM THE BRINK....AND SO CAN THE PEOPLE OF METROPOLIS.
YOU NEVER APPRECIATE LIFE SO MUCH AS WHEN YOU'VE TASTED DEATH.
SOMETHING SUPERMAN CAN RELATE TO, GREEN ARROW.

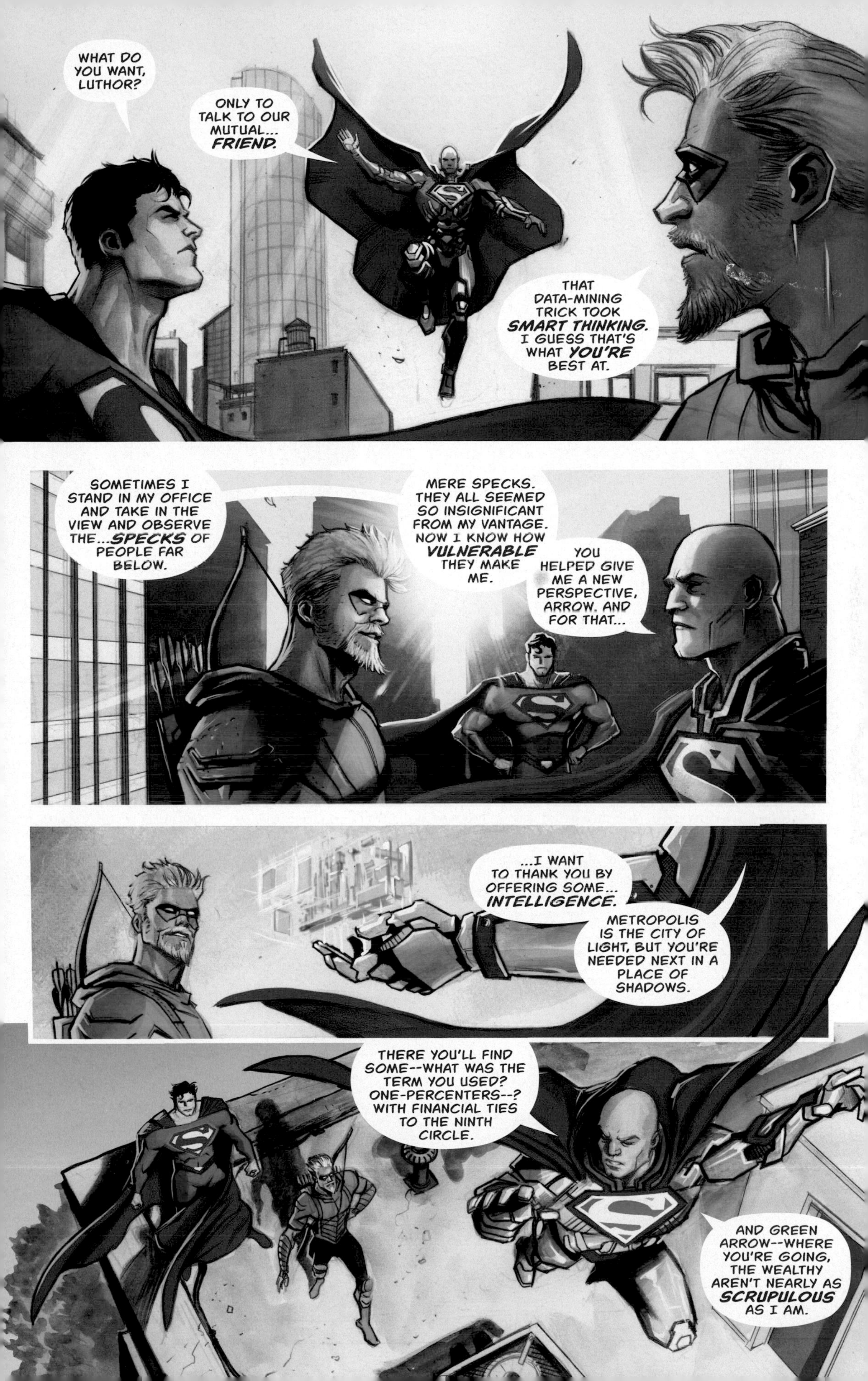
WHAT DO YOU WANT, LUTHOR?
ONLY TO TALK TO OUR MUTUAL... FRIEND.
THAT DATA-MINING TRICK TOOK SMART THINKING. I GUESS THAT'S WHAT YOU'RE BEST AT.
SOMETIMES I STAND IN MY OFFICE AND TAKE IN THE VIEW AND OBSERVE THE...SPECKS OF PEOPLE FAR BELOW.
MERE SPECKS. THEY ALL SEEMED SO INSIGNIFICANT FROM MY VANTAGE. NOW I KNOW HOW VULNERABLE THEY MAKE ME.
YOU HELPED GIVE ME A NEW PERSPECTIVE, ARROW. AND FOR THAT...
...I WANT TO THANK YOU BY OFFERING SOME... INTELLIGENCE.
METROPOLIS IS THE CITY OF LIGHT, BUT YOU'RE NEEDED NEXT IN A PLACE OF SHADOWS.
THERE YOU'LL FIND SOME--WHAT WAS THE TERM YOU USED? ONE-PERCENTERS--? WITH FINANCIAL TIES TO THE NINTH CIRCLE.
AND GREEN ARROW--WHERE YOU'RE GOING, THE WEALTHY AREN'T NEARLY AS SCRUPULOUS AS I AM.

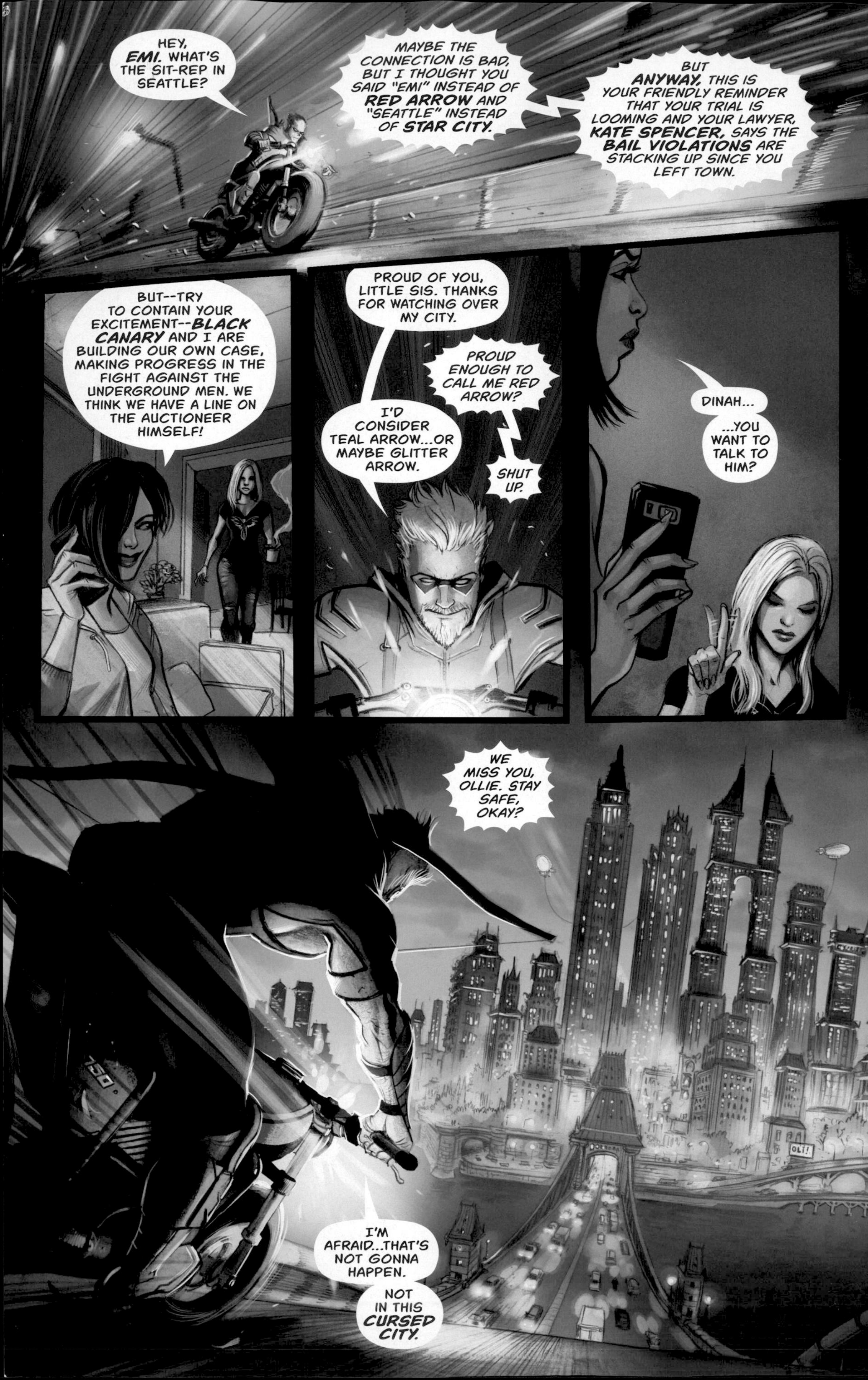
HEY, EMI. WHAT'S THE SIT-REP IN SEATTLE?
MAYBE THE CONNECTION IS BAD, BUT I THOUGHT YOU SAID "EMI" INSTEAD OF RED ARROW AND "SEATTLE" INSTEAD OF STAR CITY.
BUT ANYWAY, THIS IS YOUR FRIENDLY REMINDER THAT YOUR TRIAL IS LOOMING AND YOUR LAWYER, KATE SPENCER, SAYS THE BAIL VIOLATIONS ARE STACKING UP SINCE YOU LEFT TOWN.
BUT--TRY TO CONTAIN YOUR EXCITEMENT--BLACK CANARY AND I ARE BUILDING OUR OWN CASE, MAKING PROGRESS IN THE FIGHT AGAINST THE UNDERGROUND MEN. WE THINK WE HAVE A LINE ON THE AUCTIONEER HIMSELF!
PROUD OF YOU, LITTLE SIS. THANKS FOR WATCHING OVER MY CITY.
PROUD ENOUGH TO CALL ME RED ARROW?
I'D CONSIDER TEAL ARROW...OR MAYBE GLITTER ARROW.
SHUT UP.
DINAH...
...YOU WANT TO TALK TO HIM?
WE MISS YOU, OLLIE. STAY SAFE, OKAY?
I'M AFRAID...THAT'S NOT GONNA HAPPEN.
NOT IN THIS CURSED CITY.

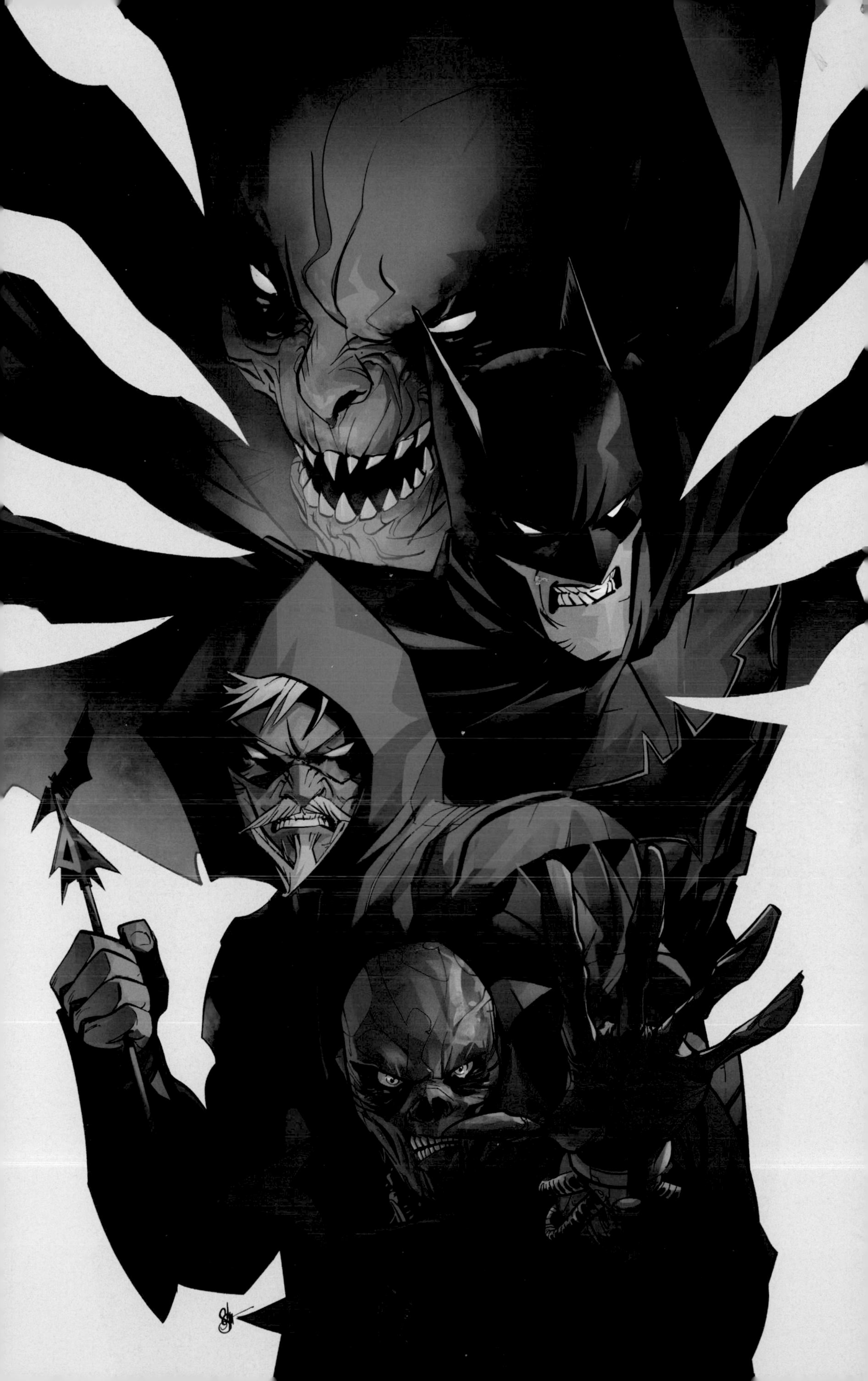

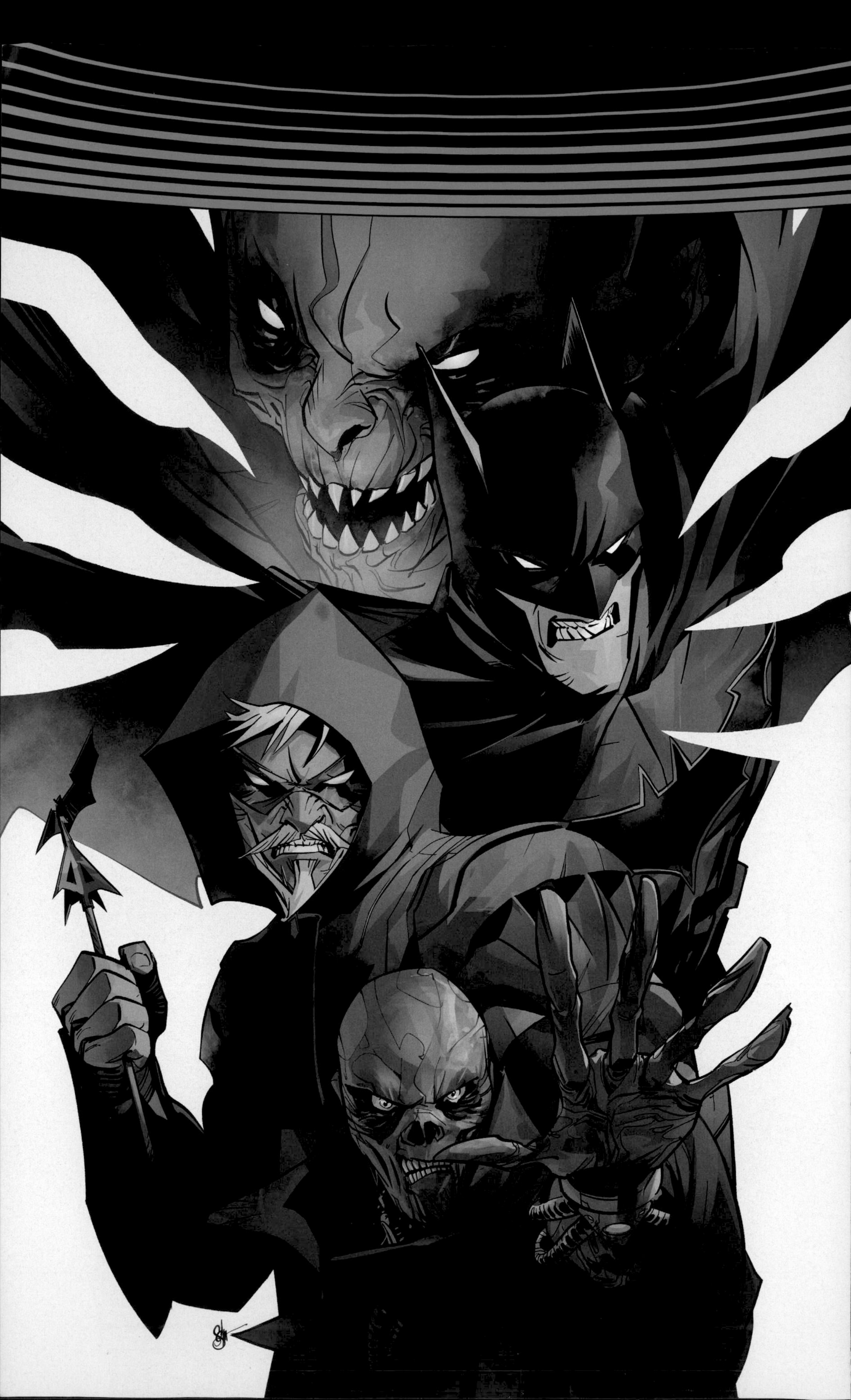

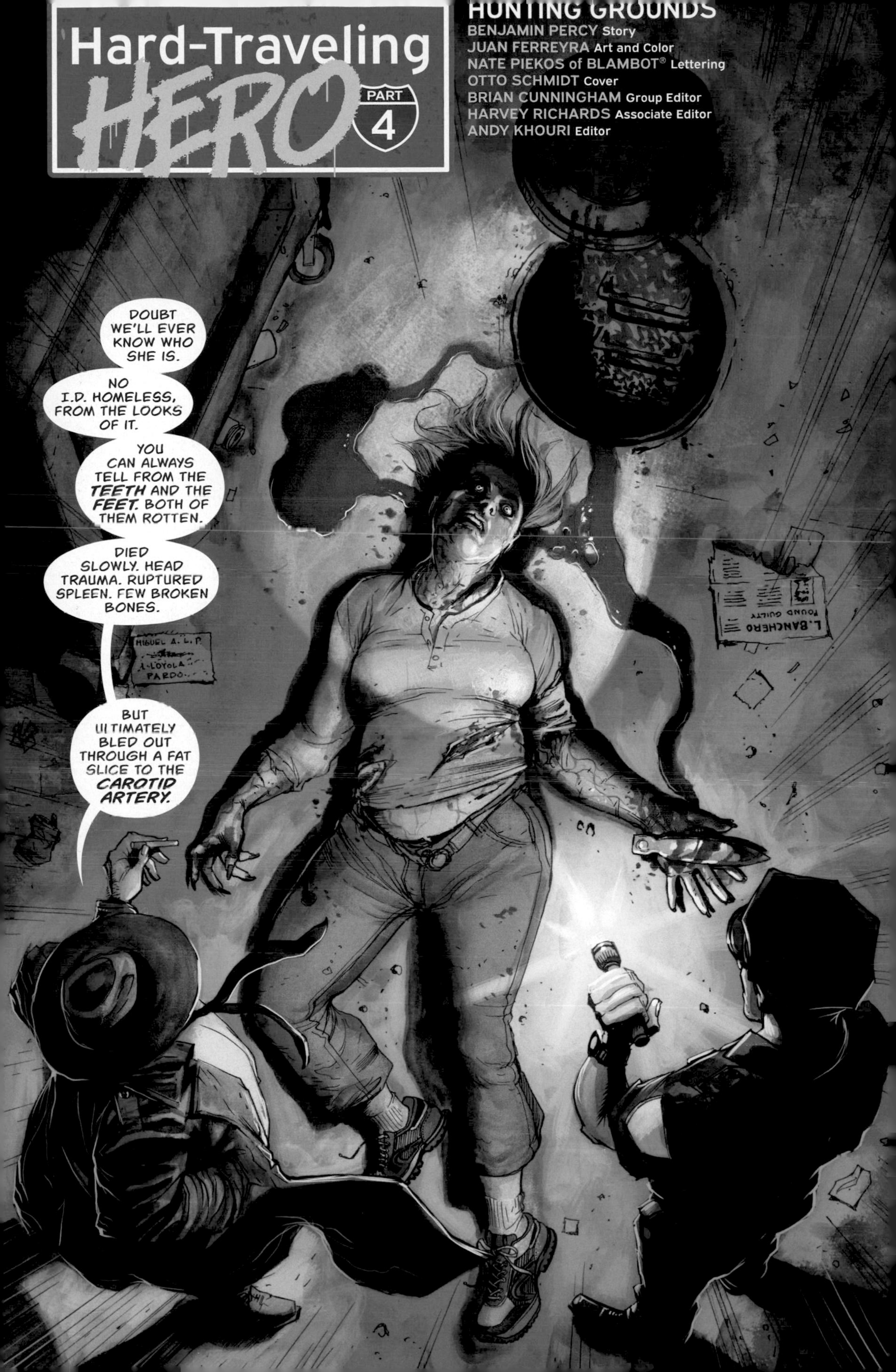
Hard-Traveling HERO PART 4
HUNTING GROUNDS
BENJAMIN PERCY Story
JUAN FERREYRA Art and Color
NATE PIEKOS of BLAMBOT® Lettering
OTTO SCHMIDT Cover
BRIAN CUNNINGHAM Group Editor
HARVEY RICHARDS Associate Editor
ANDY KHOURI Editor
DOUBT WE'LL EVER KNOW WHO SHE IS.
NO I.D. HOMELESS, FROM THE LOOKS OF IT.
YOU CAN ALWAYS TELL FROM THE *TEETH* AND THE *FEET.* BOTH OF THEM ROTTEN.
DIED SLOWLY. HEAD TRAUMA. RUPTURED SPLEEN. FEW BROKEN BONES.
BUT ULTIMATELY BLED OUT THROUGH A FAT SLICE TO THE *CAROTID ARTERY.*

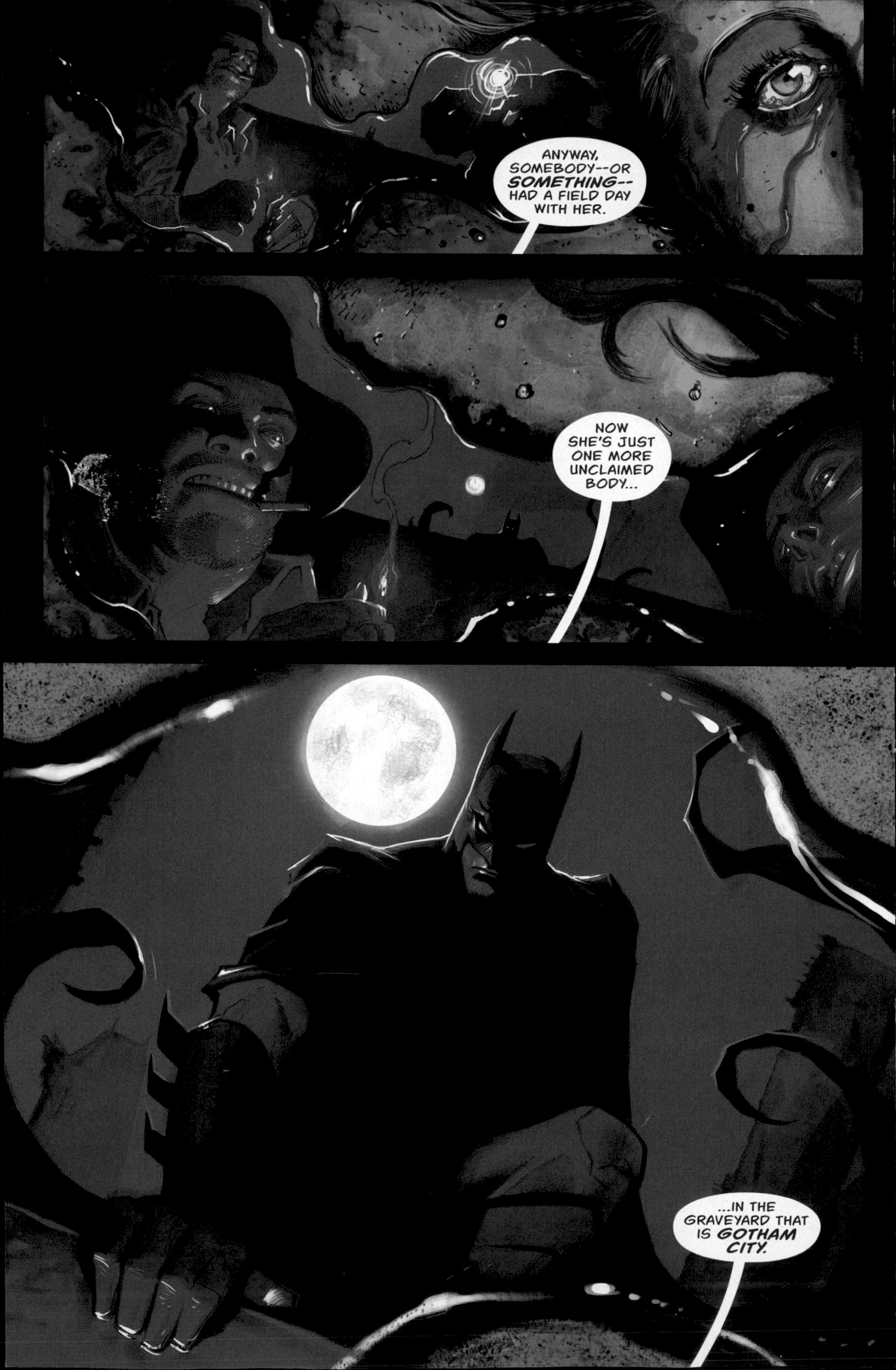
ANYWAY, SOMEBODY--OR SOMETHING--HAD A FIELD DAY WITH HER.
NOW SHE'S JUST ONE MORE UNCLAIMED BODY...
...IN THE GRAVEYARD THAT IS GOTHAM CITY.

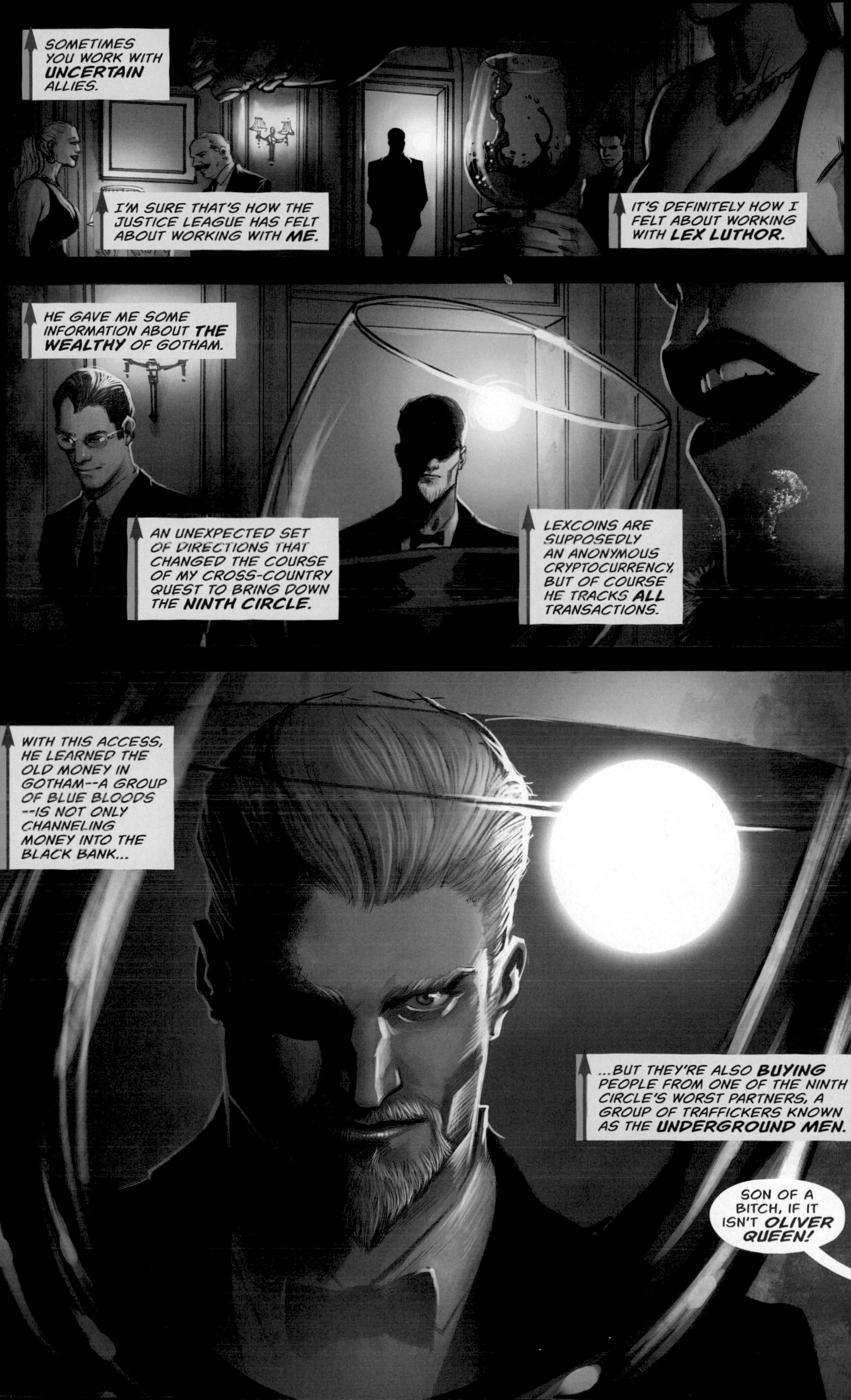
SOMETIMES YOU WORK WITH UNCERTAIN ALLIES.
I'M SURE THAT'S HOW THE JUSTICE LEAGUE HAS FELT ABOUT WORKING WITH ME.
IT'S DEFINITELY HOW I FELT ABOUT WORKING WITH LEX LUTHOR.
HE GAVE ME SOME INFORMATION ABOUT THE WEALTHY OF GOTHAM.
AN UNEXPECTED SET OF DIRECTIONS THAT CHANGED THE COURSE OF MY CROSS-COUNTRY QUEST TO BRING DOWN THE NINTH CIRCLE.
LEXCOINS ARE SUPPOSEDLY AN ANONYMOUS CRYPTOCURRENCY, BUT OF COURSE HE TRACKS ALL TRANSACTIONS.
WITH THIS ACCESS, HE LEARNED THE OLD MONEY IN GOTHAM--A GROUP OF BLUE BLOODS --IS NOT ONLY CHANNELING MONEY INTO THE BLACK BANK...
...BUT THEY'RE ALSO BUYING PEOPLE FROM ONE OF THE NINTH CIRCLE'S WORST PARTNERS, A GROUP OF TRAFFICKERS KNOWN AS THE UNDERGROUND MEN.
SON OF A BITCH, IF IT ISN'T OLIVER QUEEN!

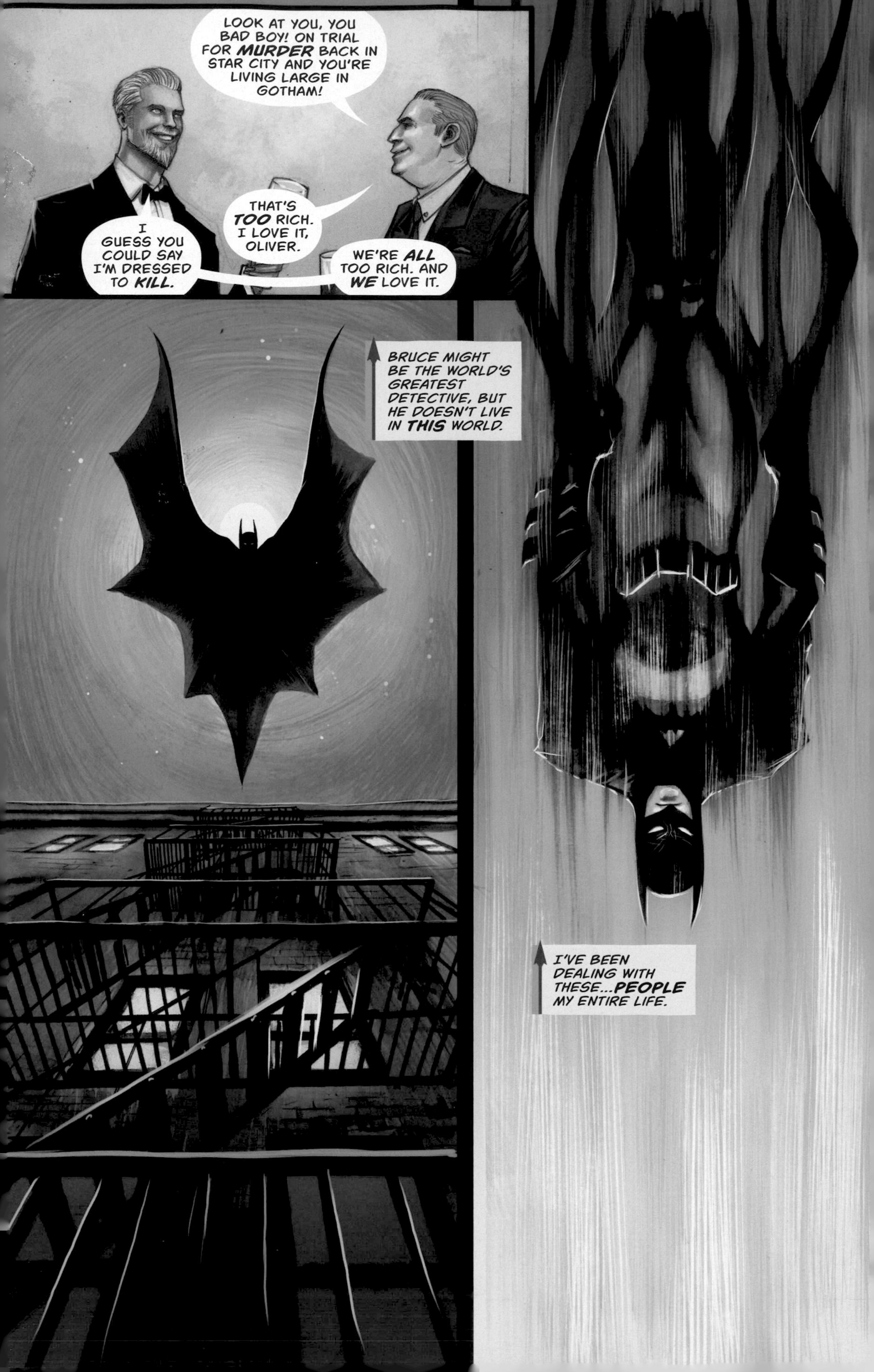
LOOK AT YOU, YOU BAD BOY! ON TRIAL FOR MURDER BACK IN STAR CITY AND YOU'RE LIVING LARGE IN GOTHAM!
I GUESS YOU COULD SAY I'M DRESSED TO KILL.
THAT'S TOO RICH. I LOVE IT, OLIVER.
WE'RE ALL TOO RICH. AND WE LOVE IT.
BRUCE MIGHT BE THE WORLD'S GREATEST DETECTIVE, BUT HE DOESN'T LIVE IN THIS WORLD.
I'VE BEEN DEALING WITH THESE...PEOPLE MY ENTIRE LIFE.

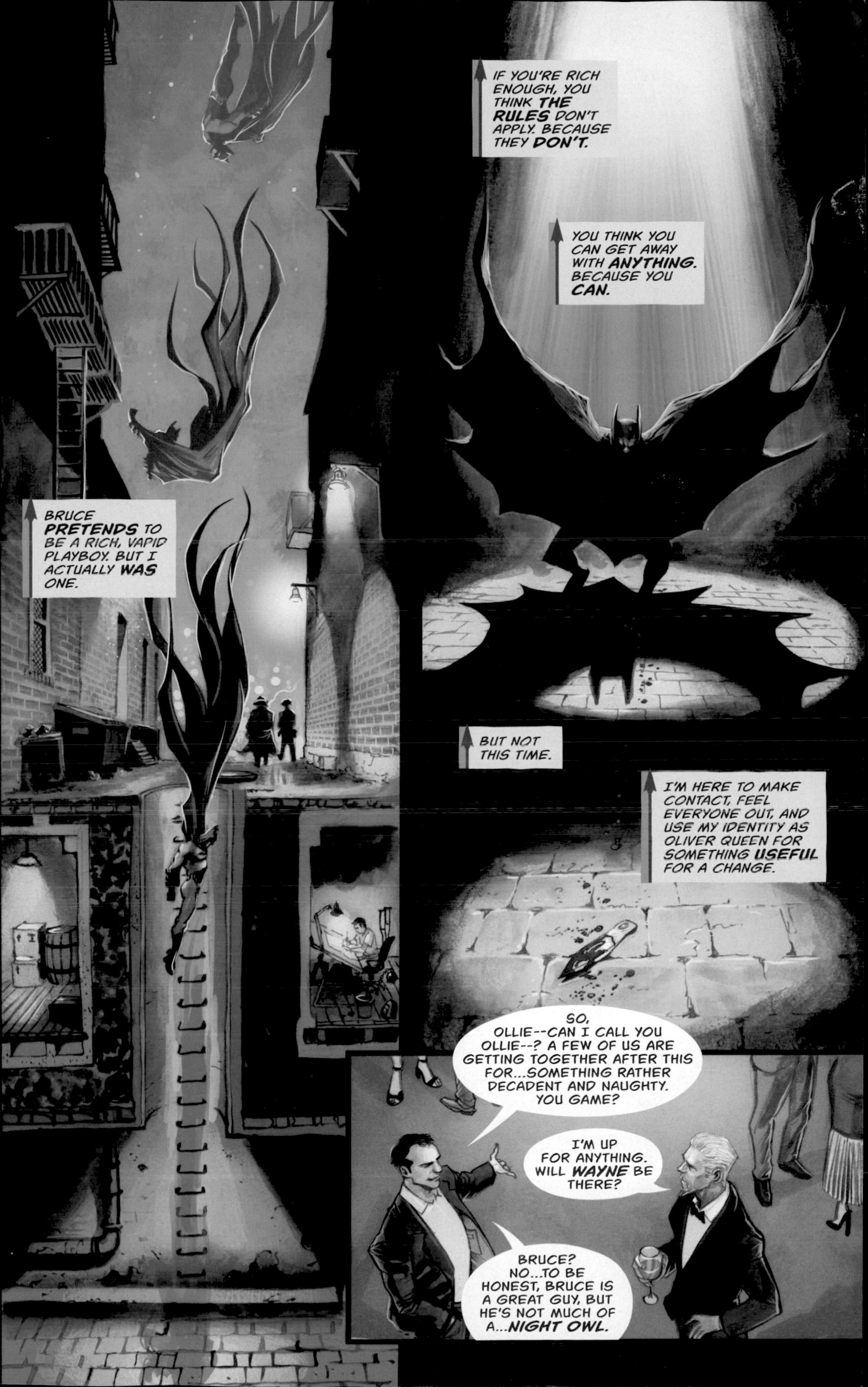
BRUCE PRETENDS TO BE A RICH, VAPID PLAYBOY. BUT I ACTUALLY WAS ONE.
IF YOU'RE RICH ENOUGH, YOU THINK THE RULES DON'T APPLY. BECAUSE THEY DON'T.
YOU THINK YOU CAN GET AWAY WITH ANYTHING. BECAUSE YOU CAN.
BUT NOT THIS TIME.
I'M HERE TO MAKE CONTACT, FEEL EVERYONE OUT, AND USE MY IDENTITY AS OLIVER QUEEN FOR SOMETHING USEFUL FOR A CHANGE.
SO, OLLIE--CAN I CALL YOU OLLIE--? A FEW OF US ARE GETTING TOGETHER AFTER THIS FOR...SOMETHING RATHER DECADENT AND NAUGHTY. YOU GAME?
I'M UP FOR ANYTHING. WILL WAYNE BE THERE?
BRUCE? NO...TO BE HONEST, BRUCE IS A GREAT GUY, BUT HE'S NOT MUCH OF A...NIGHT OWL.

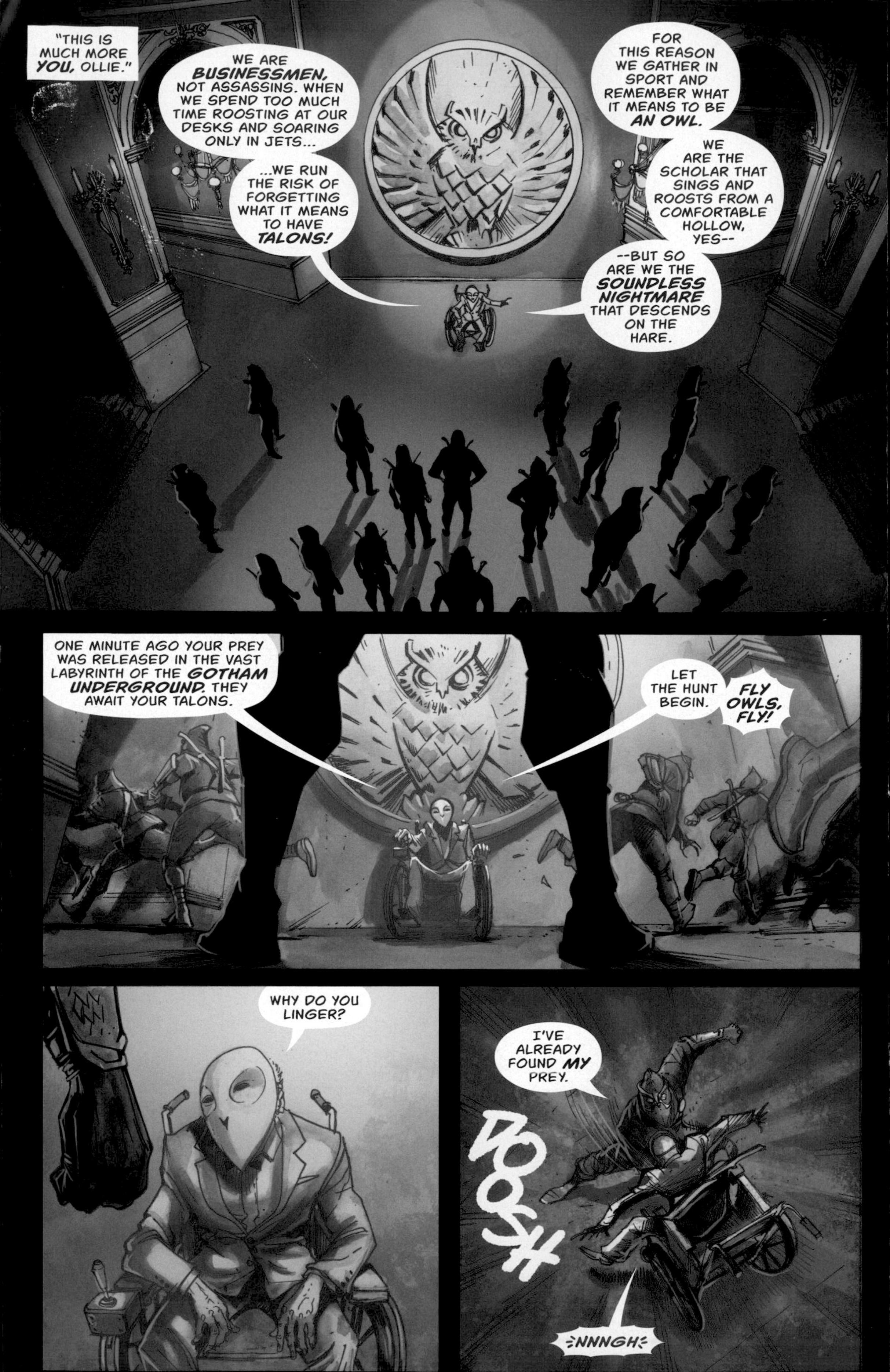
"THIS IS MUCH MORE YOU, OLLIE."
WE ARE BUSINESSMEN, NOT ASSASSINS. WHEN WE SPEND TOO MUCH TIME ROOSTING AT OUR DESKS AND SOARING ONLY IN JETS...
...WE RUN THE RISK OF FORGETTING WHAT IT MEANS TO HAVE TALONS!
FOR THIS REASON WE GATHER IN SPORT AND REMEMBER WHAT IT MEANS TO BE AN OWL.
WE ARE THE SCHOLAR THAT SINGS AND ROOSTS FROM A COMFORTABLE HOLLOW, YES--
--BUT SO ARE WE THE SOUNDLESS NIGHTMARE THAT DESCENDS ON THE HARE.
ONE MINUTE AGO YOUR PREY WAS RELEASED IN THE VAST LABYRINTH OF THE GOTHAM UNDERGROUND. THEY AWAIT YOUR TALONS.
LET THE HUNT BEGIN.
FLY OWLS, FLY!
WHY DO YOU LINGER?
I'VE ALREADY FOUND MY PREY.
DOOSH
NNNGH

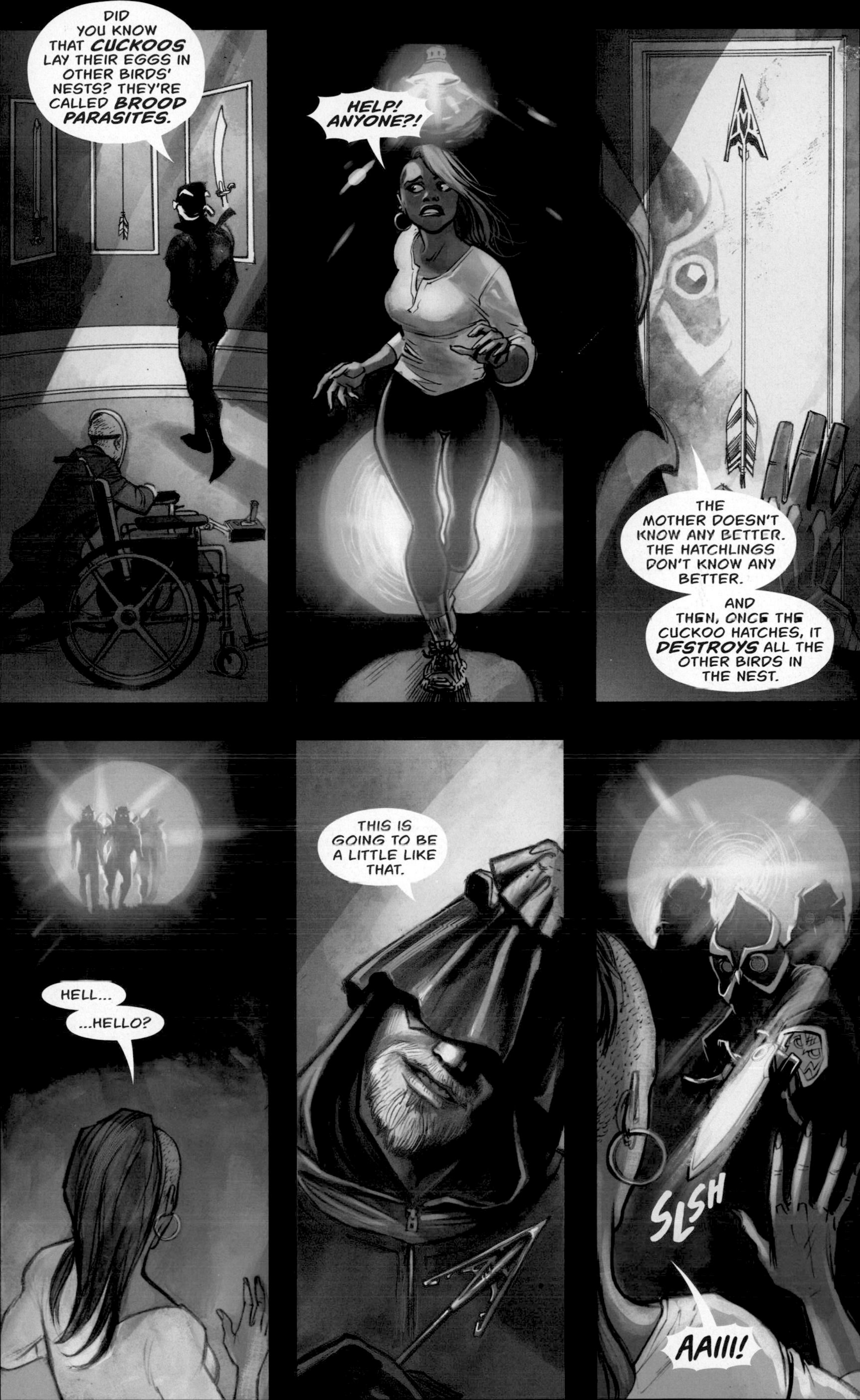
DID YOU KNOW THAT CUCKOOS LAY THEIR EGGS IN OTHER BIRDS' NESTS? THEY'RE CALLED BROOD PARASITES.
HELP! ANYONE?!
THE MOTHER DOESN'T KNOW ANY BETTER. THE HATCHLINGS DON'T KNOW ANY BETTER.
AND THEN, ONCE THE CUCKOO HATCHES, IT DESTROYS ALL THE OTHER BIRDS IN THE NEST.
HELL...
...HELLO?
THIS IS GOING TO BE A LITTLE LIKE THAT.
SLSH
AAIII!

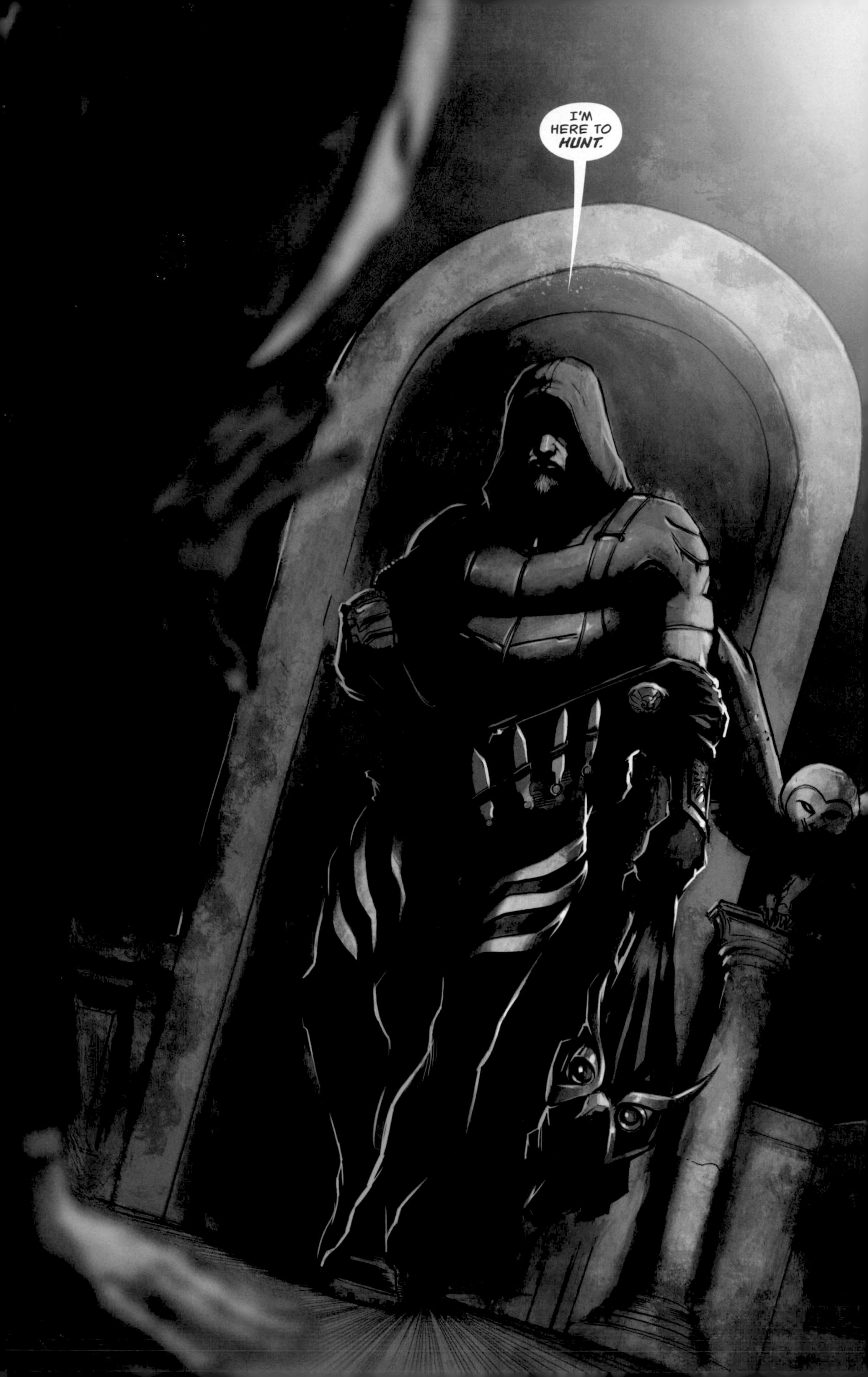
I'M HERE TO HUNT.

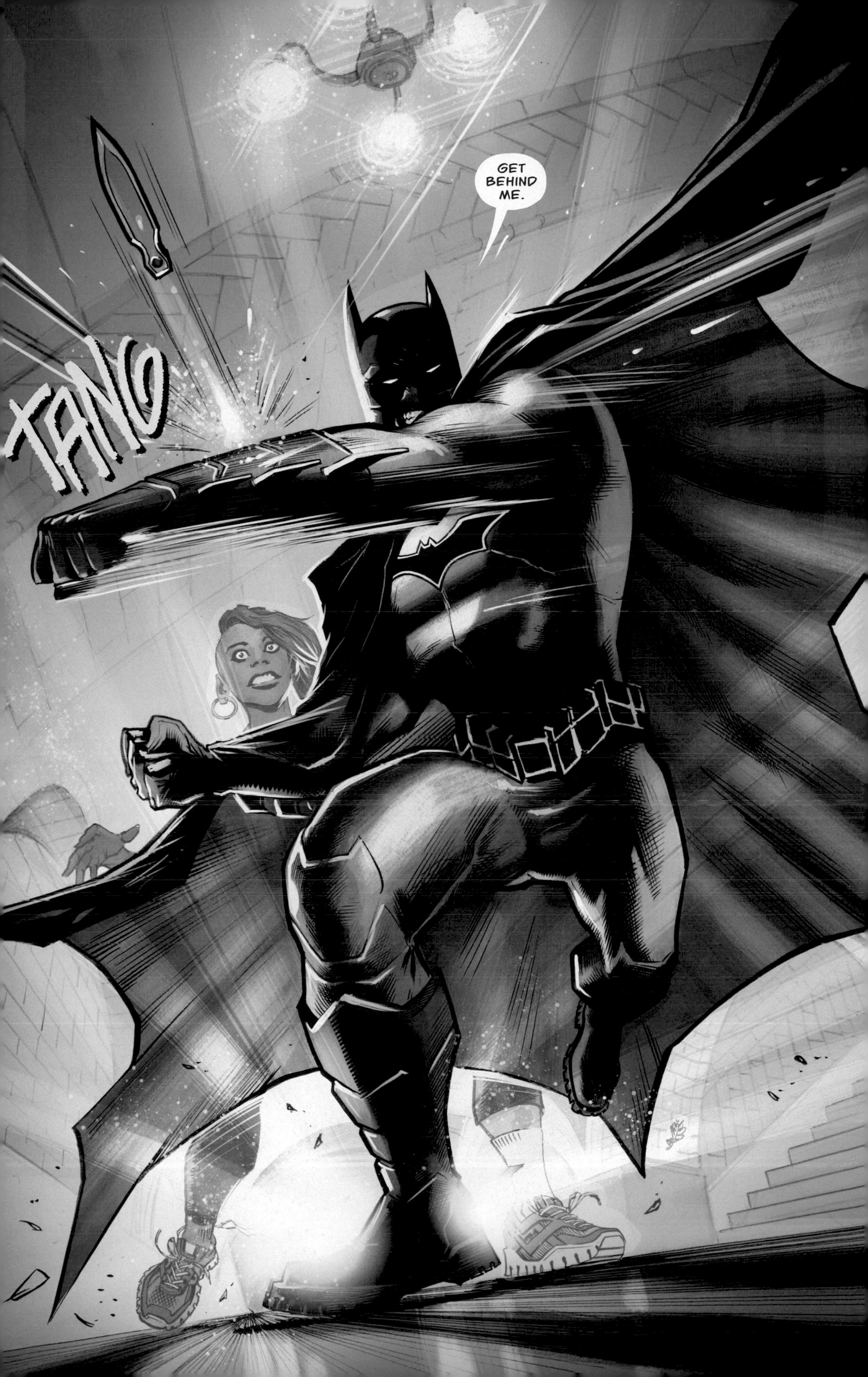
GET BEHIND ME.
TANG

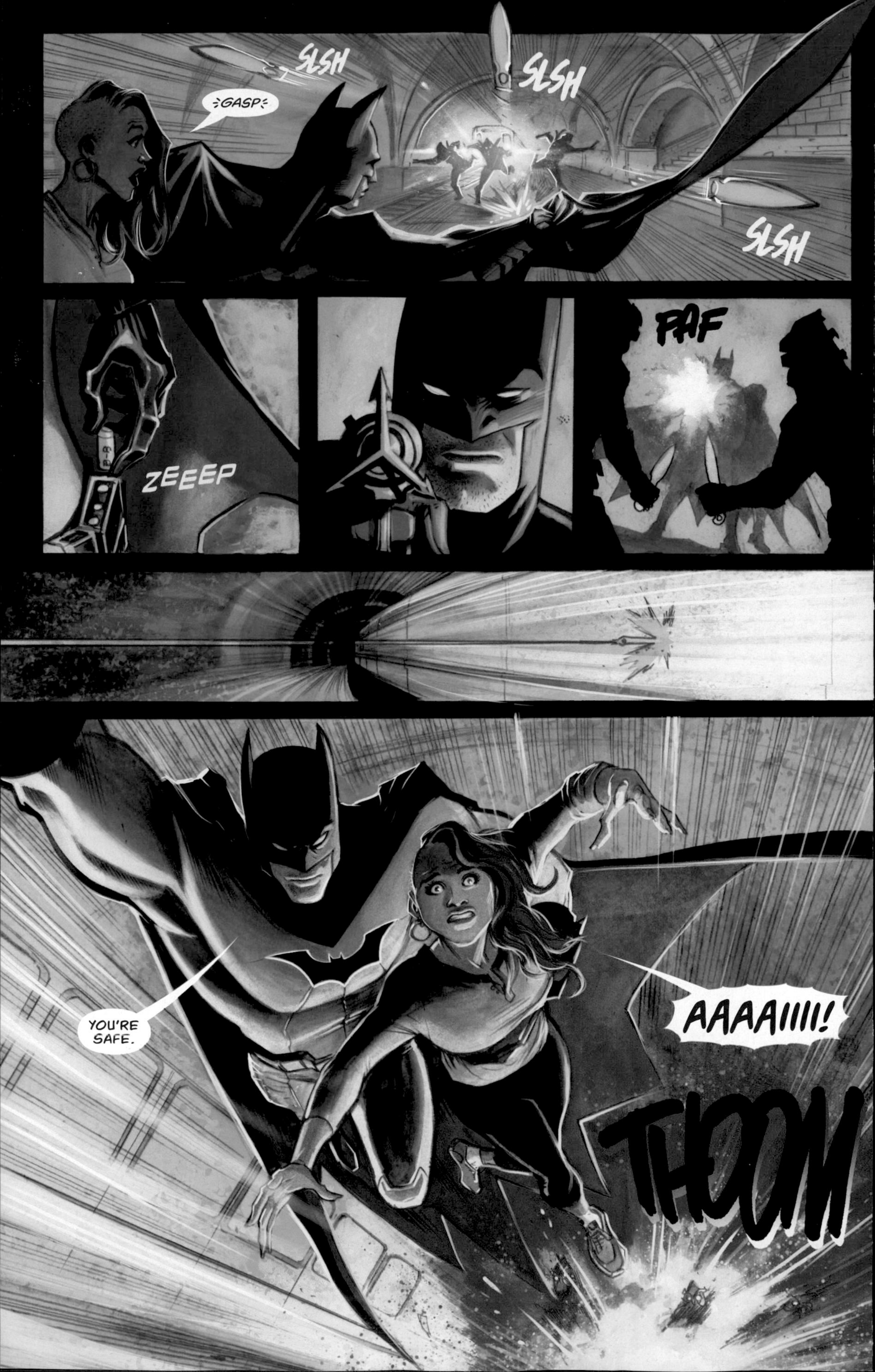
SLSH
GASP
SLSH
SLSH
ZEEEP
PAF
YOU'RE SAFE.
AAAAIIII!
THOOM

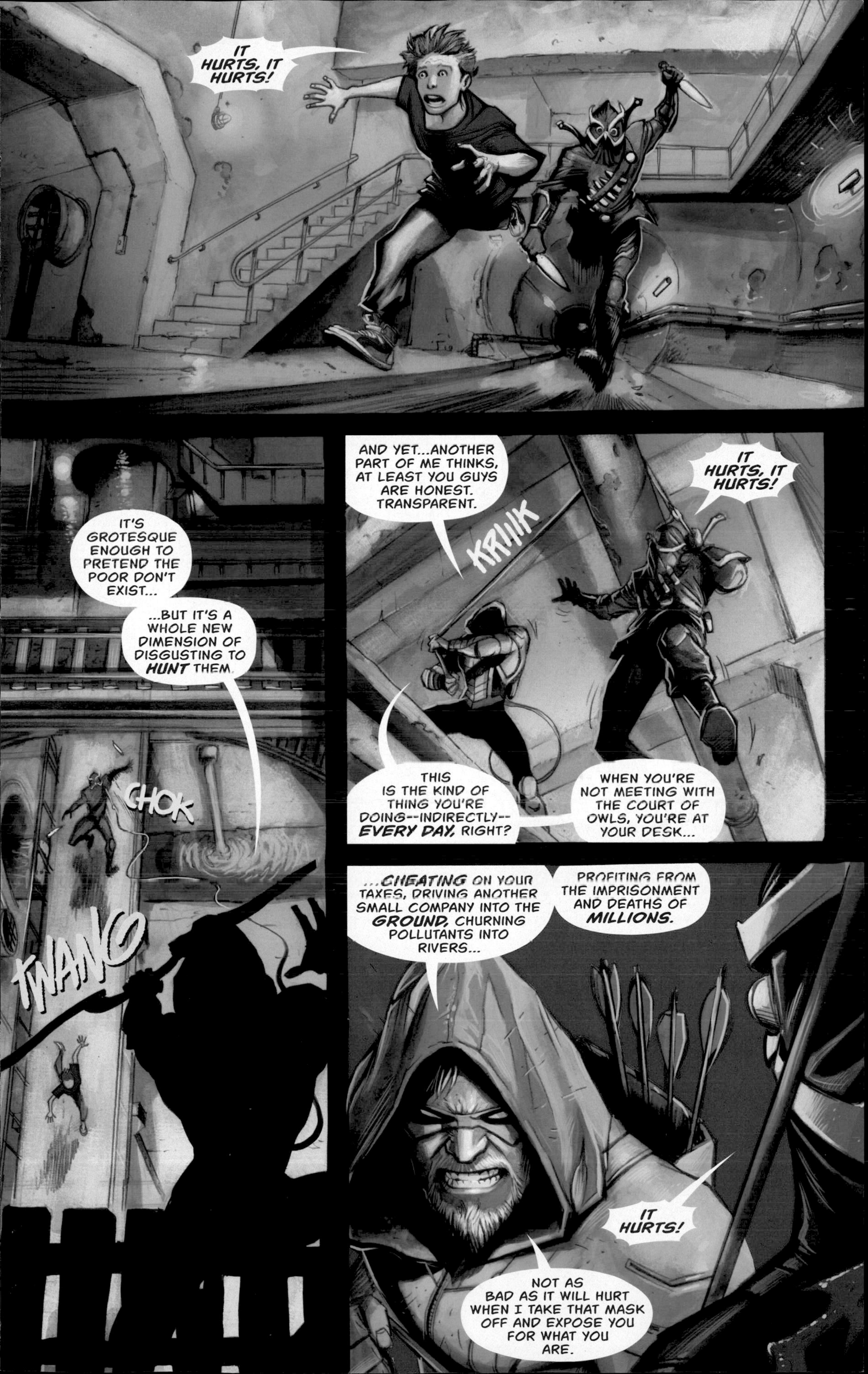
IT HURTS, IT HURTS!
IT'S GROTESQUE ENOUGH TO PRETEND THE POOR DON'T EXIST...
...BUT IT'S A WHOLE NEW DIMENSION OF DISGUSTING TO HUNT THEM.
CHOK
TWANG
AND YET...ANOTHER PART OF ME THINKS, AT LEAST YOU GUYS ARE HONEST. TRANSPARENT.
KRIIIK
IT HURTS, IT HURTS!
THIS IS THE KIND OF THING YOU'RE DOING--INDIRECTLY--EVERY DAY, RIGHT?
WHEN YOU'RE NOT MEETING WITH THE COURT OF OWLS, YOU'RE AT YOUR DESK...
...CHEATING ON YOUR TAXES, DRIVING ANOTHER SMALL COMPANY INTO THE GROUND, CHURNING POLLUTANTS INTO RIVERS...
PROFITING FROM THE IMPRISONMENT AND DEATHS OF MILLIONS.
IT HURTS!
NOT AS BAD AS IT WILL HURT WHEN I TAKE THAT MASK OFF AND EXPOSE YOU FOR WHAT YOU ARE.

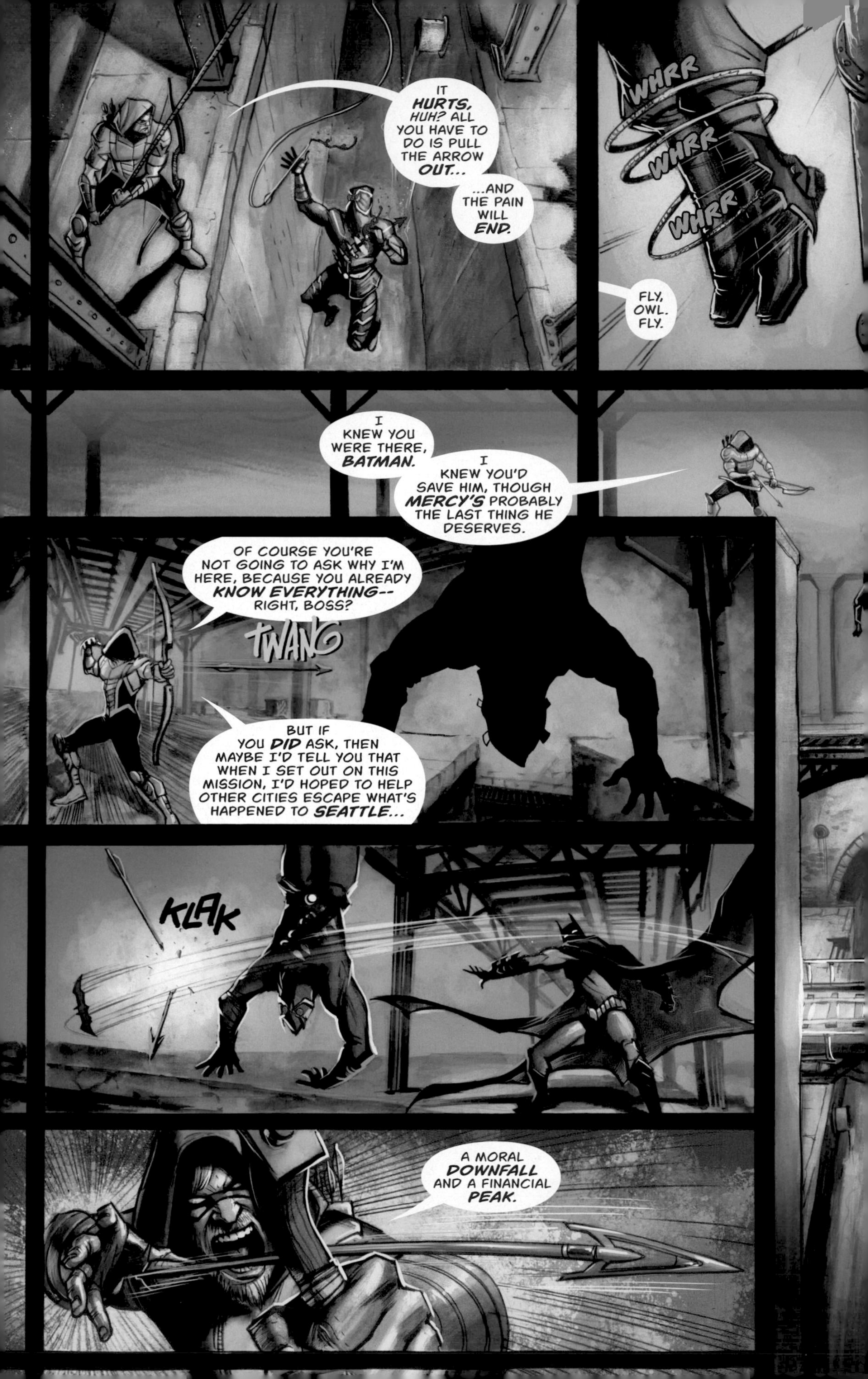

IT HURTS, HUH? ALL YOU HAVE TO DO IS PULL THE ARROW OUT...
...AND THE PAIN WILL END.
WHRR
WHRR
WHRR
FLY, OWL. FLY.
I KNEW YOU WERE THERE, BATMAN.
I KNEW YOU'D SAVE HIM, THOUGH MERCY'S PROBABLY THE LAST THING HE DESERVES.
OF COURSE YOU'RE NOT GOING TO ASK WHY I'M HERE, BECAUSE YOU ALREADY KNOW EVERYTHING-- RIGHT, BOSS?
TWANG
BUT IF YOU DID ASK, THEN MAYBE I'D TELL YOU THAT WHEN I SET OUT ON THIS MISSION, I'D HOPED TO HELP OTHER CITIES ESCAPE WHAT'S HAPPENED TO SEATTLE...
KLAK
A MORAL DOWNFALL AND A FINANCIAL PEAK.

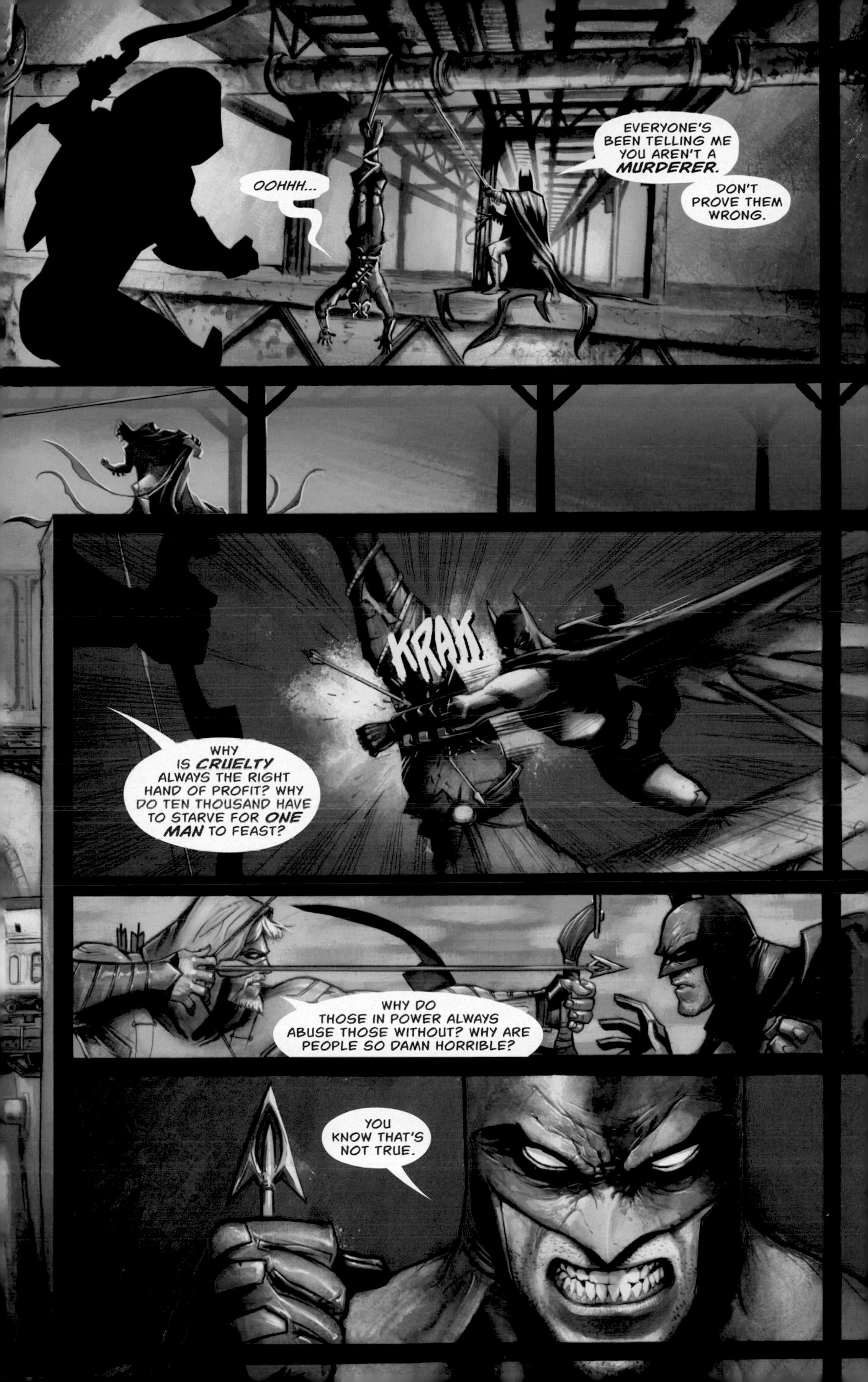
OOHHH...
EVERYONE'S BEEN TELLING ME YOU AREN'T A MURDERER.
DON'T PROVE THEM WRONG.
KRAK
WHY IS CRUELTY ALWAYS THE RIGHT HAND OF PROFIT? WHY DO TEN THOUSAND HAVE TO STARVE FOR ONE MAN TO FEAST?
WHY DO THOSE IN POWER ALWAYS ABUSE THOSE WITHOUT? WHY ARE PEOPLE SO DAMN HORRIBLE?
YOU KNOW THAT'S NOT TRUE.

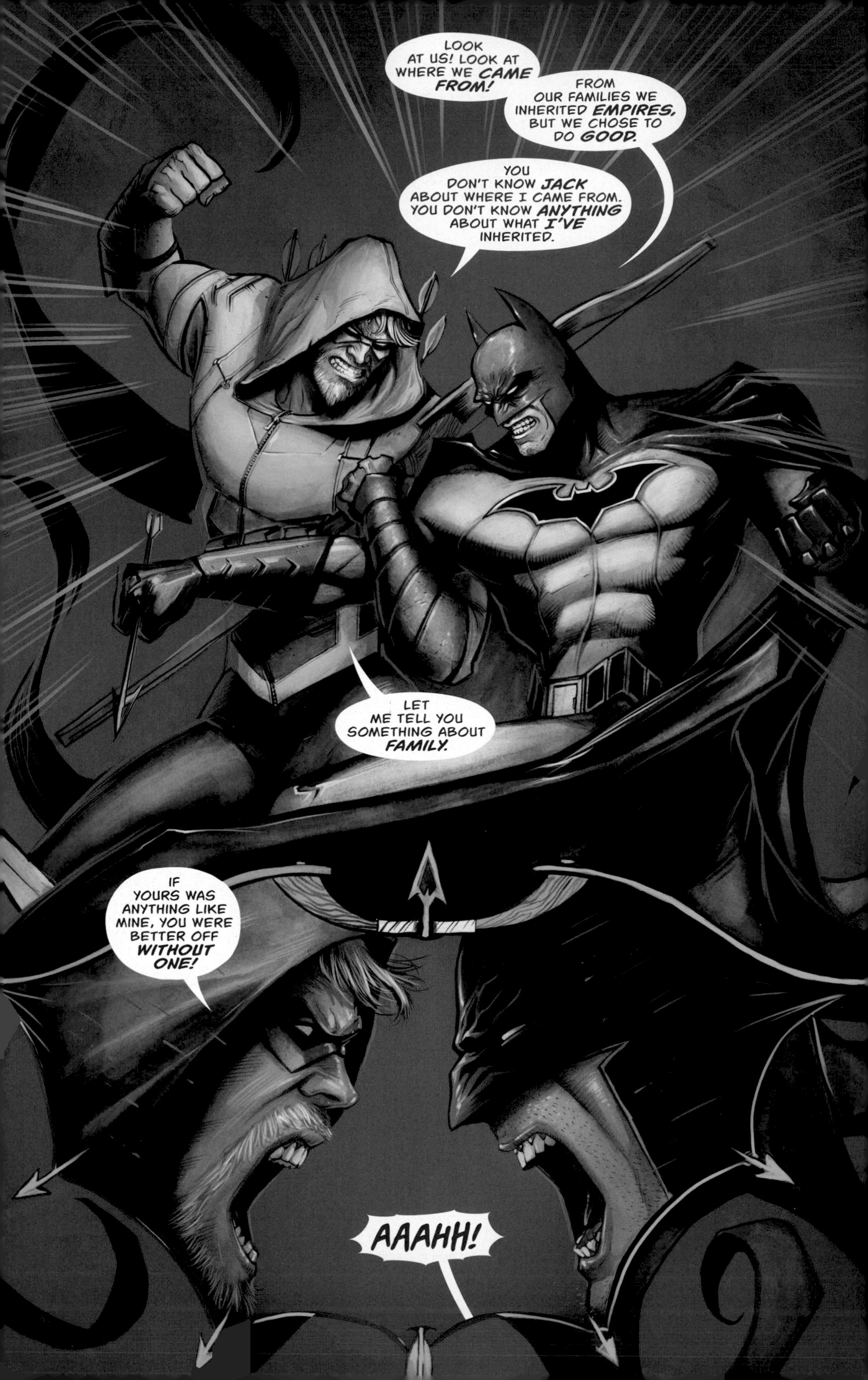
LOOK AT US! LOOK AT WHERE WE CAME FROM!
FROM OUR FAMILIES WE INHERITED EMPIRES, BUT WE CHOSE TO DO GOOD.
YOU DON'T KNOW JACK ABOUT WHERE I CAME FROM. YOU DON'T KNOW ANYTHING ABOUT WHAT I'VE INHERITED.
LET ME TELL YOU SOMETHING ABOUT FAMILY.
IF YOURS WAS ANYTHING LIKE MINE, YOU WERE BETTER OFF WITHOUT ONE!
AAAHH!

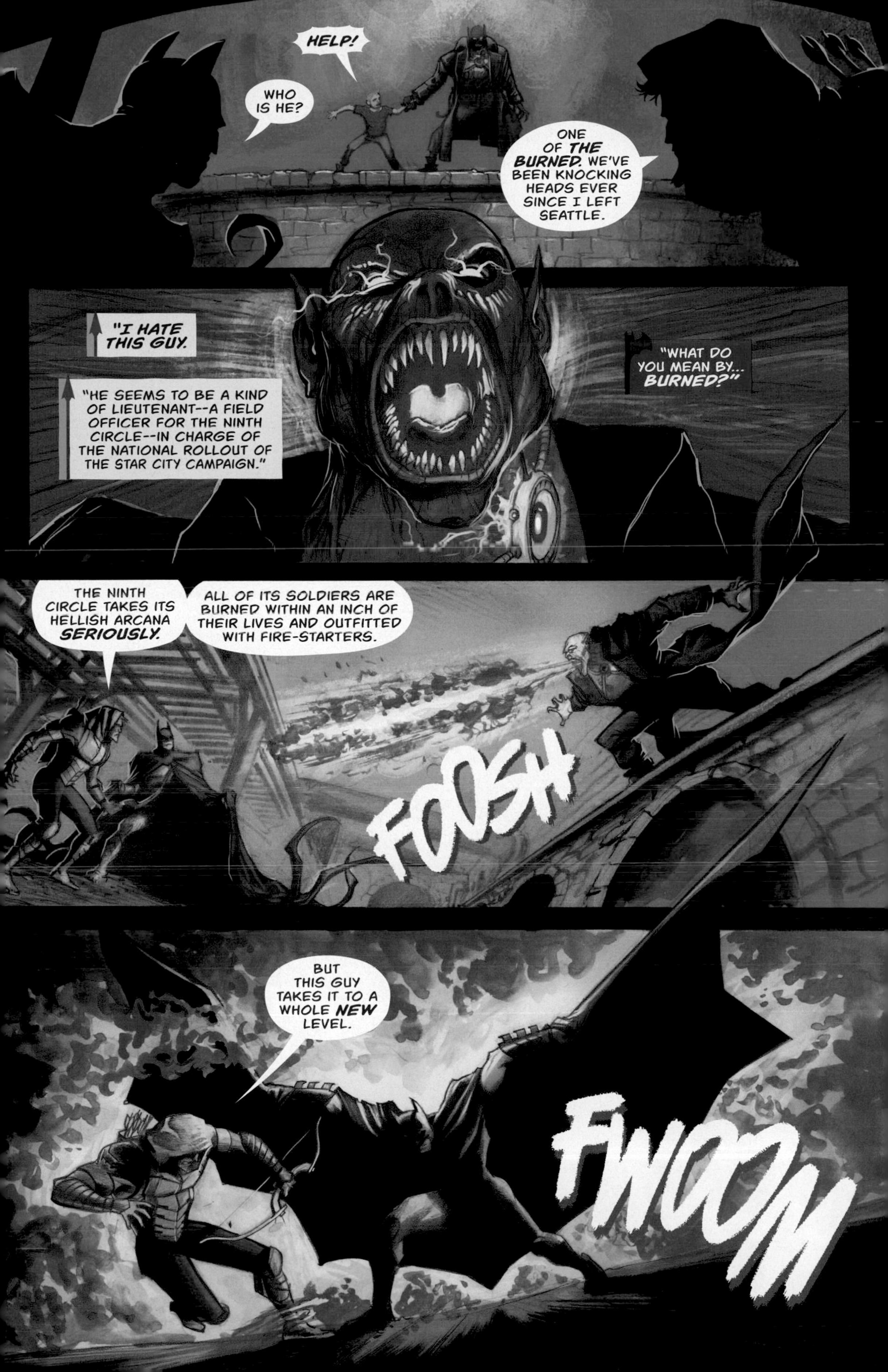
HELP!
WHO IS HE?
ONE OF THE BURNED. WE'VE BEEN KNOCKING HEADS EVER SINCE I LEFT SEATTLE.
"I HATE THIS GUY.
"HE SEEMS TO BE A KIND OF LIEUTENANT--A FIELD OFFICER FOR THE NINTH CIRCLE--IN CHARGE OF THE NATIONAL ROLLOUT OF THE STAR CITY CAMPAIGN."
"WHAT DO YOU MEAN BY... BURNED?"
THE NINTH CIRCLE TAKES ITS HELLISH ARCANA SERIOUSLY.
ALL OF ITS SOLDIERS ARE BURNED WITHIN AN INCH OF THEIR LIVES AND OUTFITTED WITH FIRE-STARTERS.
FOOSH
BUT THIS GUY TAKES IT TO A WHOLE NEW LEVEL.
FWOOM

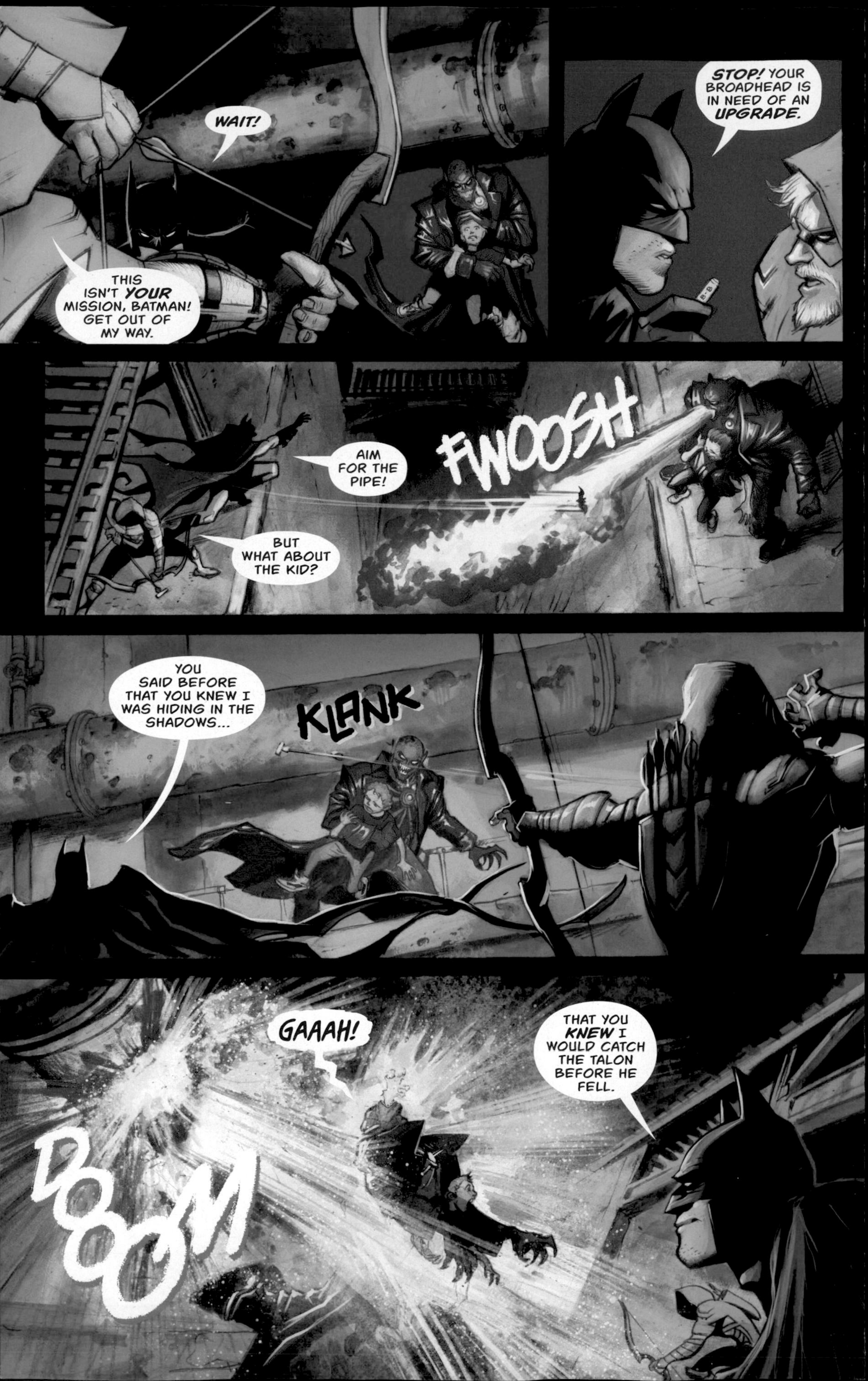
WAIT!
THIS ISN'T YOUR MISSION, BATMAN! GET OUT OF MY WAY.
STOP! YOUR BROADHEAD IS IN NEED OF AN UPGRADE.
B-B
AIM FOR THE PIPE!
FWOOSH
BUT WHAT ABOUT THE KID?
YOU SAID BEFORE THAT YOU KNEW I WAS HIDING IN THE SHADOWS...
KLANK
GAAAH!
THAT YOU KNEW I WOULD CATCH THE TALON BEFORE HE FELL.
DOOOM

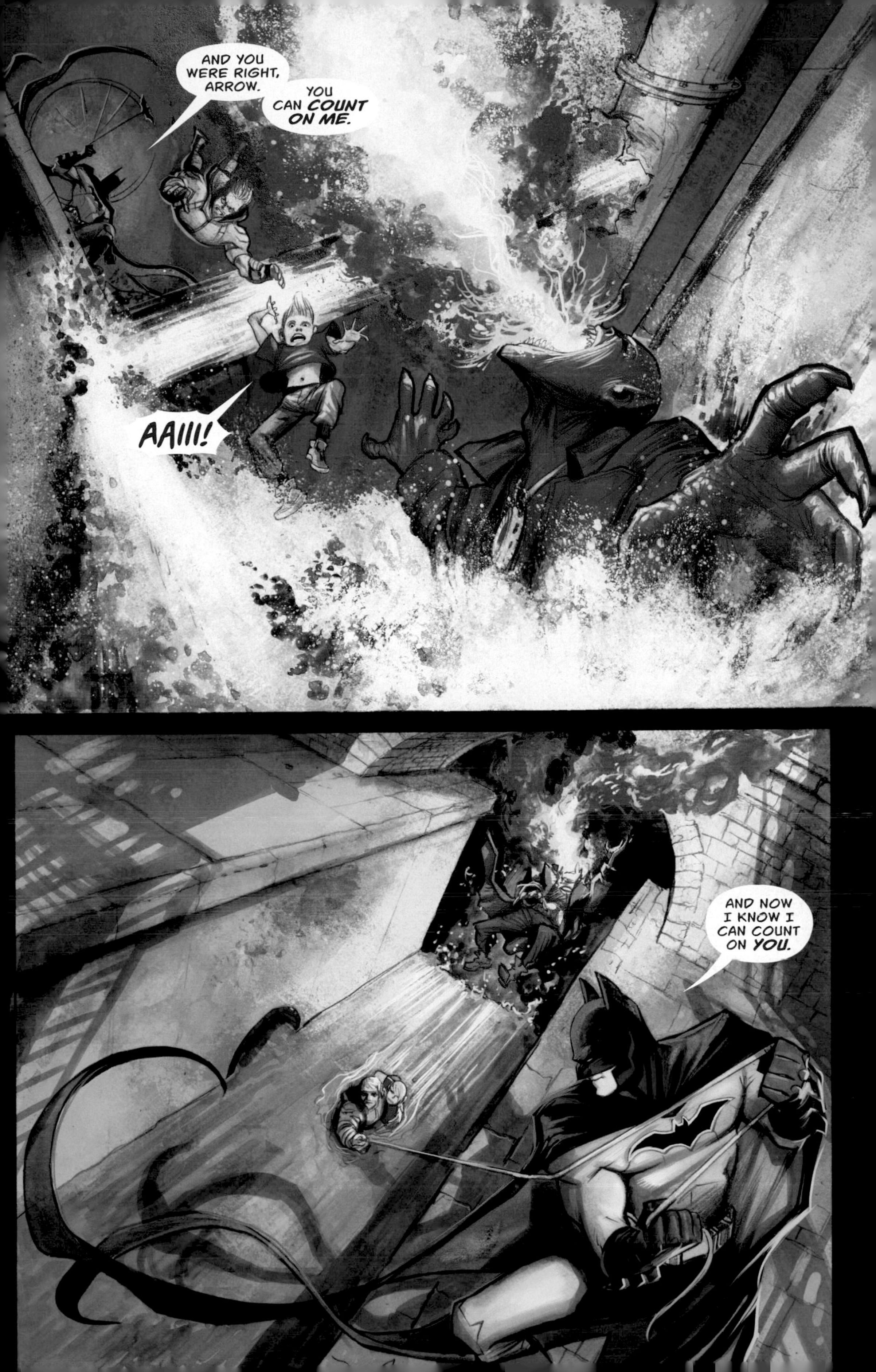
AND YOU WERE RIGHT, ARROW.
YOU CAN COUNT ON ME.
AAIII!
AND NOW I KNOW I CAN COUNT ON YOU.

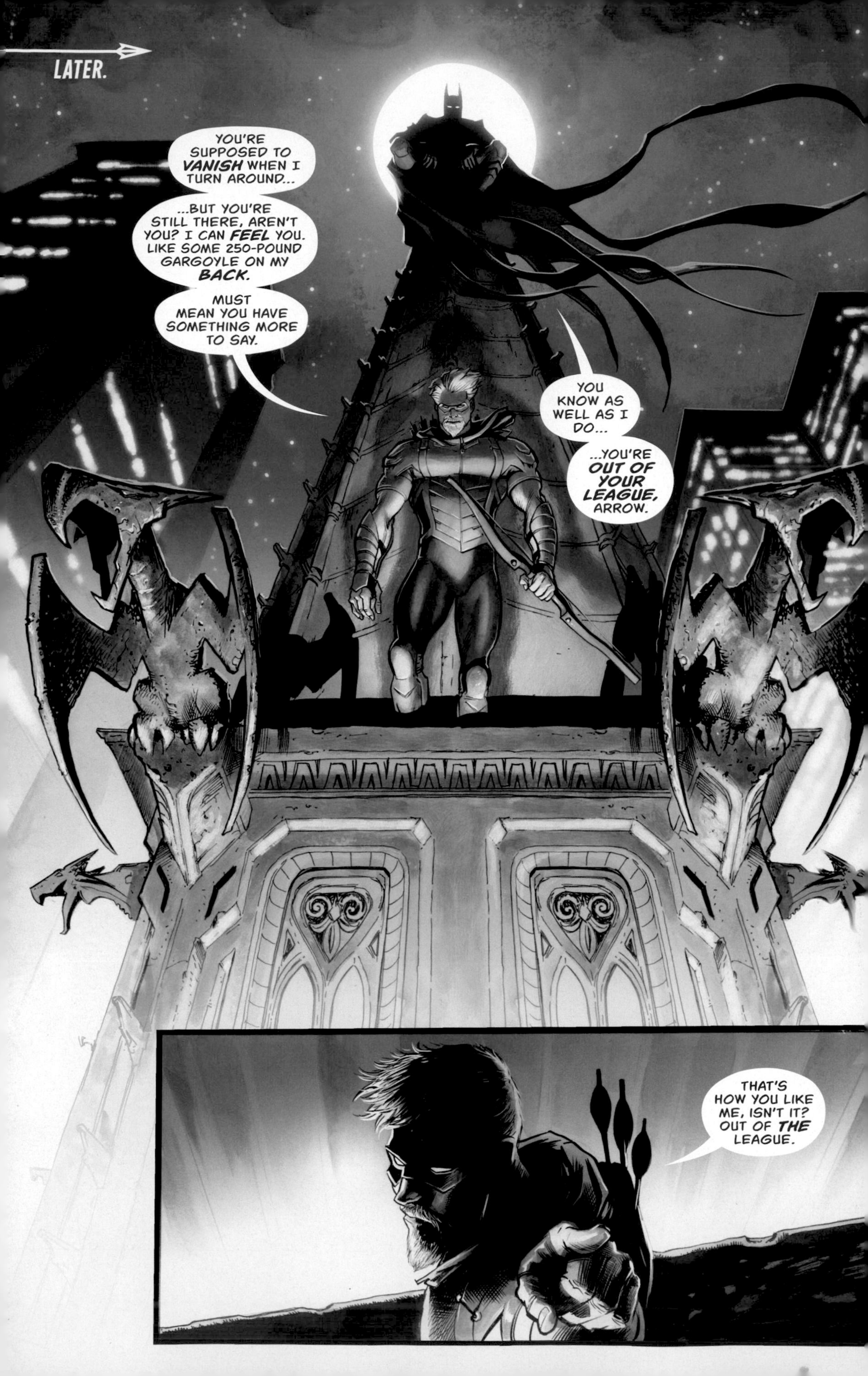
LATER.
YOU'RE SUPPOSED TO VANISH WHEN I TURN AROUND...
...BUT YOU'RE STILL THERE, AREN'T YOU? I CAN FEEL YOU. LIKE SOME 250-POUND GARGOYLE ON MY BACK.
MUST MEAN YOU HAVE SOMETHING MORE TO SAY.
YOU KNOW AS WELL AS I DO...
...YOU'RE OUT OF YOUR LEAGUE, ARROW.
THAT'S HOW YOU LIKE ME, ISN'T IT? OUT OF THE LEAGUE.

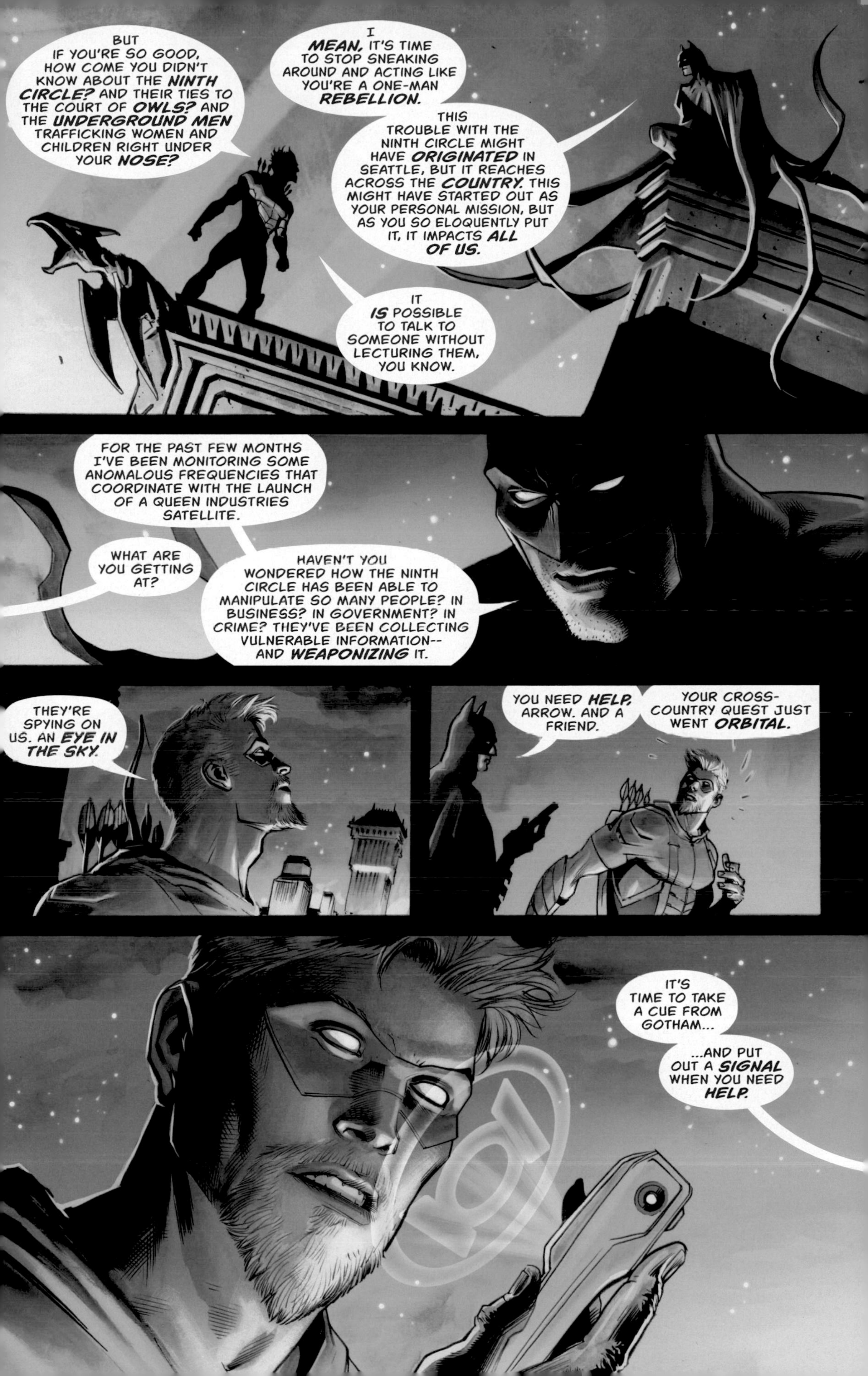
BUT IF YOU'RE SO GOOD, HOW COME YOU DIDN'T KNOW ABOUT THE NINTH CIRCLE? AND THEIR TIES TO THE COURT OF OWLS? AND THE UNDERGROUND MEN TRAFFICKING WOMEN AND CHILDREN RIGHT UNDER YOUR NOSE?
I MEAN, IT'S TIME TO STOP SNEAKING AROUND AND ACTING LIKE YOU'RE A ONE-MAN REBELLION.
THIS TROUBLE WITH THE NINTH CIRCLE MIGHT HAVE ORIGINATED IN SEATTLE, BUT IT REACHES ACROSS THE COUNTRY. THIS MIGHT HAVE STARTED OUT AS YOUR PERSONAL MISSION, BUT AS YOU SO ELOQUENTLY PUT IT, IT IMPACTS ALL OF US.
IT IS POSSIBLE TO TALK TO SOMEONE WITHOUT LECTURING THEM, YOU KNOW.
FOR THE PAST FEW MONTHS I'VE BEEN MONITORING SOME ANOMALOUS FREQUENCIES THAT COORDINATE WITH THE LAUNCH OF A QUEEN INDUSTRIES SATELLITE.
WHAT ARE YOU GETTING AT?
HAVEN'T YOU WONDERED HOW THE NINTH CIRCLE HAS BEEN ABLE TO MANIPULATE SO MANY PEOPLE? IN BUSINESS? IN GOVERNMENT? IN CRIME? THEY'VE BEEN COLLECTING VULNERABLE INFORMATION-- AND WEAPONIZING IT.
THEY'RE SPYING ON US. AN EYE IN THE SKY.
YOU NEED HELP, ARROW. AND A FRIEND.
YOUR CROSS-COUNTRY QUEST JUST WENT ORBITAL.
IT'S TIME TO TAKE A CUE FROM GOTHAM...
...AND PUT OUT A SIGNAL WHEN YOU NEED HELP.

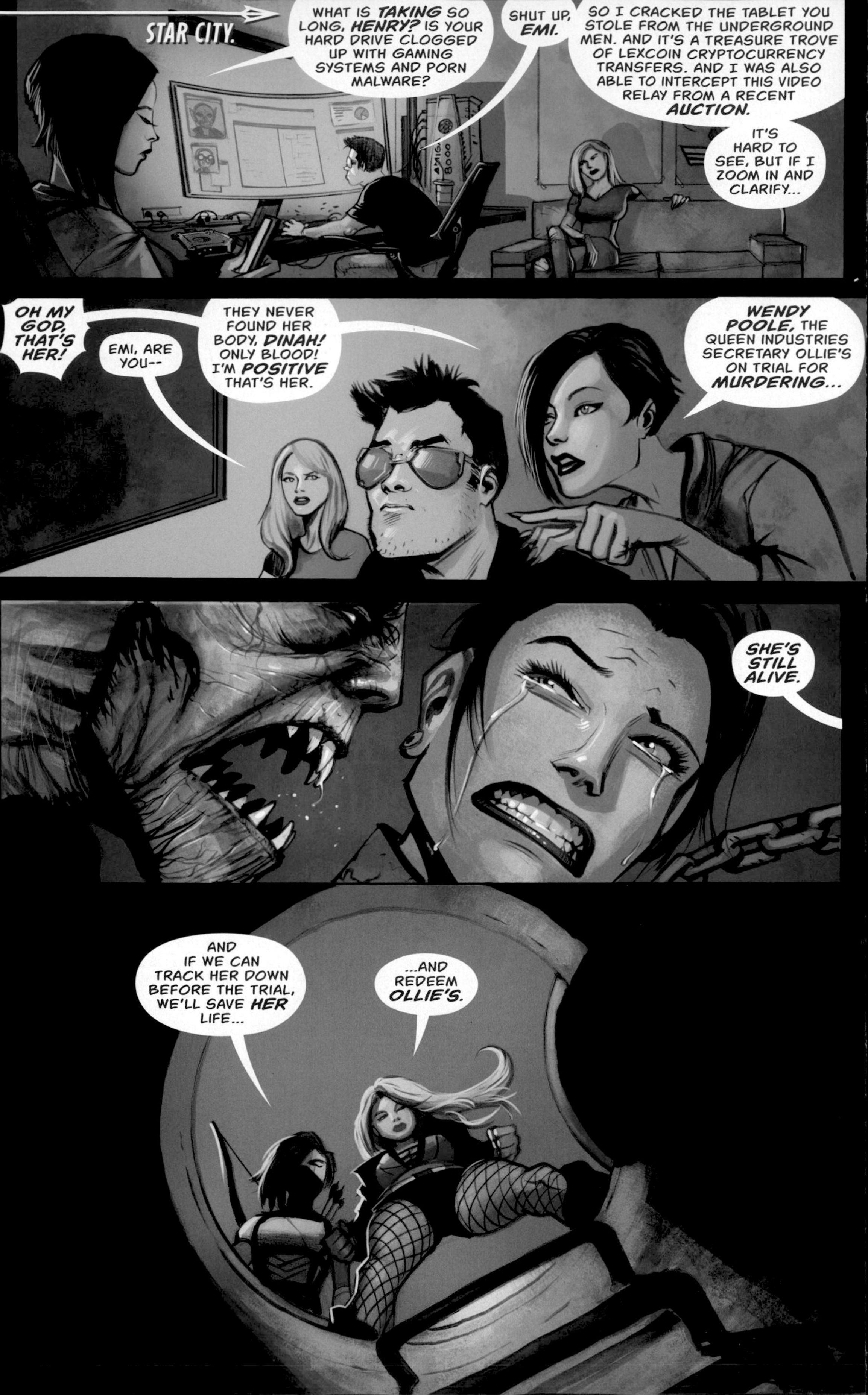
STAR CITY.
WHAT IS TAKING SO LONG, HENRY? IS YOUR HARD DRIVE CLOGGED UP WITH GAMING SYSTEMS AND PORN MALWARE?
SHUT UP, EMI.
SO I CRACKED THE TABLET YOU STOLE FROM THE UNDERGROUND MEN. AND IT'S A TREASURE TROVE OF LEXCOIN CRYPTOCURRENCY TRANSFERS. AND I WAS ALSO ABLE TO INTERCEPT THIS VIDEO RELAY FROM A RECENT AUCTION.
IT'S HARD TO SEE, BUT IF I ZOOM IN AND CLARIFY...
OH MY GOD, THAT'S HER!
EMI, ARE YOU--
THEY NEVER FOUND HER BODY, DINAH! ONLY BLOOD! I'M POSITIVE THAT'S HER.
WENDY POOLE, THE QUEEN INDUSTRIES SECRETARY OLLIE'S ON TRIAL FOR MURDERING...
SHE'S STILL ALIVE.
AND IF WE CAN TRACK HER DOWN BEFORE THE TRIAL, WE'LL SAVE HER LIFE...
...AND REDEEM OLLIE'S.

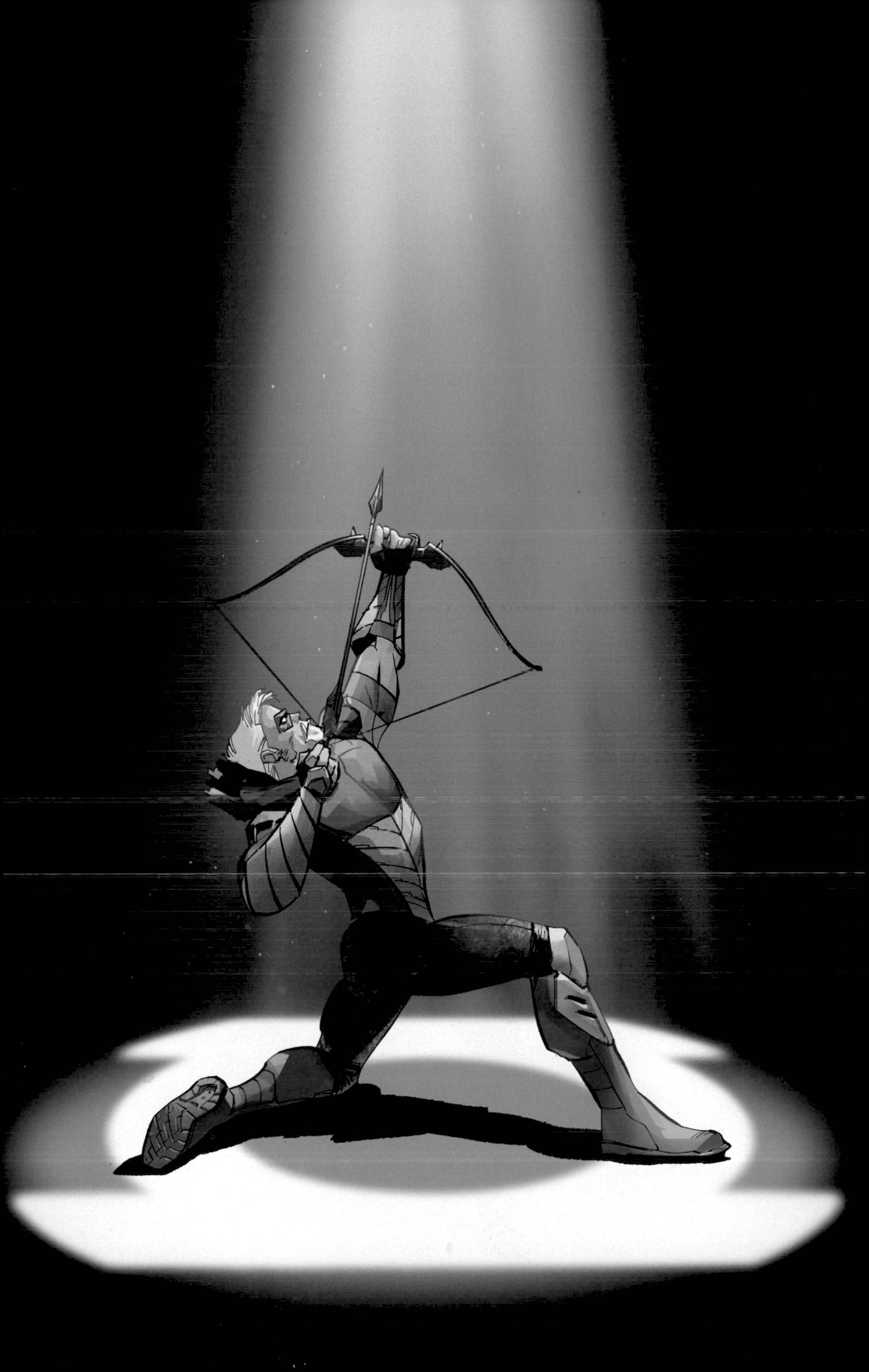

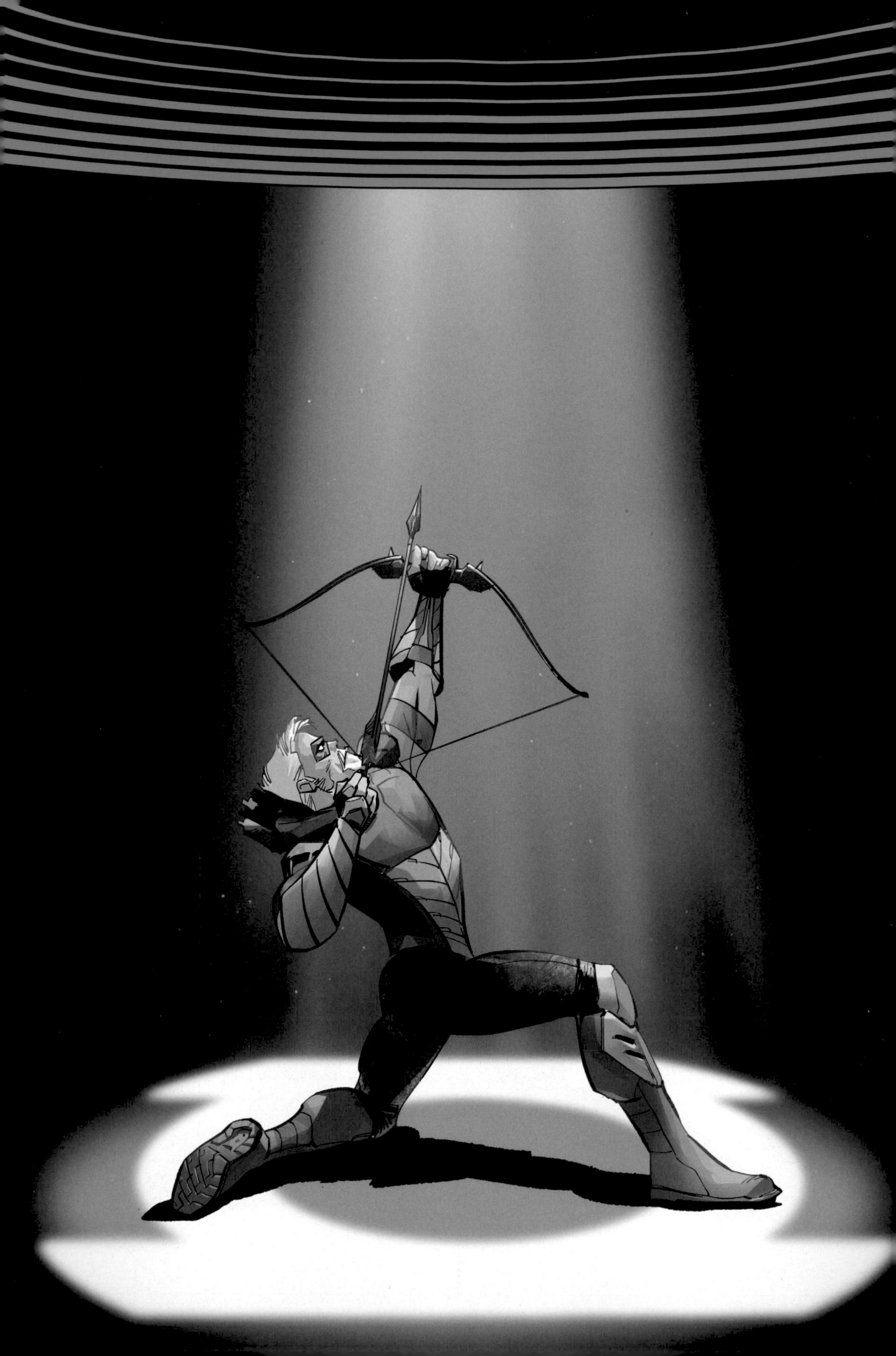

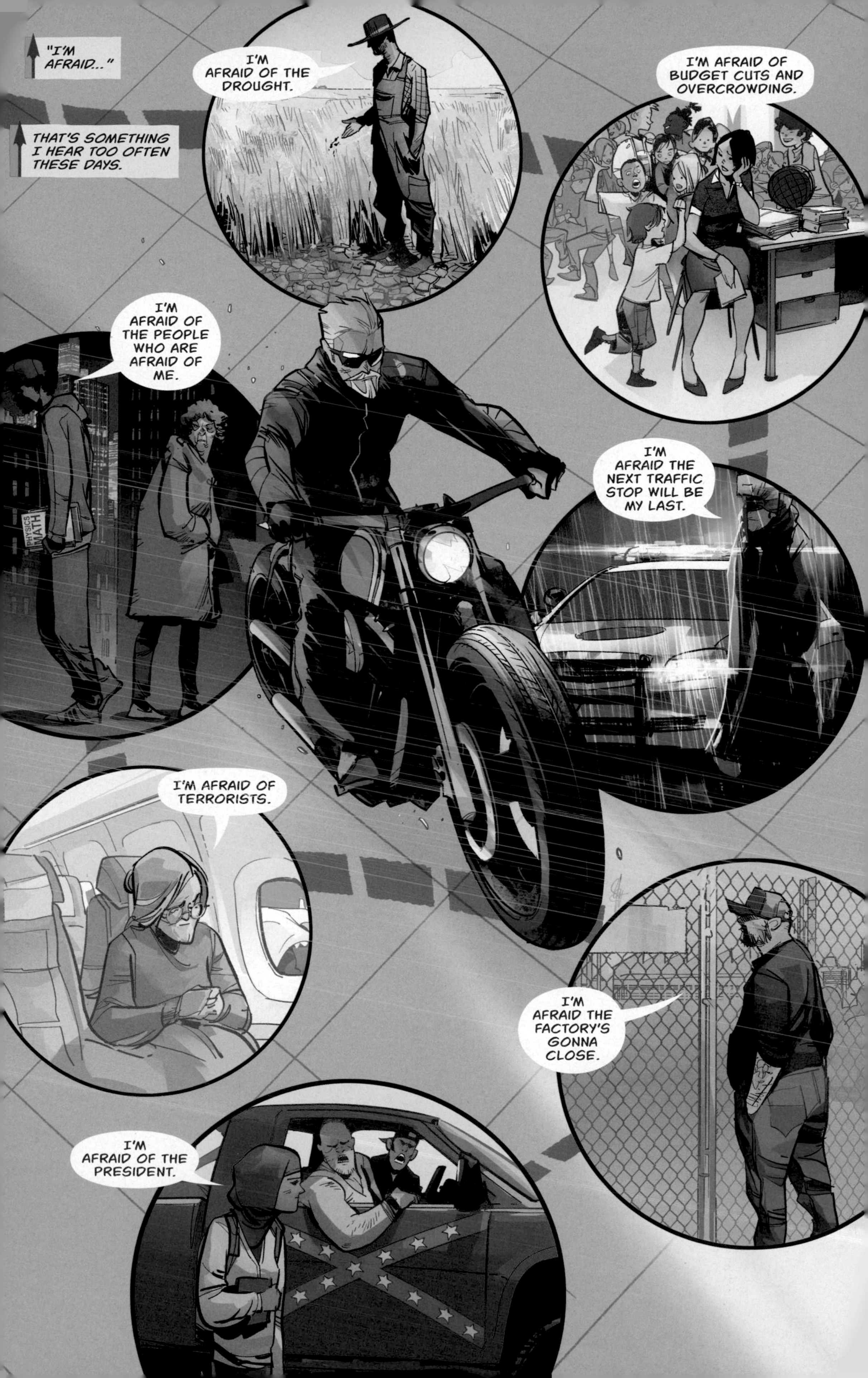
"I'M AFRAID..."
THAT'S SOMETHING I HEAR TOO OFTEN THESE DAYS.
I'M AFRAID OF THE DROUGHT.
I'M AFRAID OF BUDGET CUTS AND OVERCROWDING.
I'M AFRAID OF THE PEOPLE WHO ARE AFRAID OF ME.
PHYSICS
MATH
I'M AFRAID THE NEXT TRAFFIC STOP WILL BE MY LAST.
I'M AFRAID OF TERRORISTS.
I'M AFRAID THE FACTORY'S GONNA CLOSE.
I'M AFRAID OF THE PRESIDENT.

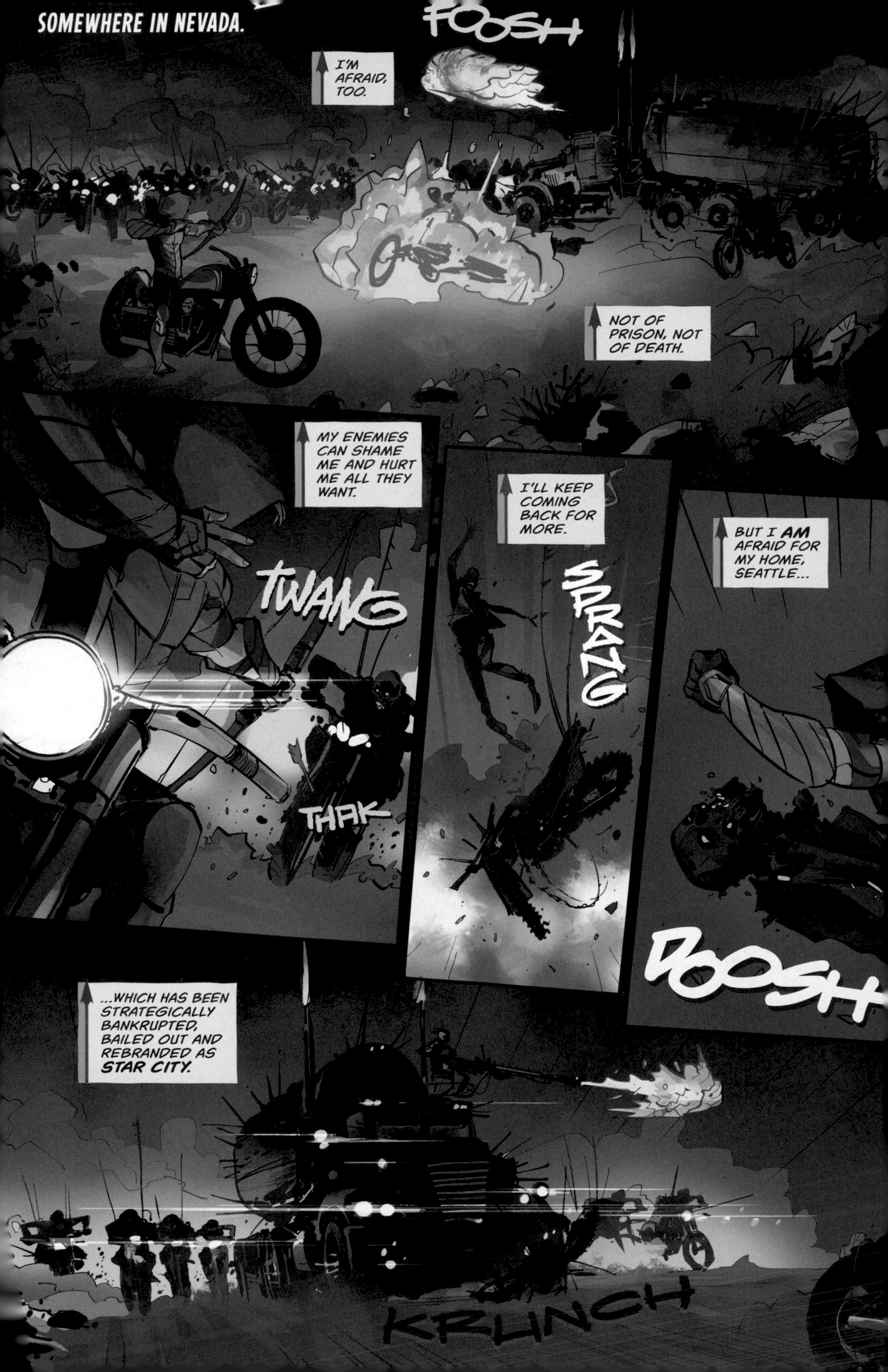
SOMEWHERE IN NEVADA.
FOOSH
I'M AFRAID, TOO.
NOT OF PRISON, NOT OF DEATH.
MY ENEMIES CAN SHAME ME AND HURT ME ALL THEY WANT.
TWANG
THAK
I'LL KEEP COMING BACK FOR MORE.
SPRANG
BUT I **AM** AFRAID FOR MY HOME, SEATTLE...
DOOSH
...WHICH HAS BEEN STRATEGICALLY BANKRUPTED, BAILED OUT AND REBRANDED AS **STAR CITY**.
KRUNCH

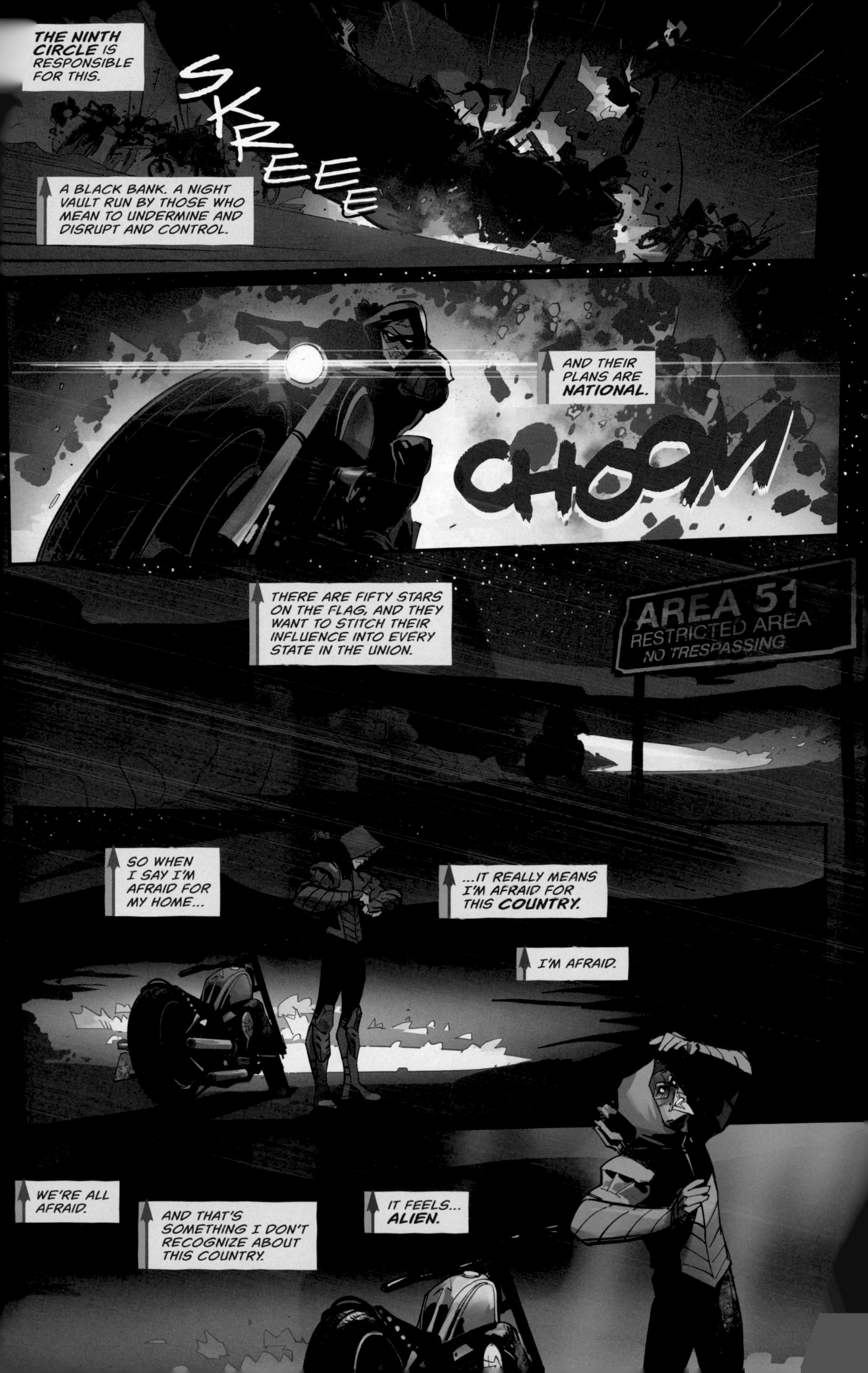
THE NINTH CIRCLE IS RESPONSIBLE FOR THIS.
SKREEEE
A BLACK BANK. A NIGHT VAULT RUN BY THOSE WHO MEAN TO UNDERMINE AND DISRUPT AND CONTROL.
AND THEIR PLANS ARE NATIONAL.
CHOOM
THERE ARE FIFTY STARS ON THE FLAG, AND THEY WANT TO STITCH THEIR INFLUENCE INTO EVERY STATE IN THE UNION.
AREA 51
RESTRICTED AREA
NO TRESPASSING
SO WHEN I SAY I'M AFRAID FOR MY HOME...
...IT REALLY MEANS I'M AFRAID FOR THIS COUNTRY.
I'M AFRAID.
WE'RE ALL AFRAID.
AND THAT'S SOMETHING I DON'T RECOGNIZE ABOUT THIS COUNTRY.
IT FEELS... ALIEN.

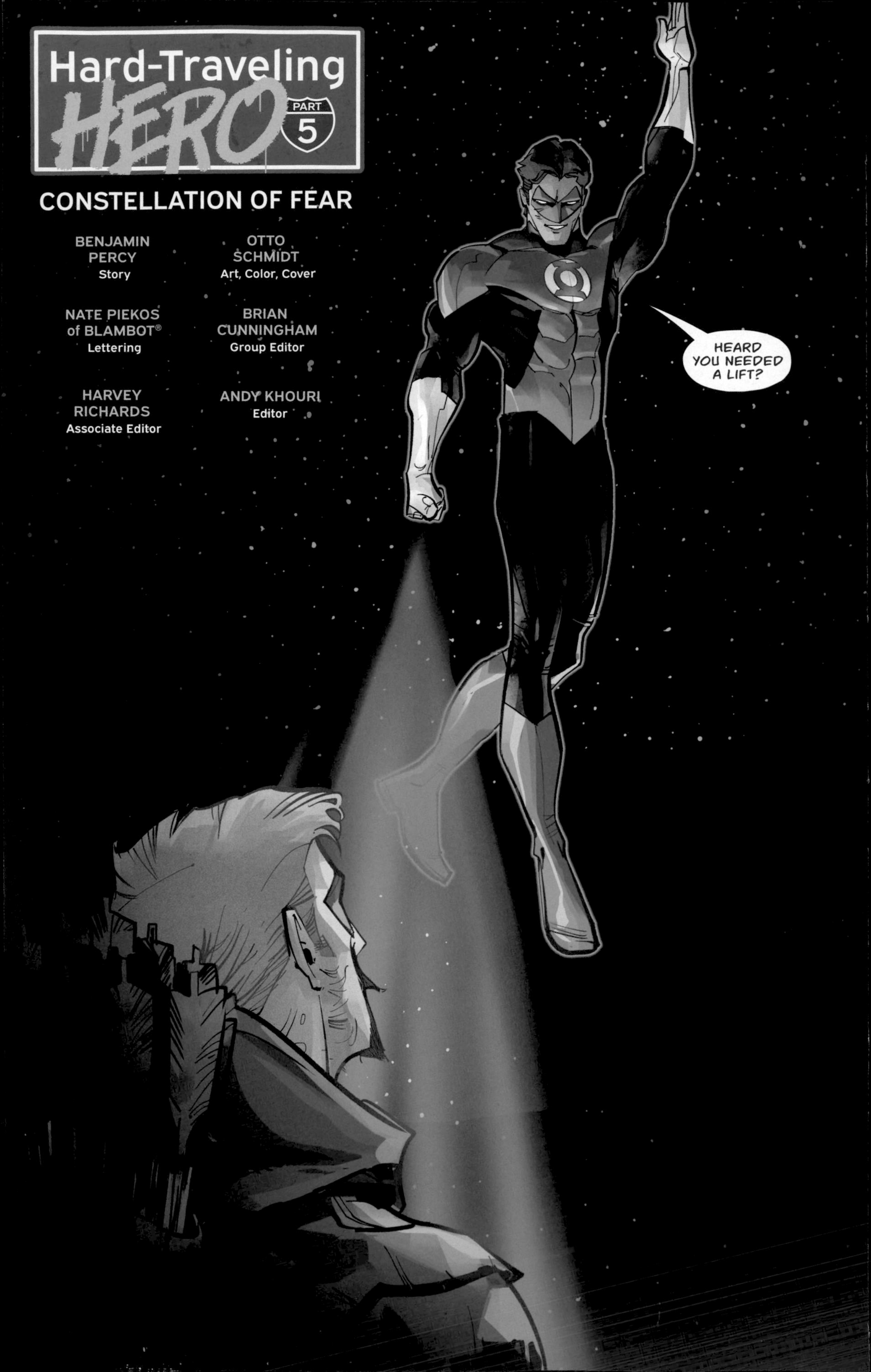
Hard-Traveling
HERO
PART
5
CONSTELLATION OF FEAR
BENJAMIN PERCY Story
OTTO SCHMIDT Art, Color, Cover
NATE PIEKOS of BLAMBOT® Lettering
BRIAN CUNNINGHAM Group Editor
HARVEY RICHARDS Associate Editor
ANDY KHOURI Editor
HEARD YOU NEEDED A LIFT?

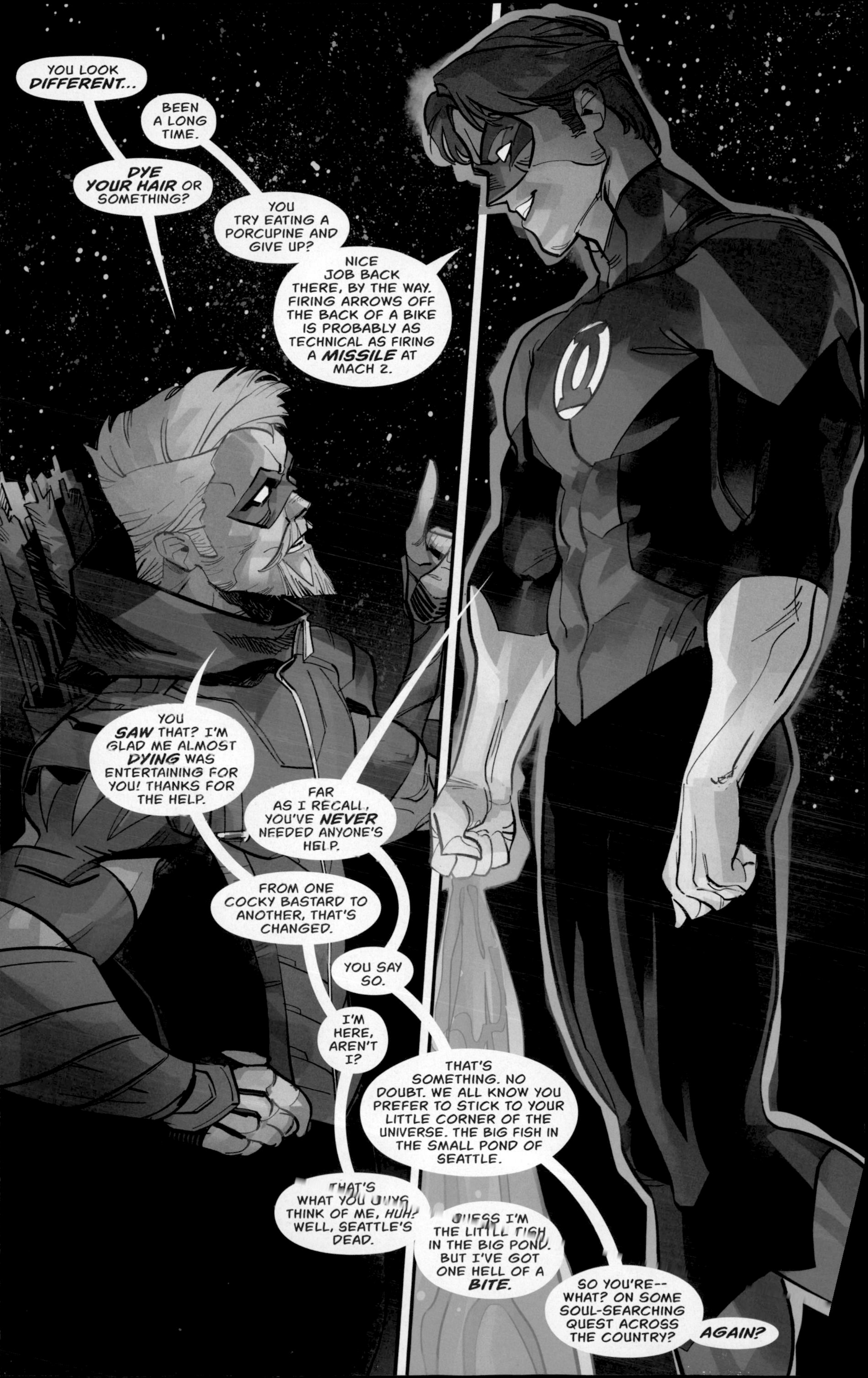
YOU LOOK *DIFFERENT...*
BEEN A LONG TIME.
*DYE YOUR HAIR* OR SOMETHING?
YOU TRY EATING A PORCUPINE AND GIVE UP?
NICE JOB BACK THERE, BY THE WAY. FIRING ARROWS OFF THE BACK OF A BIKE IS PROBABLY AS TECHNICAL AS FIRING A *MISSILE* AT MACH 2.
YOU *SAW* THAT? I'M GLAD ME ALMOST *DYING* WAS ENTERTAINING FOR YOU! THANKS FOR THE HELP.
FAR AS I RECALL, YOU'VE *NEVER* NEEDED ANYONE'S HELP.
FROM ONE COCKY BASTARD TO ANOTHER, THAT'S CHANGED.
YOU SAY SO.
I'M HERE, AREN'T I?
THAT'S SOMETHING. NO DOUBT. WE ALL KNOW YOU PREFER TO STICK TO YOUR LITTLE CORNER OF THE UNIVERSE. THE BIG FISH IN THE SMALL POND OF SEATTLE.
THAT'S WHAT YOU GUYS THINK OF ME, *HUH?* WELL, SEATTLE'S DEAD.
GUESS I'M THE LITTLE FISH IN THE BIG POND. BUT I'VE GOT ONE HELL OF A *BITE.*
SO YOU'RE-- WHAT? ON SOME SOUL-SEARCHING QUEST ACROSS THE COUNTRY? *AGAIN?*

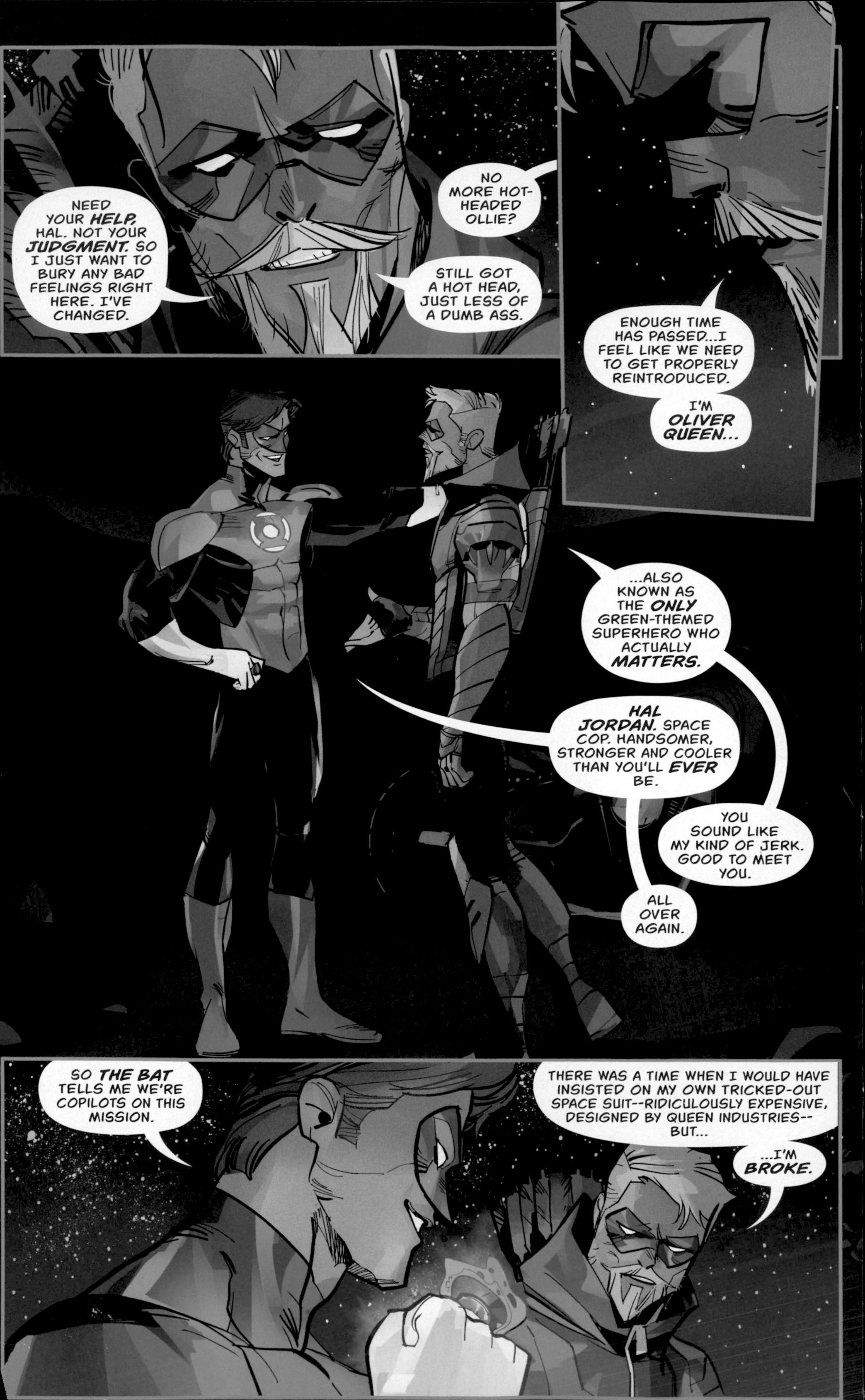
NEED YOUR HELP, HAL. NOT YOUR JUDGMENT. SO I JUST WANT TO BURY ANY BAD FEELINGS RIGHT HERE. I'VE CHANGED.
NO MORE HOT-HEADED OLLIE?
STILL GOT A HOT HEAD, JUST LESS OF A DUMB ASS.
ENOUGH TIME HAS PASSED...I FEEL LIKE WE NEED TO GET PROPERLY REINTRODUCED.
I'M OLIVER QUEEN...
...ALSO KNOWN AS THE ONLY GREEN-THEMED SUPERHERO WHO ACTUALLY MATTERS.
HAL JORDAN. SPACE COP. HANDSOMER, STRONGER AND COOLER THAN YOU'LL EVER BE.
YOU SOUND LIKE MY KIND OF JERK. GOOD TO MEET YOU.
ALL OVER AGAIN.
SO THE BAT TELLS ME WE'RE COPILOTS ON THIS MISSION.
THERE WAS A TIME WHEN I WOULD HAVE INSISTED ON MY OWN TRICKED-OUT SPACE SUIT--RIDICULOUSLY EXPENSIVE, DESIGNED BY QUEEN INDUSTRIES--BUT...
...I'M BROKE.

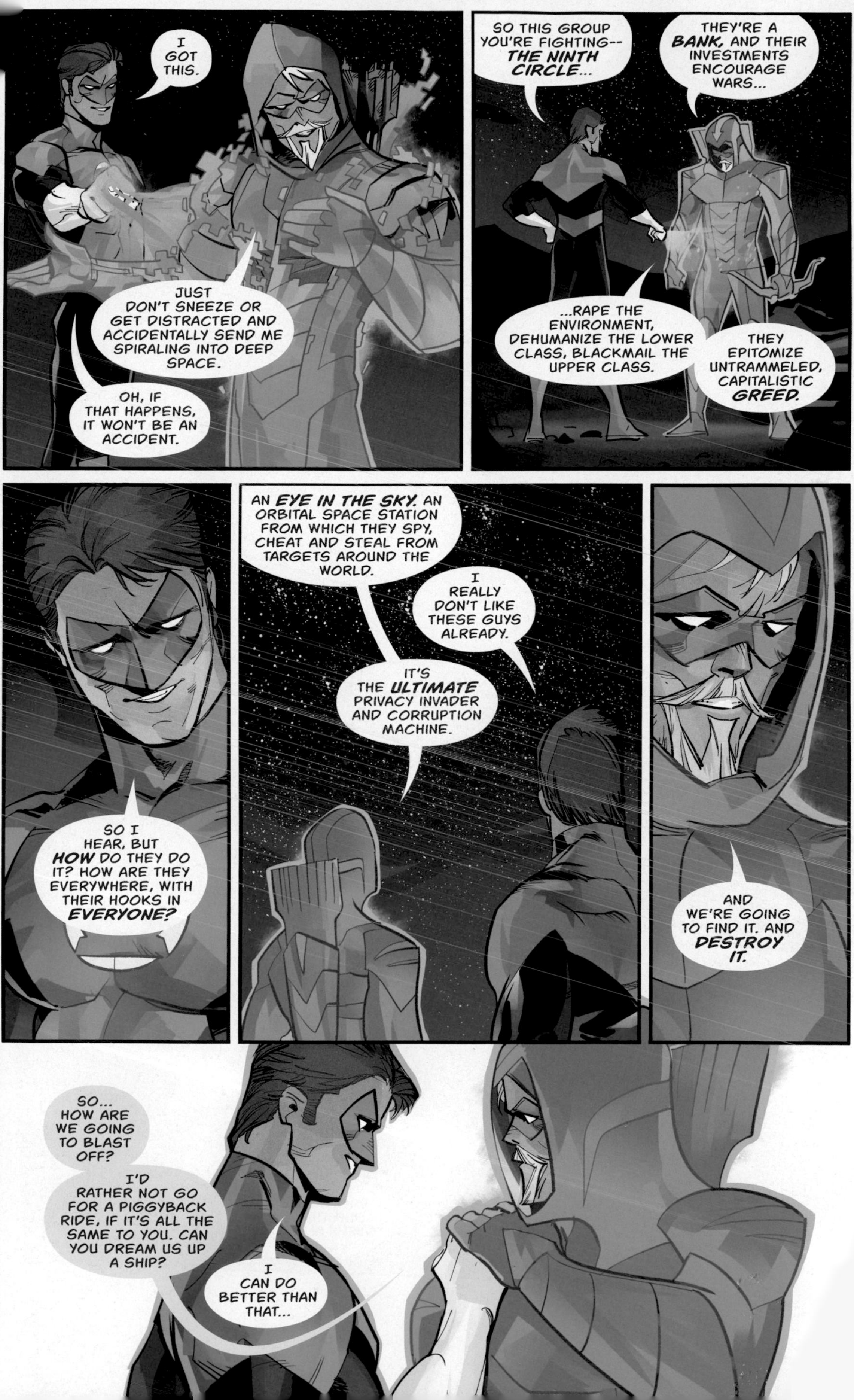
I GOT THIS.
JUST DON'T SNEEZE OR GET DISTRACTED AND ACCIDENTALLY SEND ME SPIRALING INTO DEEP SPACE.
OH, IF THAT HAPPENS, IT WON'T BE AN ACCIDENT.
SO THIS GROUP YOU'RE FIGHTING-- THE NINTH CIRCLE...
THEY'RE A BANK, AND THEIR INVESTMENTS ENCOURAGE WARS...
...RAPE THE ENVIRONMENT, DEHUMANIZE THE LOWER CLASS, BLACKMAIL THE UPPER CLASS.
THEY EPITOMIZE UNTRAMMELED, CAPITALISTIC GREED.
SO I HEAR, BUT HOW DO THEY DO IT? HOW ARE THEY EVERYWHERE, WITH THEIR HOOKS IN EVERYONE?
AN EYE IN THE SKY. AN ORBITAL SPACE STATION FROM WHICH THEY SPY, CHEAT AND STEAL FROM TARGETS AROUND THE WORLD.
I REALLY DON'T LIKE THESE GUYS ALREADY.
IT'S THE ULTIMATE PRIVACY INVADER AND CORRUPTION MACHINE.
AND WE'RE GOING TO FIND IT. AND DESTROY IT.
SO... HOW ARE WE GOING TO BLAST OFF?
I'D RATHER NOT GO FOR A PIGGYBACK RIDE, IF IT'S ALL THE SAME TO YOU. CAN YOU DREAM US UP A SHIP?
I CAN DO BETTER THAN THAT...

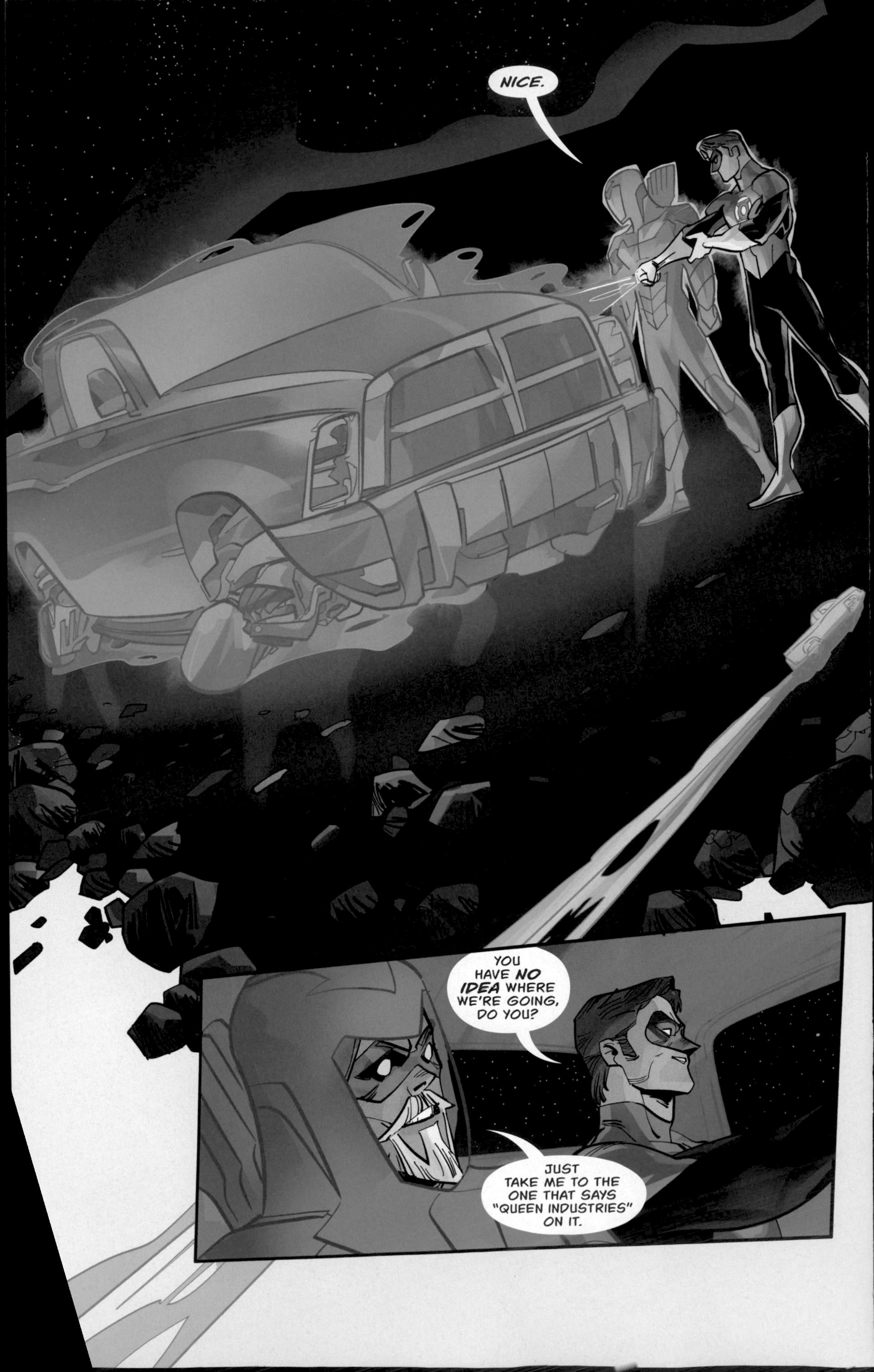
NICE.
YOU HAVE NO IDEA WHERE WE'RE GOING, DO YOU?
JUST TAKE ME TO THE ONE THAT SAYS "QUEEN INDUSTRIES" ON IT.

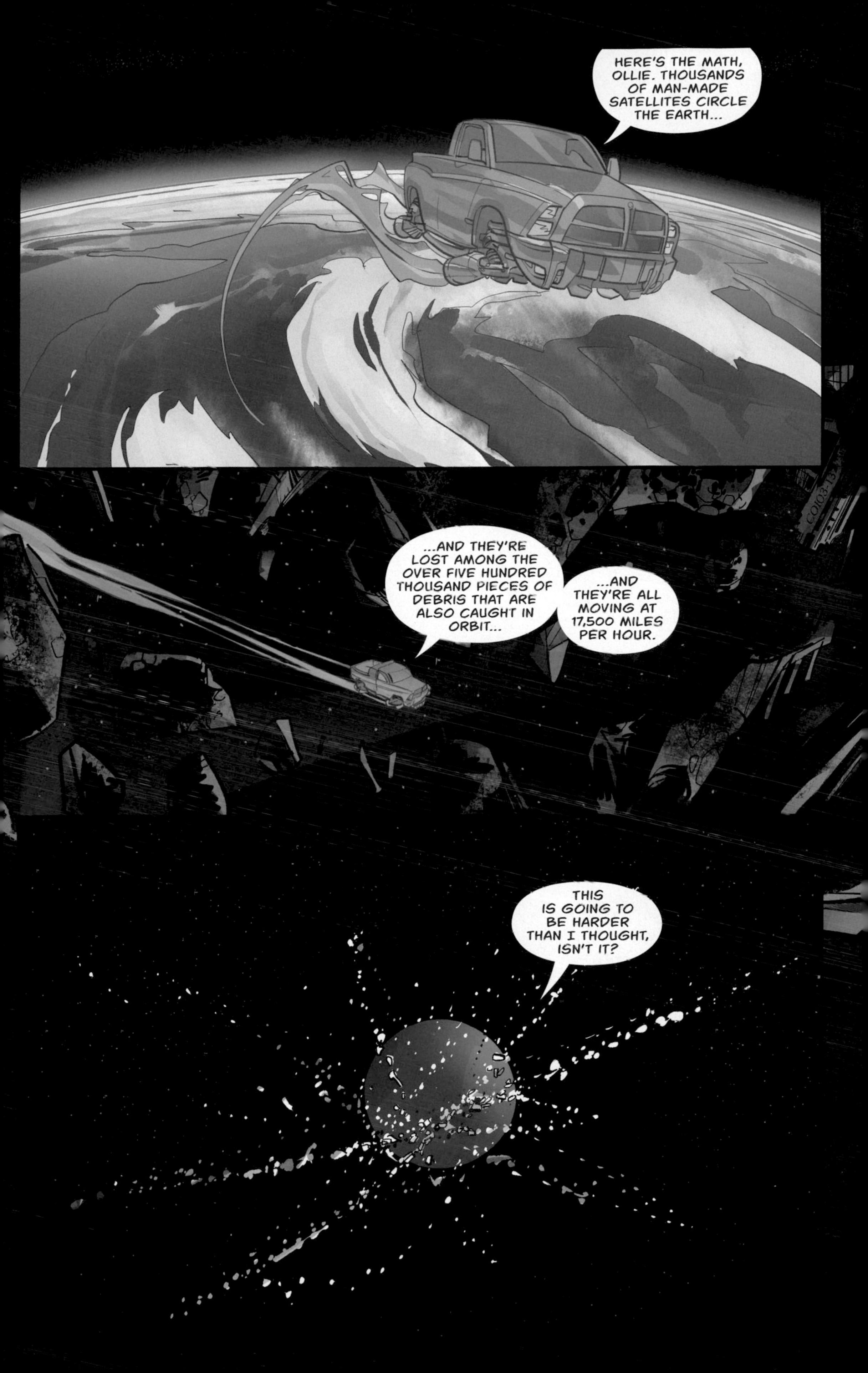
HERE'S THE MATH, OLLIE. THOUSANDS OF MAN-MADE SATELLITES CIRCLE THE EARTH...
...AND THEY'RE LOST AMONG THE OVER FIVE HUNDRED THOUSAND PIECES OF DEBRIS THAT ARE ALSO CAUGHT IN ORBIT...
...AND THEY'RE ALL MOVING AT 17,500 MILES PER HOUR.
THIS IS GOING TO BE HARDER THAN I THOUGHT, ISN'T IT?

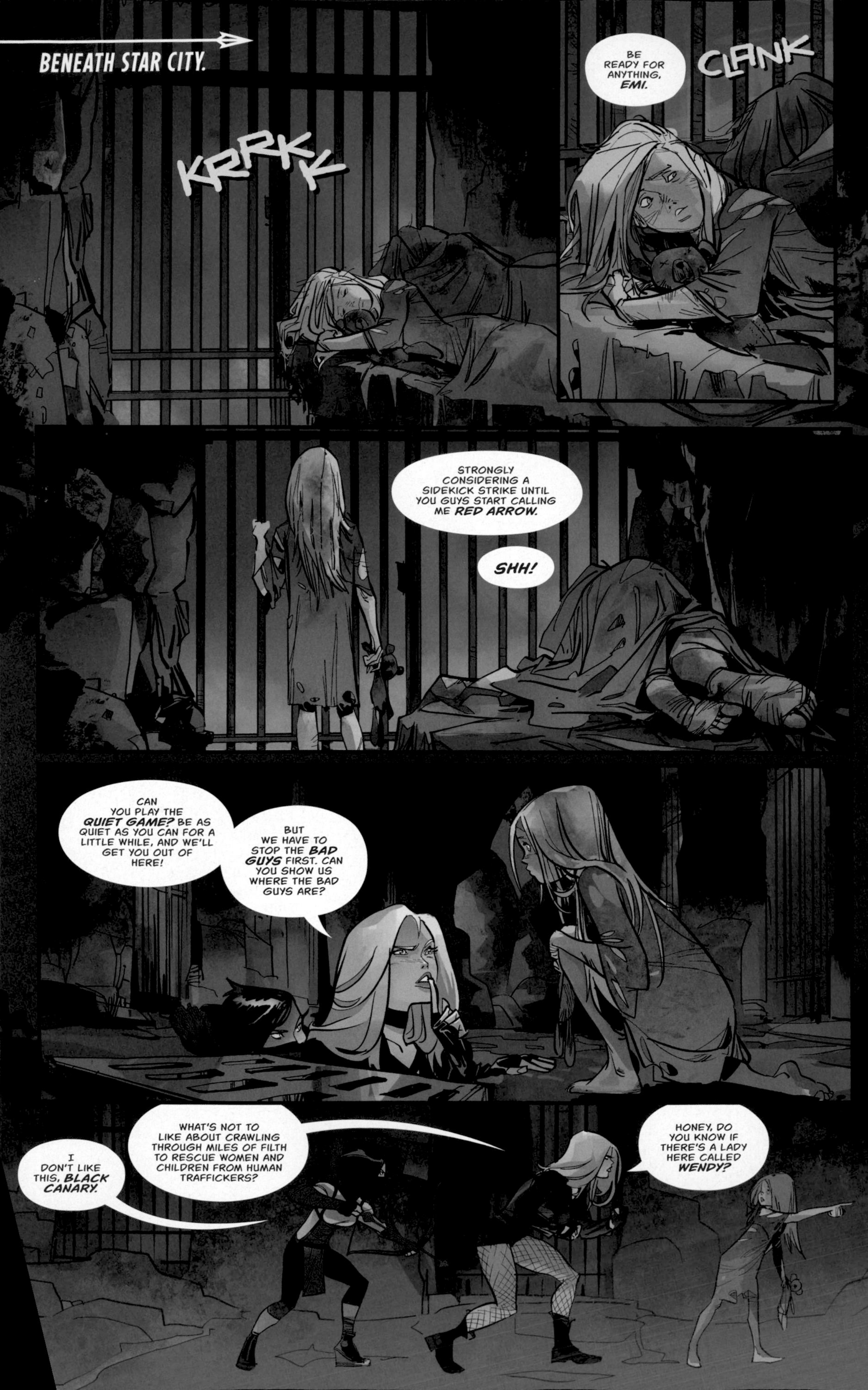
BENEATH STAR CITY.
KRRKK
BE READY FOR ANYTHING, EMI.
CLANK
STRONGLY CONSIDERING A SIDEKICK STRIKE UNTIL YOU GUYS START CALLING ME RED ARROW.
SHH!
CAN YOU PLAY THE QUIET GAME? BE AS QUIET AS YOU CAN FOR A LITTLE WHILE, AND WE'LL GET YOU OUT OF HERE!
BUT WE HAVE TO STOP THE BAD GUYS FIRST. CAN YOU SHOW US WHERE THE BAD GUYS ARE?
I DON'T LIKE THIS, BLACK CANARY.
WHAT'S NOT TO LIKE ABOUT CRAWLING THROUGH MILES OF FILTH TO RESCUE WOMEN AND CHILDREN FROM HUMAN TRAFFICKERS?
HONEY, DO YOU KNOW IF THERE'S A LADY HERE CALLED WENDY?

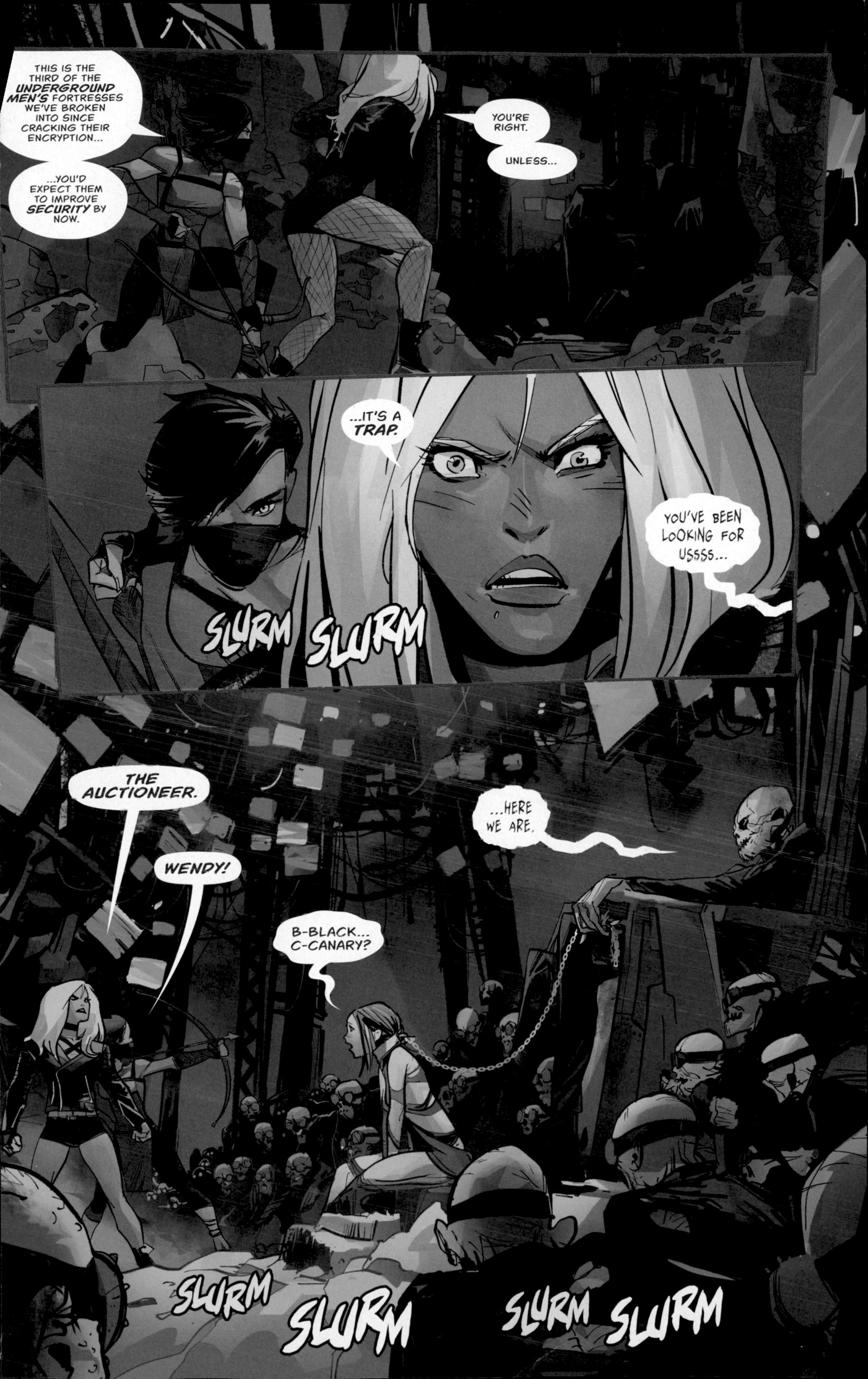
THIS IS THE THIRD OF THE UNDERGROUND MEN'S FORTRESSES WE'VE BROKEN INTO SINCE CRACKING THEIR ENCRYPTION...
...YOU'D EXPECT THEM TO IMPROVE SECURITY BY NOW.
YOU'RE RIGHT.
UNLESS...
...IT'S A TRAP.
YOU'VE BEEN LOOKING FOR USSSS...
SLURM SLURM
THE AUCTIONEER.
...HERE WE ARE.
WENDY!
B-BLACK... C-CANARY?
SLURM SLURM SLURM SLURM

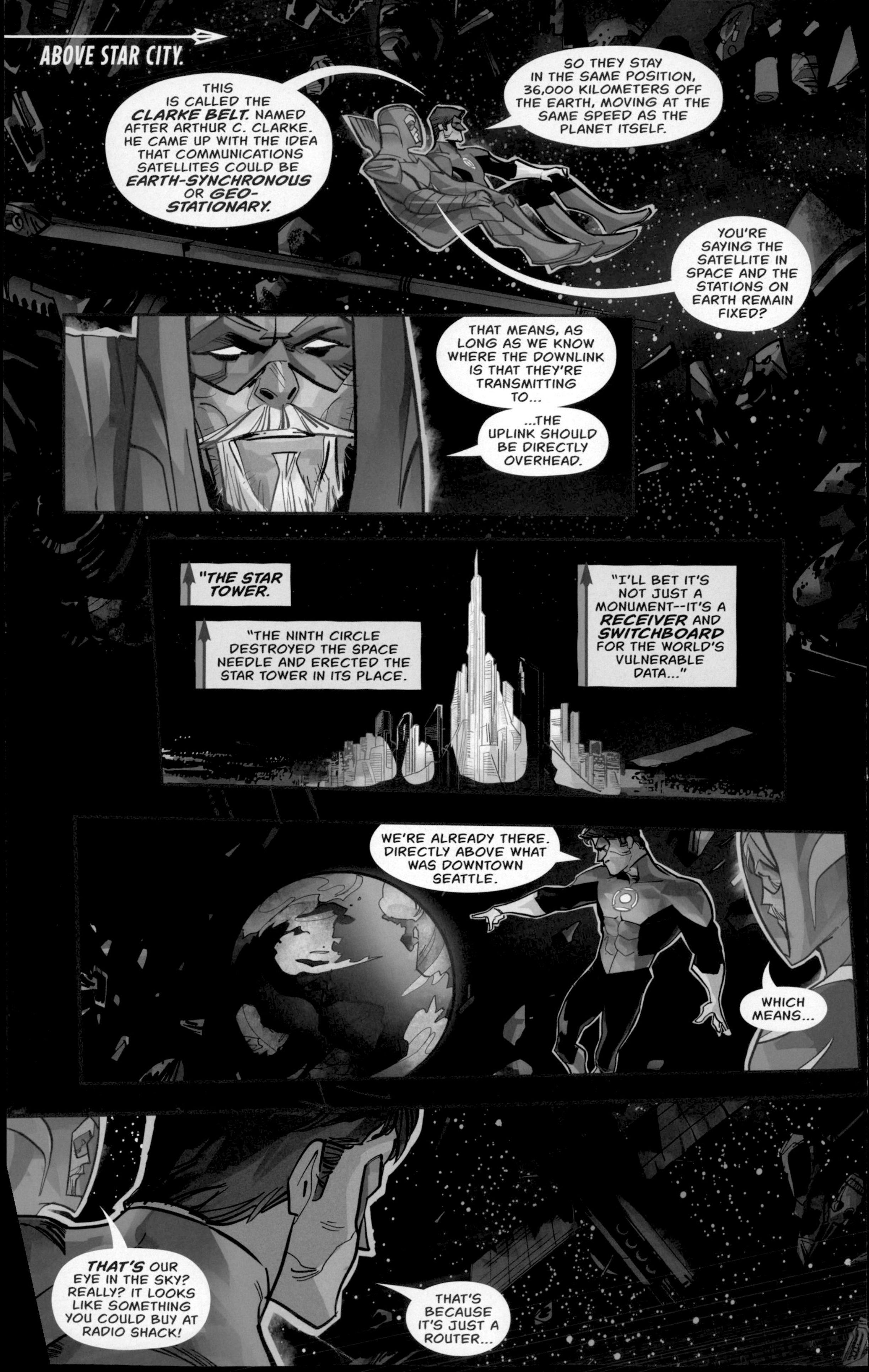
ABOVE STAR CITY.
THIS IS CALLED THE CLARKE BELT. NAMED AFTER ARTHUR C. CLARKE. HE CAME UP WITH THE IDEA THAT COMMUNICATIONS SATELLITES COULD BE EARTH-SYNCHRONOUS OR GEO-STATIONARY.
SO THEY STAY IN THE SAME POSITION, 36,000 KILOMETERS OFF THE EARTH, MOVING AT THE SAME SPEED AS THE PLANET ITSELF.
YOU'RE SAYING THE SATELLITE IN SPACE AND THE STATIONS ON EARTH REMAIN FIXED?
THAT MEANS, AS LONG AS WE KNOW WHERE THE DOWNLINK IS THAT THEY'RE TRANSMITTING TO...
...THE UPLINK SHOULD BE DIRECTLY OVERHEAD.
"THE STAR TOWER.
"THE NINTH CIRCLE DESTROYED THE SPACE NEEDLE AND ERECTED THE STAR TOWER IN ITS PLACE.
"I'LL BET IT'S NOT JUST A MONUMENT--IT'S A RECEIVER AND SWITCHBOARD FOR THE WORLD'S VULNERABLE DATA..."
WE'RE ALREADY THERE. DIRECTLY ABOVE WHAT WAS DOWNTOWN SEATTLE.
WHICH MEANS...
THAT'S OUR EYE IN THE SKY? REALLY? IT LOOKS LIKE SOMETHING YOU COULD BUY AT RADIO SHACK!
THAT'S BECAUSE IT'S JUST A ROUTER...

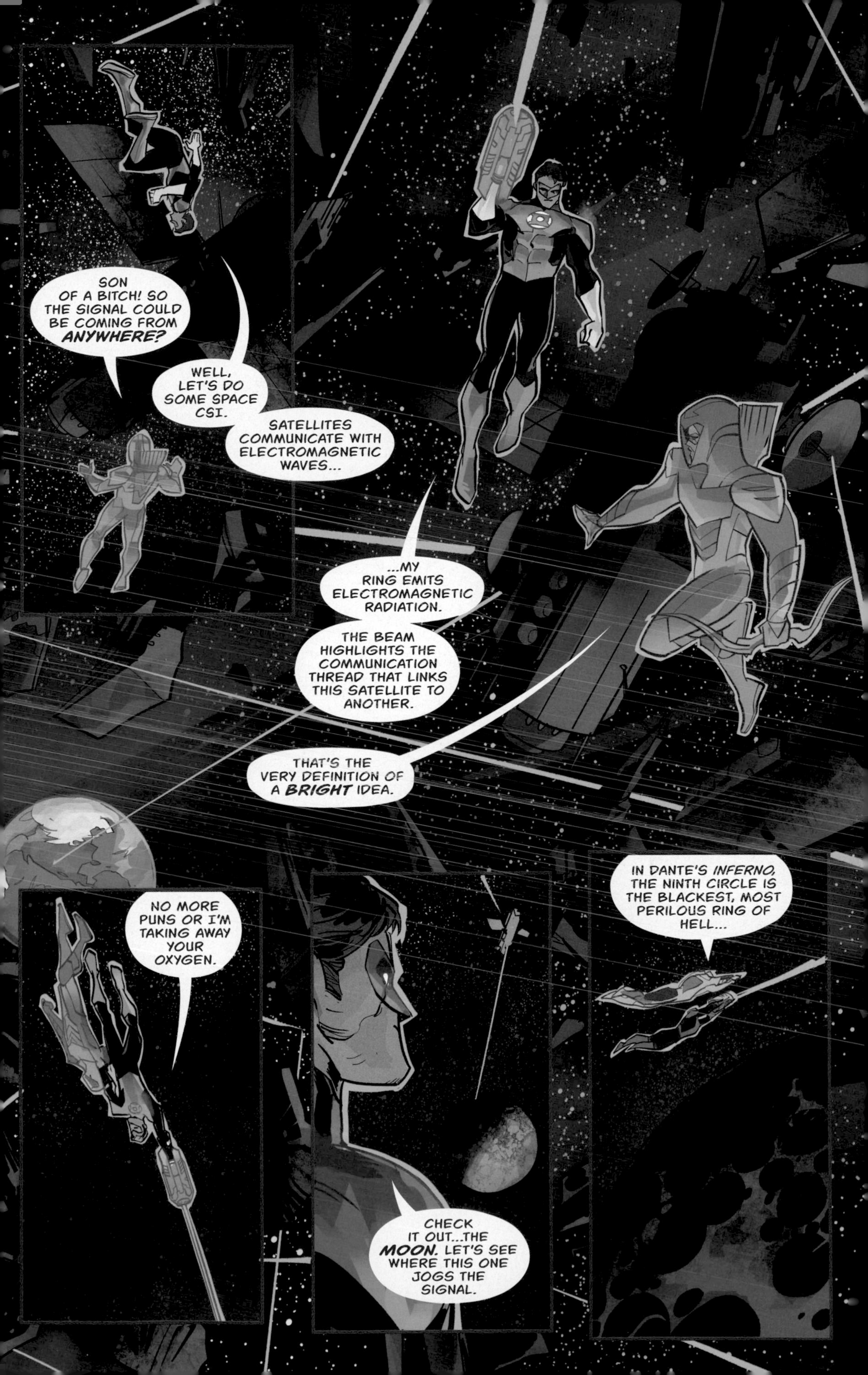
SON OF A BITCH! SO THE SIGNAL COULD BE COMING FROM ANYWHERE?
WELL, LET'S DO SOME SPACE CSI.
SATELLITES COMMUNICATE WITH ELECTROMAGNETIC WAVES...
...MY RING EMITS ELECTROMAGNETIC RADIATION.
THE BEAM HIGHLIGHTS THE COMMUNICATION THREAD THAT LINKS THIS SATELLITE TO ANOTHER.
THAT'S THE VERY DEFINITION OF A BRIGHT IDEA.
NO MORE PUNS OR I'M TAKING AWAY YOUR OXYGEN.
CHECK IT OUT...THE MOON. LET'S SEE WHERE THIS ONE JOGS THE SIGNAL.
IN DANTE'S INFERNO, THE NINTH CIRCLE IS THE BLACKEST, MOST PERILOUS RING OF HELL...

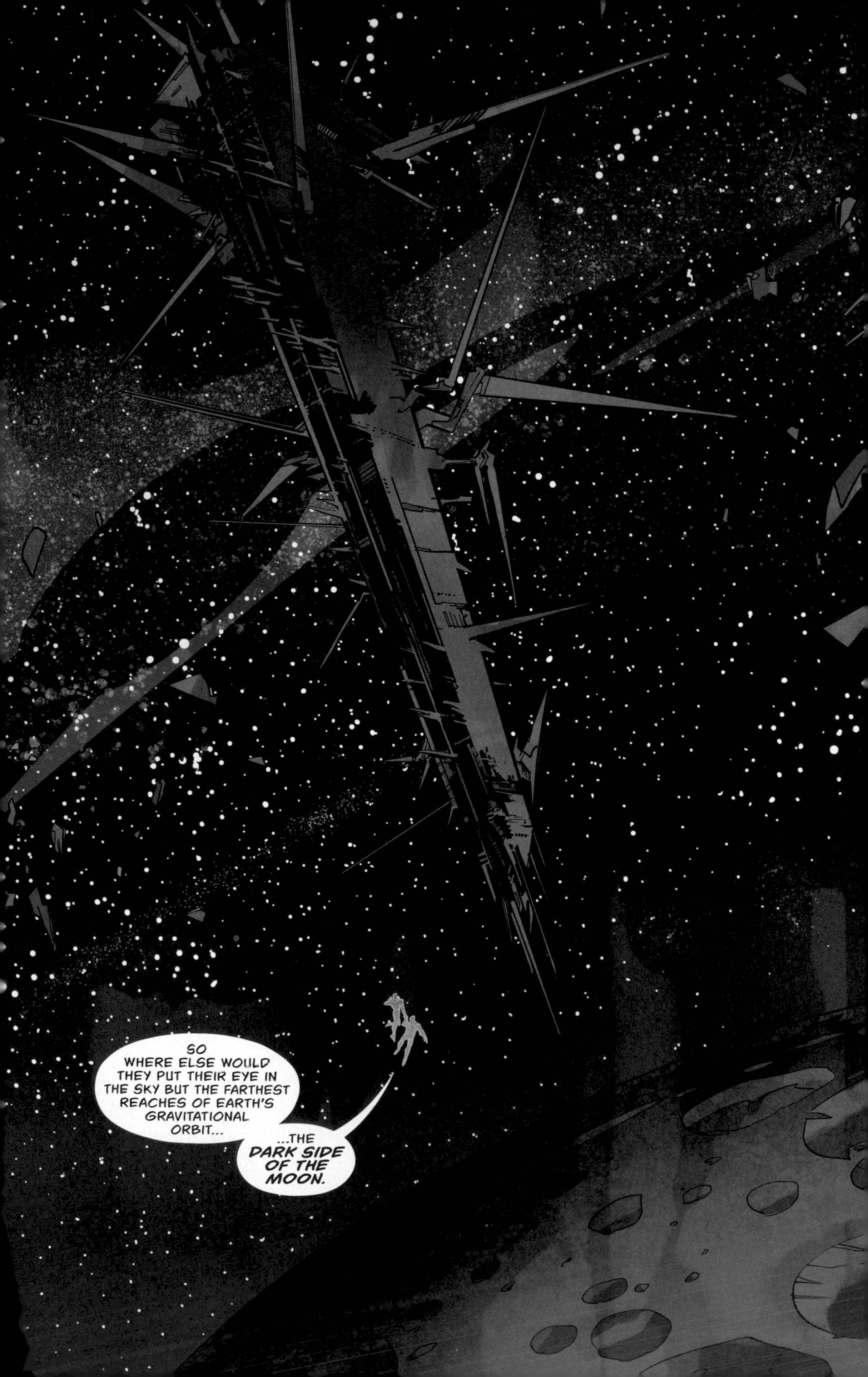
SO WHERE ELSE WOULD THEY PUT THEIR EYE IN THE SKY BUT THE FARTHEST REACHES OF EARTH'S GRAVITATIONAL ORBIT...
...THE *DARK SIDE OF THE MOON.*

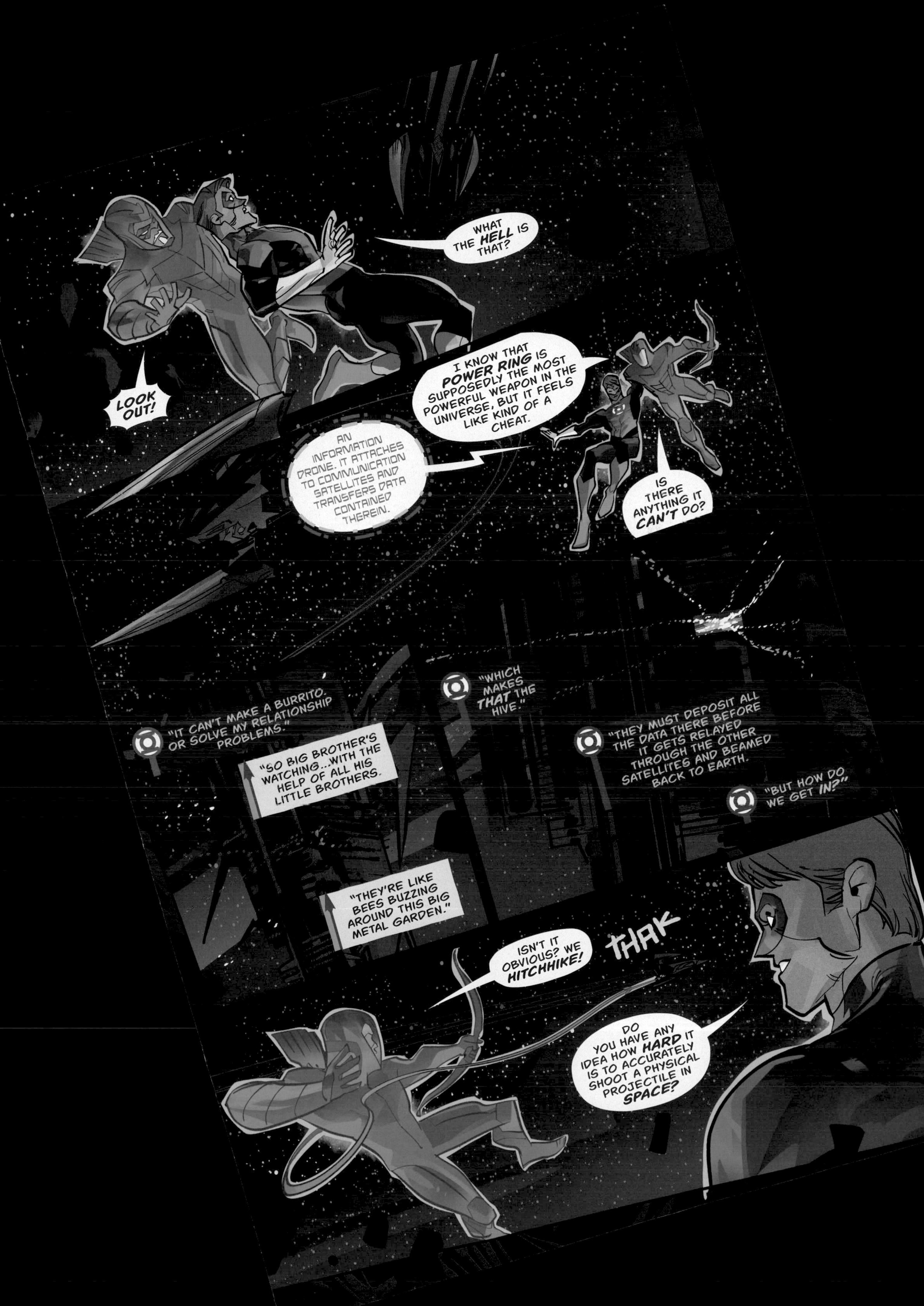
WHAT THE HELL IS THAT?
LOOK OUT!
AN INFORMATION DRONE. IT ATTACHES TO COMMUNICATION SATELLITES AND TRANSFERS DATA CONTAINED THEREIN.
I KNOW THAT POWER RING IS SUPPOSEDLY THE MOST POWERFUL WEAPON IN THE UNIVERSE, BUT IT FEELS LIKE KIND OF A CHEAT.
IS THERE ANYTHING IT CAN'T DO?
"IT CAN'T MAKE A BURRITO. OR SOLVE MY RELATIONSHIP PROBLEMS."
"SO BIG BROTHER'S WATCHING...WITH THE HELP OF ALL HIS LITTLE BROTHERS.
"WHICH MAKES THAT THE HIVE."
"THEY MUST DEPOSIT ALL THE DATA THERE BEFORE IT GETS RELAYED THROUGH THE OTHER SATELLITES AND BEAMED BACK TO EARTH.
"THEY'RE LIKE BEES BUZZING AROUND THIS BIG METAL GARDEN."
"BUT HOW DO WE GET IN?"
ISN'T IT OBVIOUS? WE HITCHHIKE!
THAK
DO YOU HAVE ANY IDEA HOW HARD IT IS TO ACCURATELY SHOOT A PHYSICAL PROJECTILE IN SPACE?

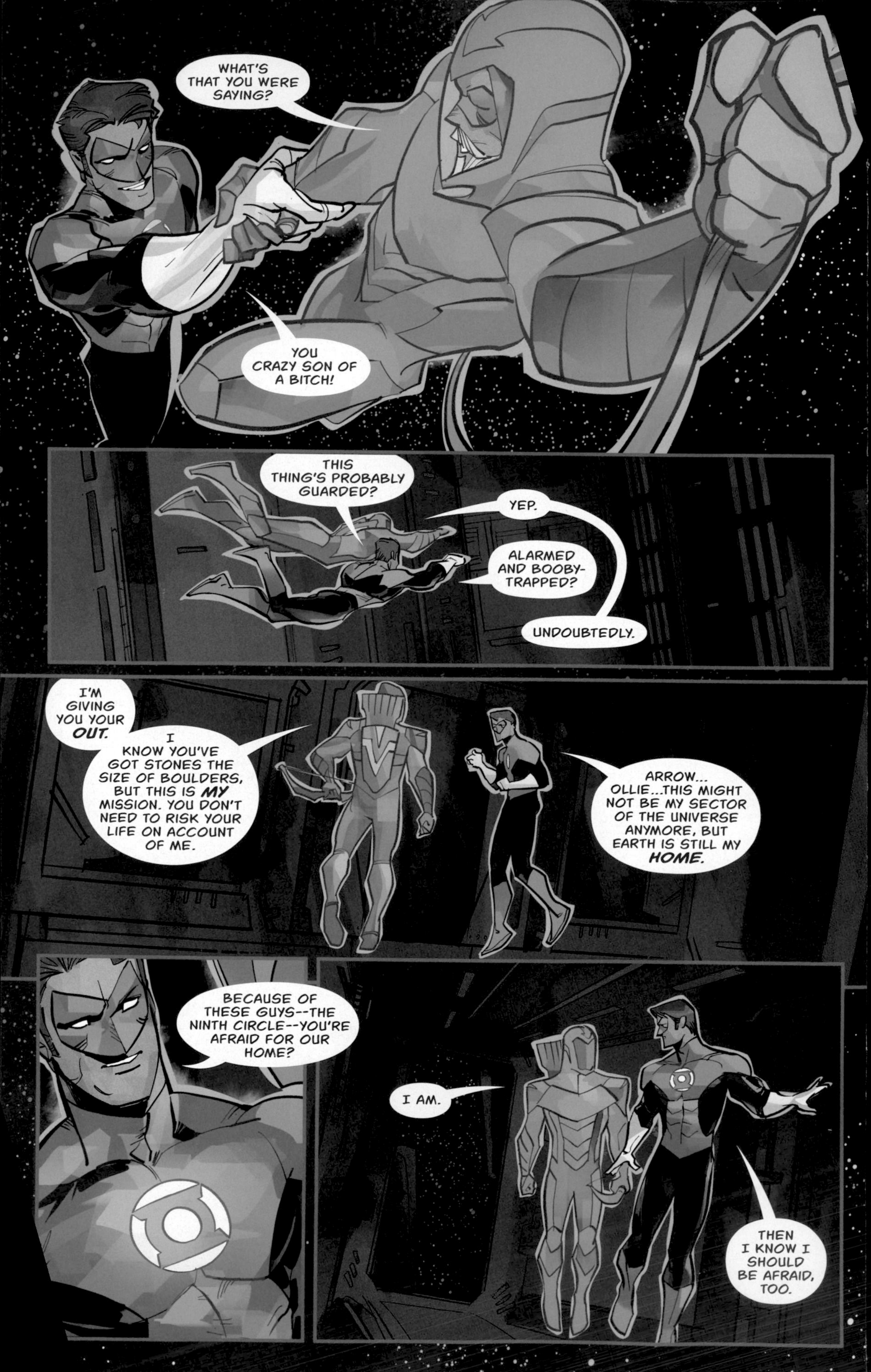
WHAT'S THAT YOU WERE SAYING?
YOU CRAZY SON OF A BITCH!
THIS THING'S PROBABLY GUARDED?
YEP.
ALARMED AND BOOBY-TRAPPED?
UNDOUBTEDLY.
I'M GIVING YOU YOUR *OUT.*
I KNOW YOU'VE GOT STONES THE SIZE OF BOULDERS, BUT THIS IS *MY* MISSION. YOU DON'T NEED TO RISK YOUR LIFE ON ACCOUNT OF ME.
ARROW... OLLIE...THIS MIGHT NOT BE MY SECTOR OF THE UNIVERSE ANYMORE, BUT EARTH IS STILL MY *HOME.*
BECAUSE OF THESE GUYS--THE NINTH CIRCLE--YOU'RE AFRAID FOR OUR HOME?
I AM.
THEN I KNOW I SHOULD BE AFRAID, TOO.

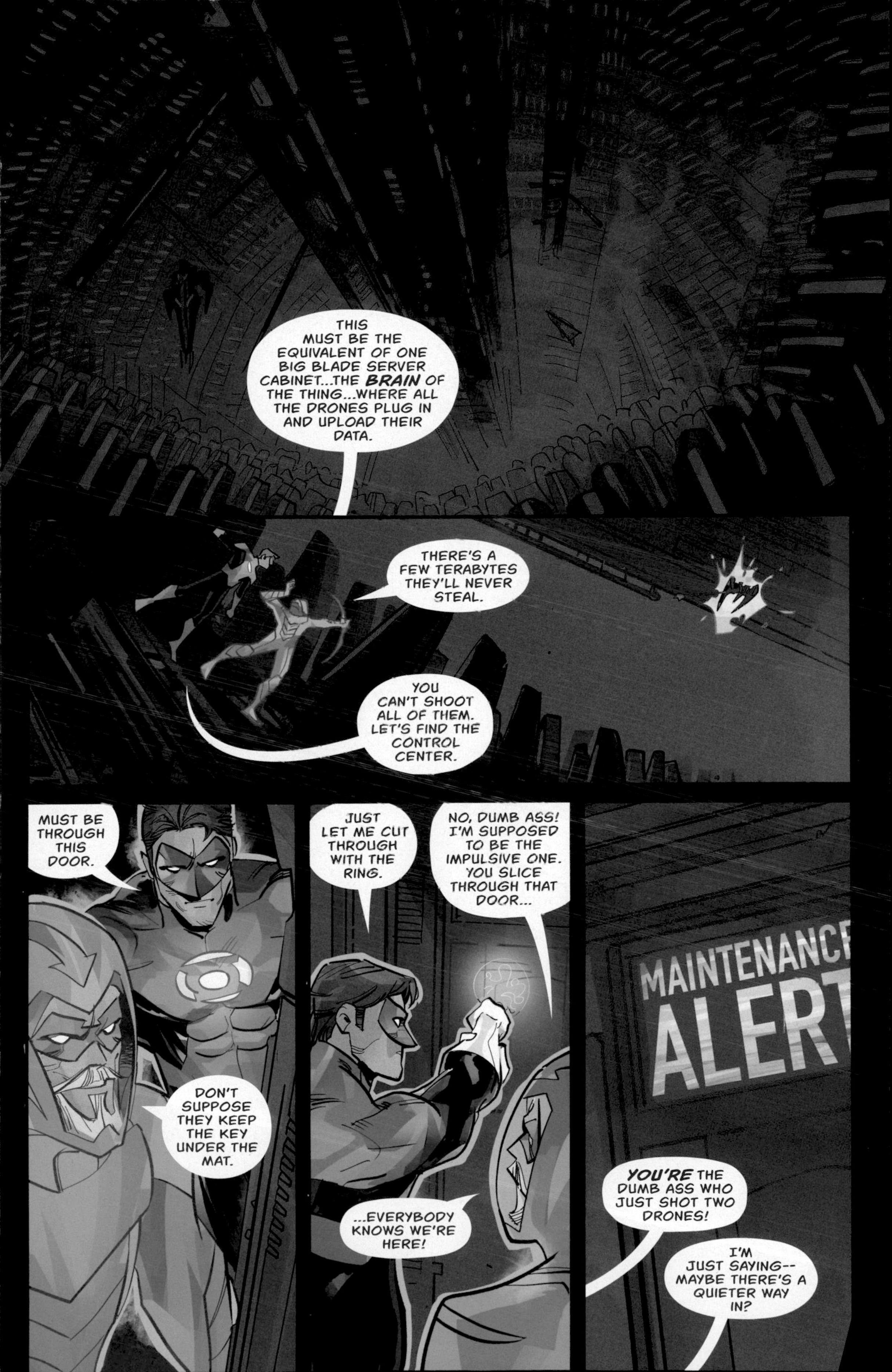

THIS MUST BE THE EQUIVALENT OF ONE BIG BLADE SERVER CABINET...THE **BRAIN** OF THE THING...WHERE ALL THE DRONES PLUG IN AND UPLOAD THEIR DATA.
THERE'S A FEW TERABYTES THEY'LL NEVER STEAL.
YOU CAN'T SHOOT ALL OF THEM. LET'S FIND THE CONTROL CENTER.
MUST BE THROUGH THIS DOOR.
DON'T SUPPOSE THEY KEEP THE KEY UNDER THE MAT.
JUST LET ME CUT THROUGH WITH THE RING.
NO, DUMB ASS! I'M SUPPOSED TO BE THE IMPULSIVE ONE. YOU SLICE THROUGH THAT DOOR...
...EVERYBODY KNOWS WE'RE HERE!
MAINTENANCE ALERT
***YOU'RE*** THE DUMB ASS WHO JUST SHOT TWO DRONES!
I'M JUST SAYING-- MAYBE THERE'S A QUIETER WAY IN?

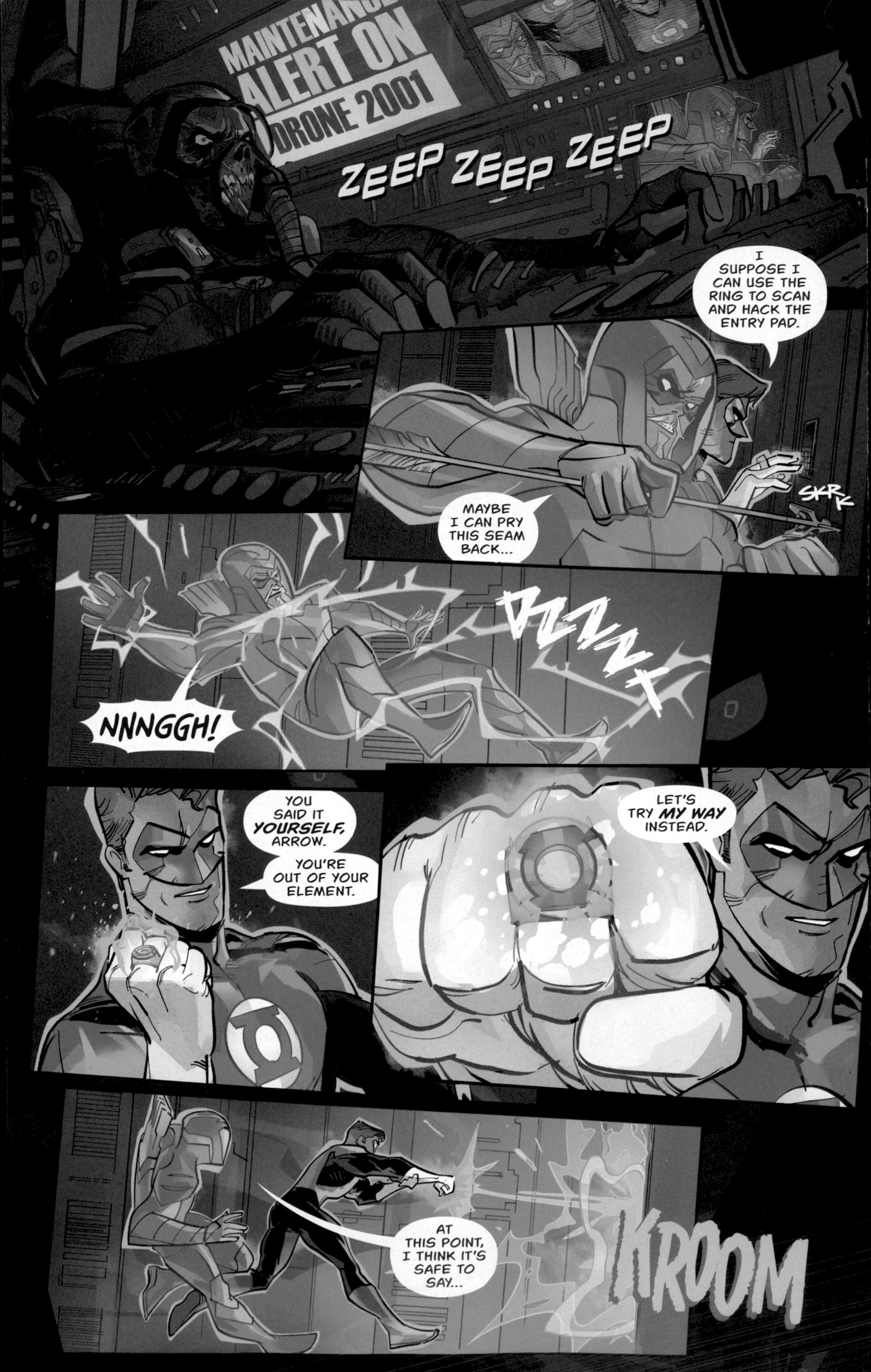
MAINTENANCE ALERT ON DRONE 2001
ZEEP ZEEP ZEEP
I SUPPOSE I CAN USE THE RING TO SCAN AND HACK THE ENTRY PAD.
SKRK
MAYBE I CAN PRY THIS SEAM BACK...
DZZZT
NNNGGH!
YOU SAID IT YOURSELF, ARROW.
YOU'RE OUT OF YOUR ELEMENT.
LET'S TRY MY WAY INSTEAD.
KROOM
AT THIS POINT, I THINK IT'S SAFE TO SAY...

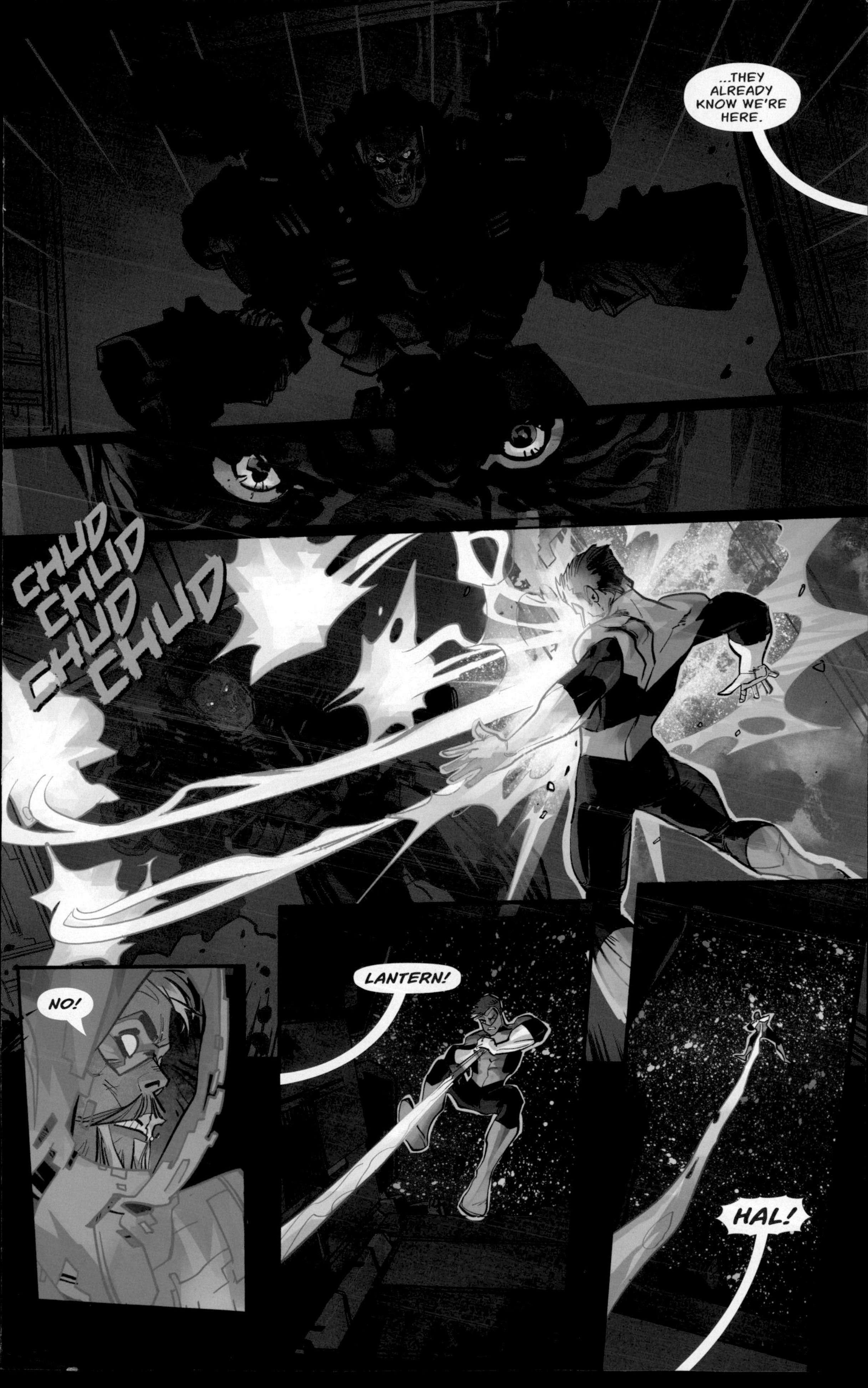
...THEY ALREADY KNOW WE'RE HERE.
CHUD CHUD CHUD CHUD
NO!
LANTERN!
HAL!

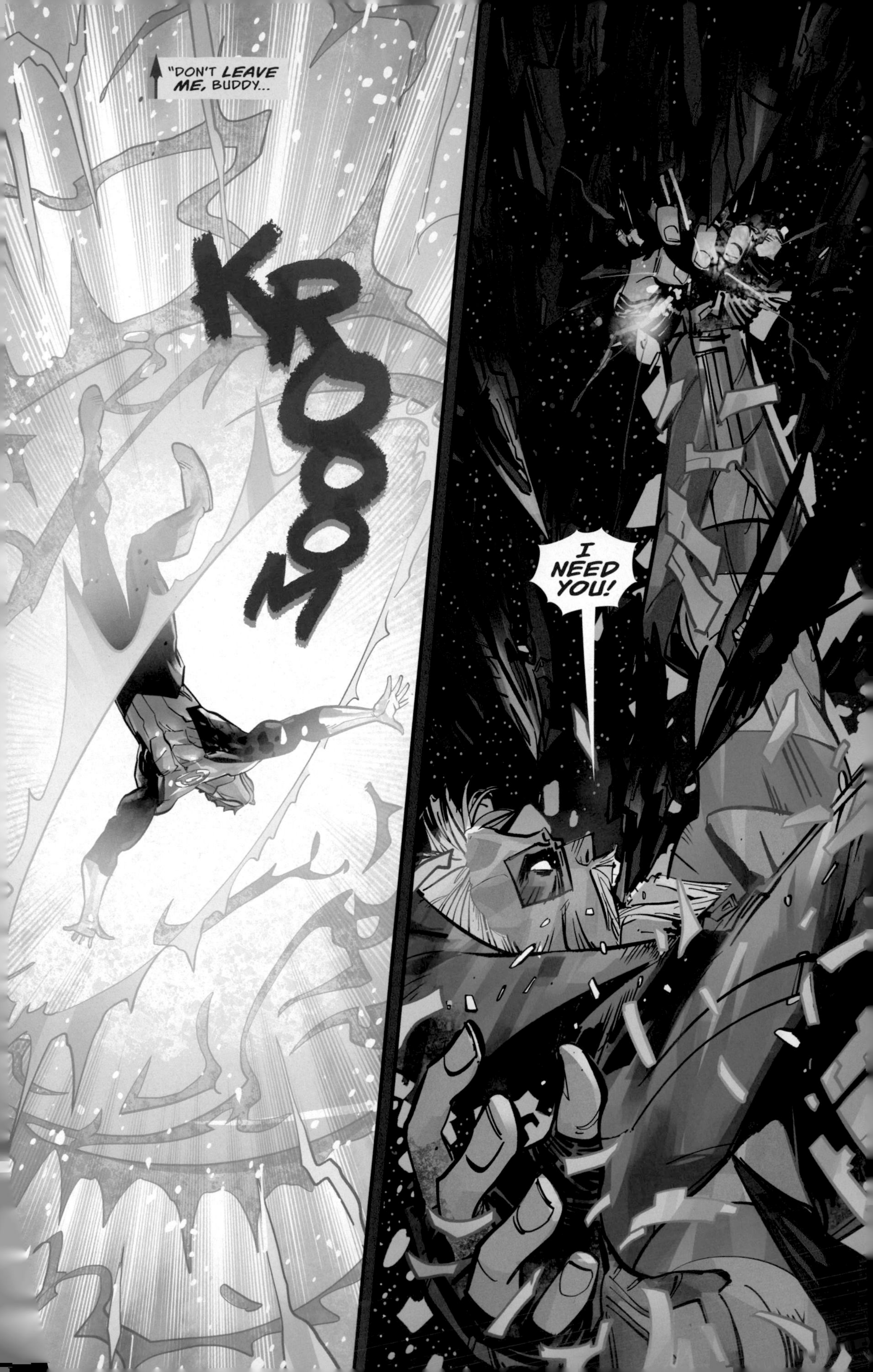
"DON'T LEAVE ME, BUDDY...
KROOOM
I NEED YOU!

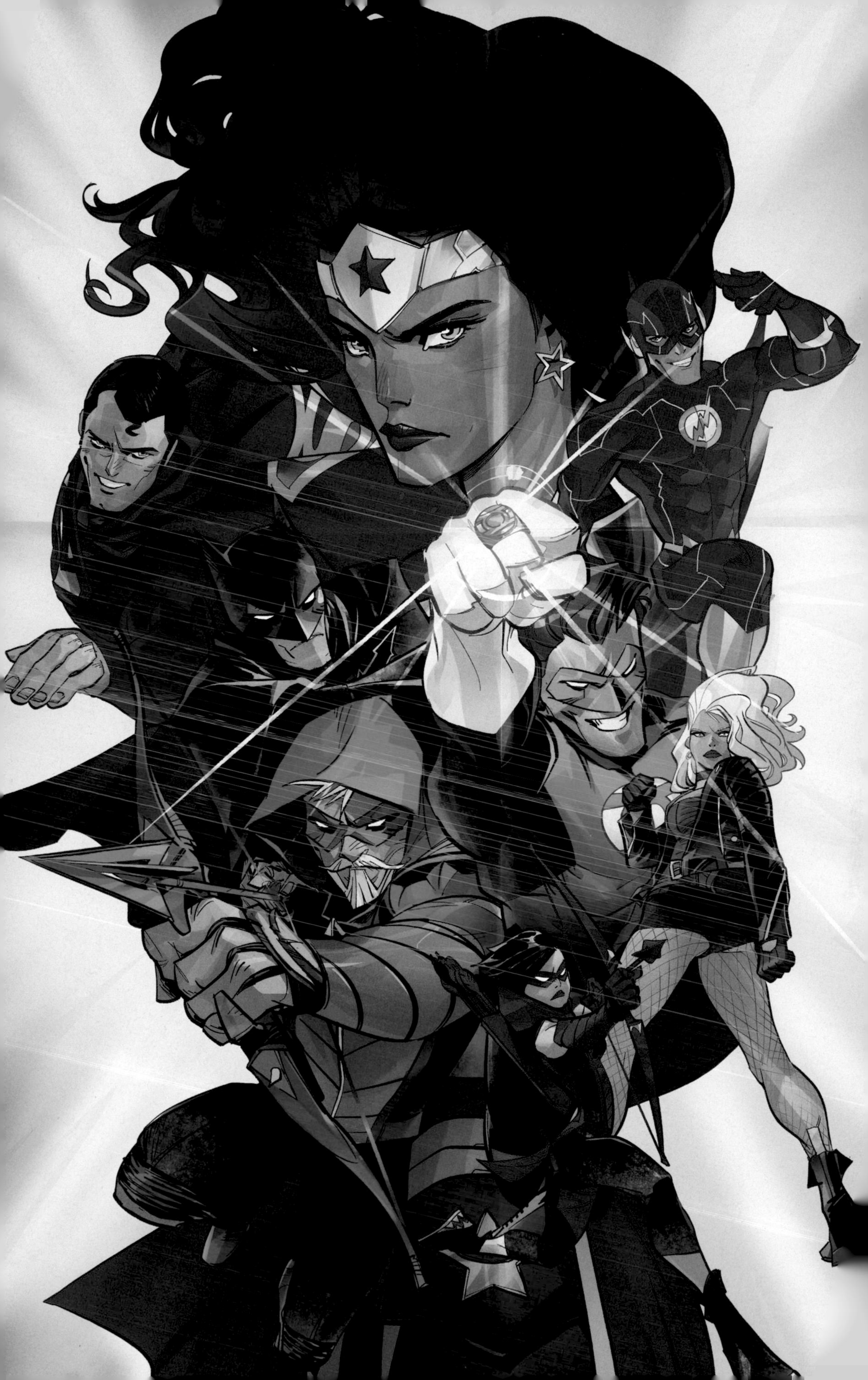

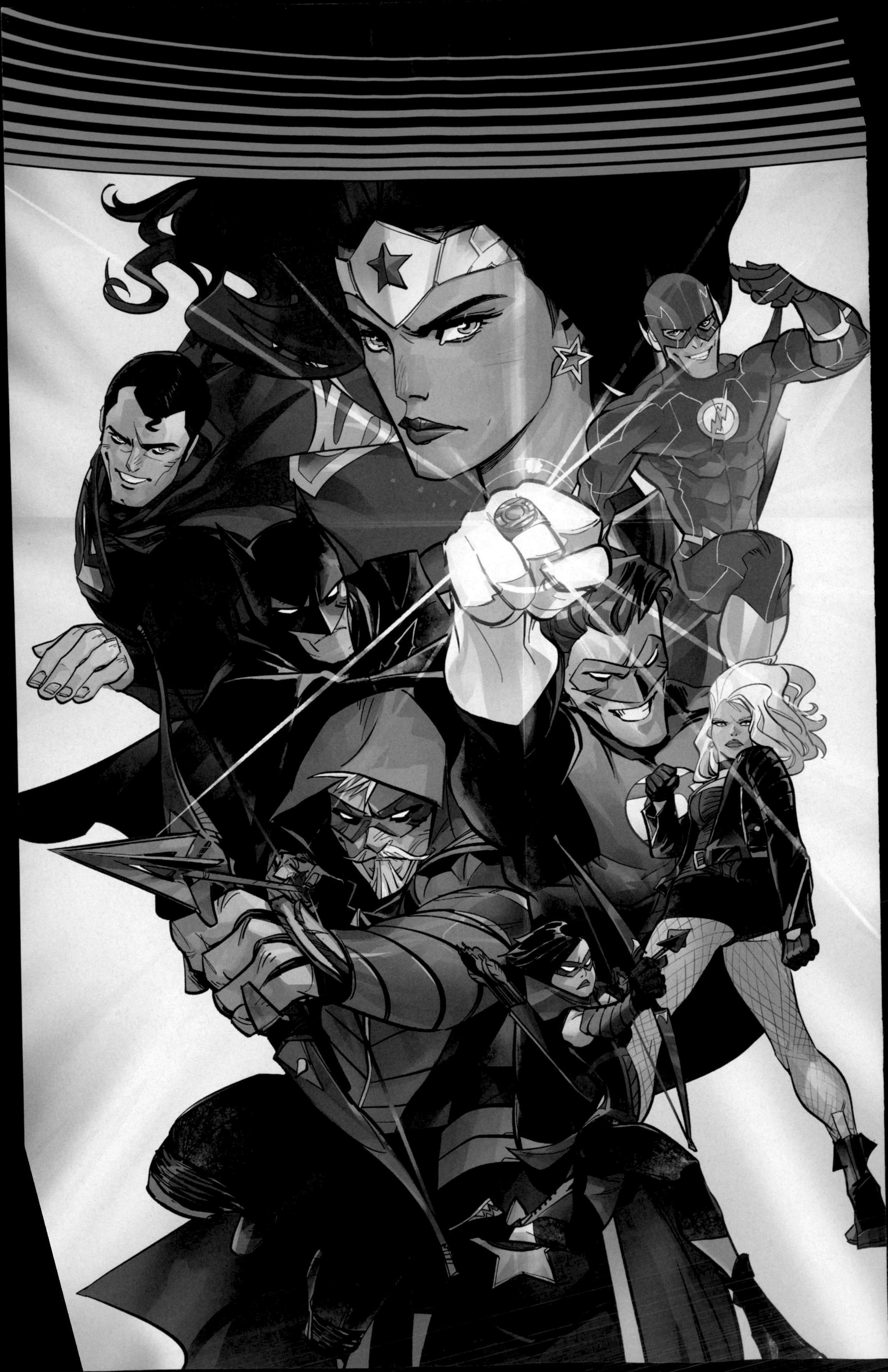

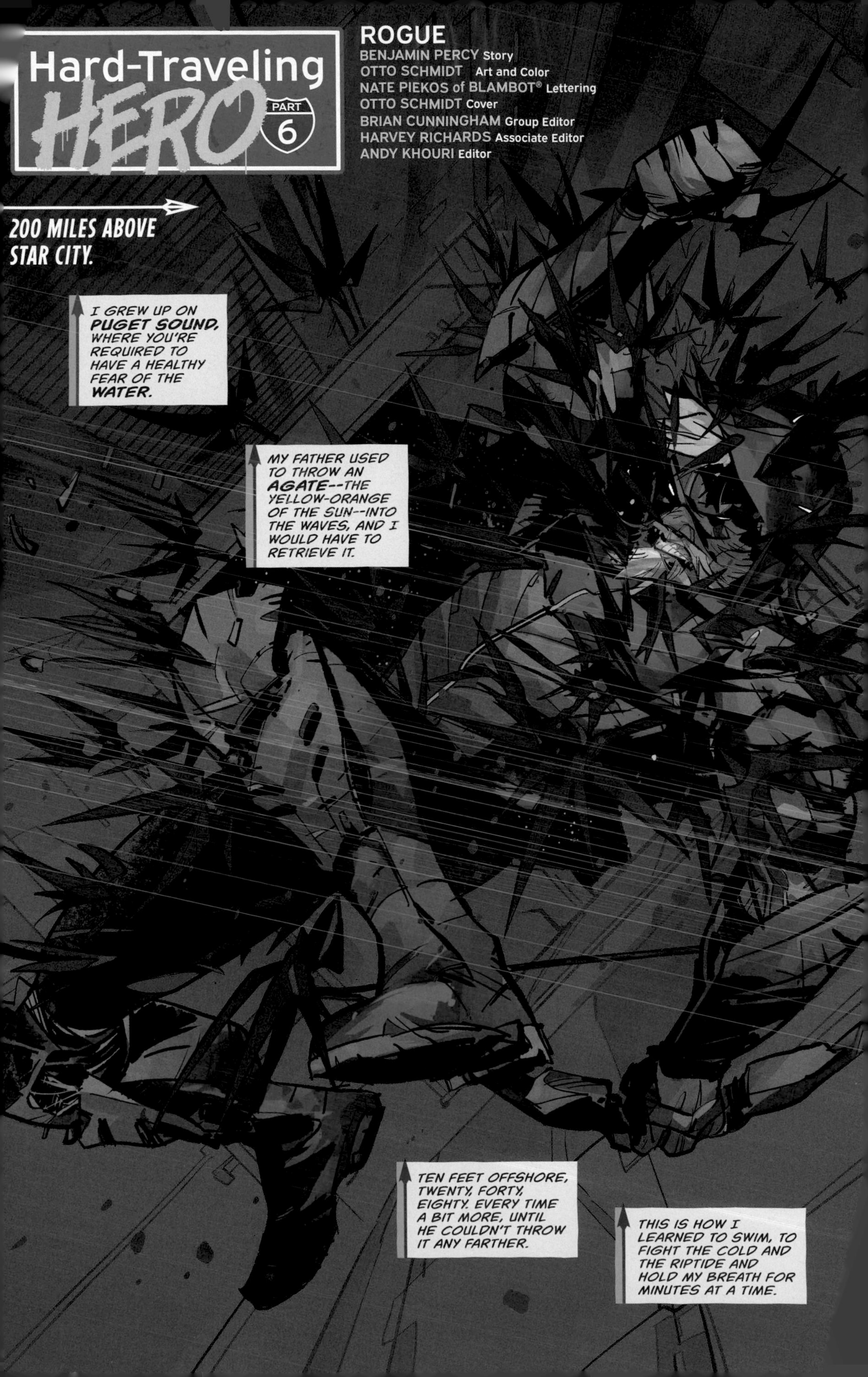
Hard-Traveling HERO
PART 6
ROGUE
BENJAMIN PERCY Story
OTTO SCHMIDT Art and Color
NATE PIEKOS of BLAMBOT® Lettering
OTTO SCHMIDT Cover
BRIAN CUNNINGHAM Group Editor
HARVEY RICHARDS Associate Editor
ANDY KHOURI Editor
200 MILES ABOVE STAR CITY.
I GREW UP ON PUGET SOUND, WHERE YOU'RE REQUIRED TO HAVE A HEALTHY FEAR OF THE WATER.
MY FATHER USED TO THROW AN AGATE--THE YELLOW-ORANGE OF THE SUN--INTO THE WAVES, AND I WOULD HAVE TO RETRIEVE IT.
TEN FEET OFFSHORE, TWENTY, FORTY, EIGHTY. EVERY TIME A BIT MORE, UNTIL HE COULDN'T THROW IT ANY FARTHER.
THIS IS HOW I LEARNED TO SWIM, TO FIGHT THE COLD AND THE RIPTIDE AND HOLD MY BREATH FOR MINUTES AT A TIME.

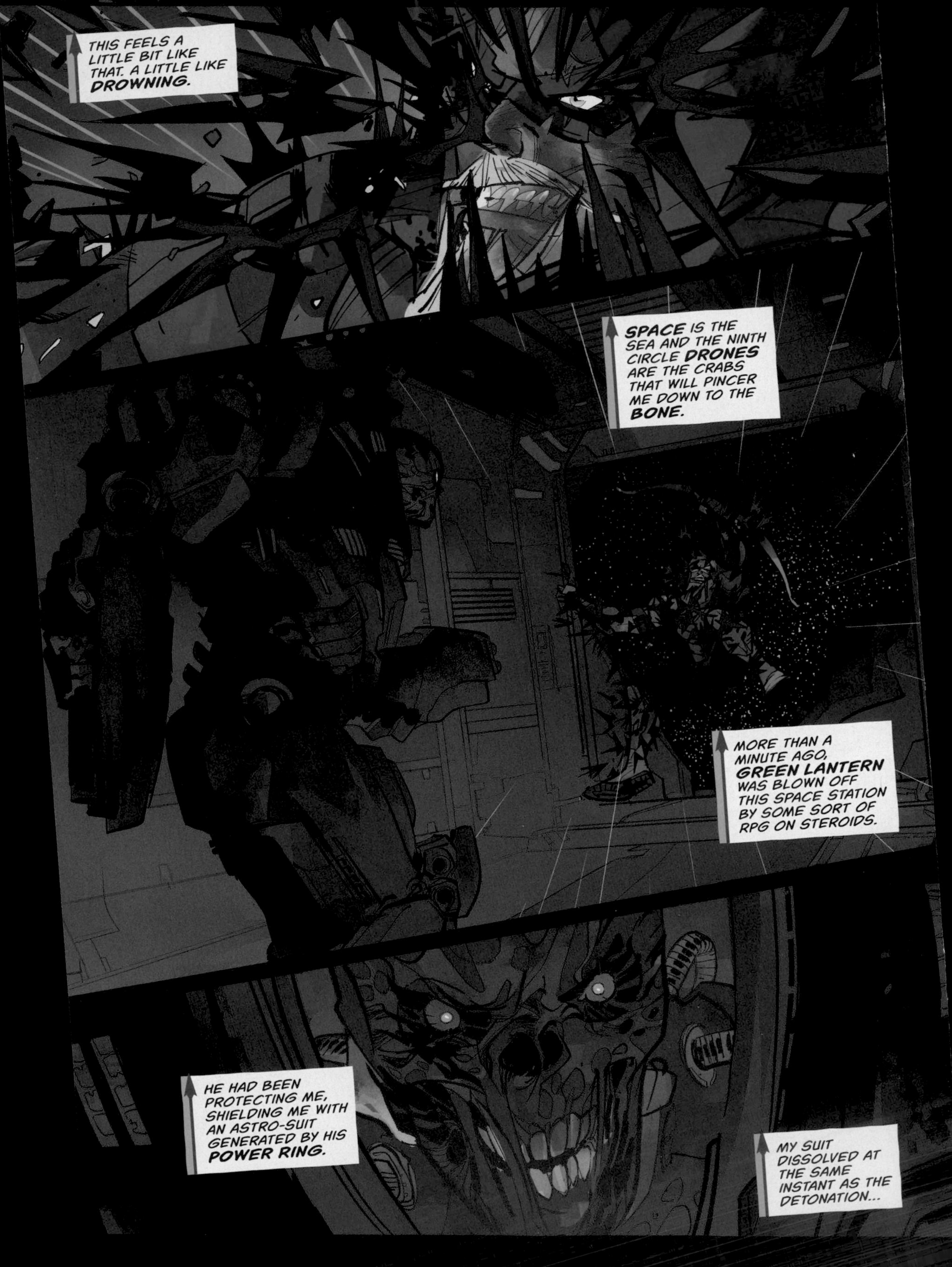
THIS FEELS A LITTLE BIT LIKE THAT. A LITTLE LIKE DROWNING.
SPACE IS THE SEA AND THE NINTH CIRCLE DRONES ARE THE CRABS THAT WILL PINCER ME DOWN TO THE BONE.
MORE THAN A MINUTE AGO, GREEN LANTERN WAS BLOWN OFF THIS SPACE STATION BY SOME SORT OF RPG ON STEROIDS.
HE HAD BEEN PROTECTING ME, SHIELDING ME WITH AN ASTRO-SUIT GENERATED BY HIS POWER RING.
MY SUIT DISSOLVED AT THE SAME INSTANT AS THE DETONATION...

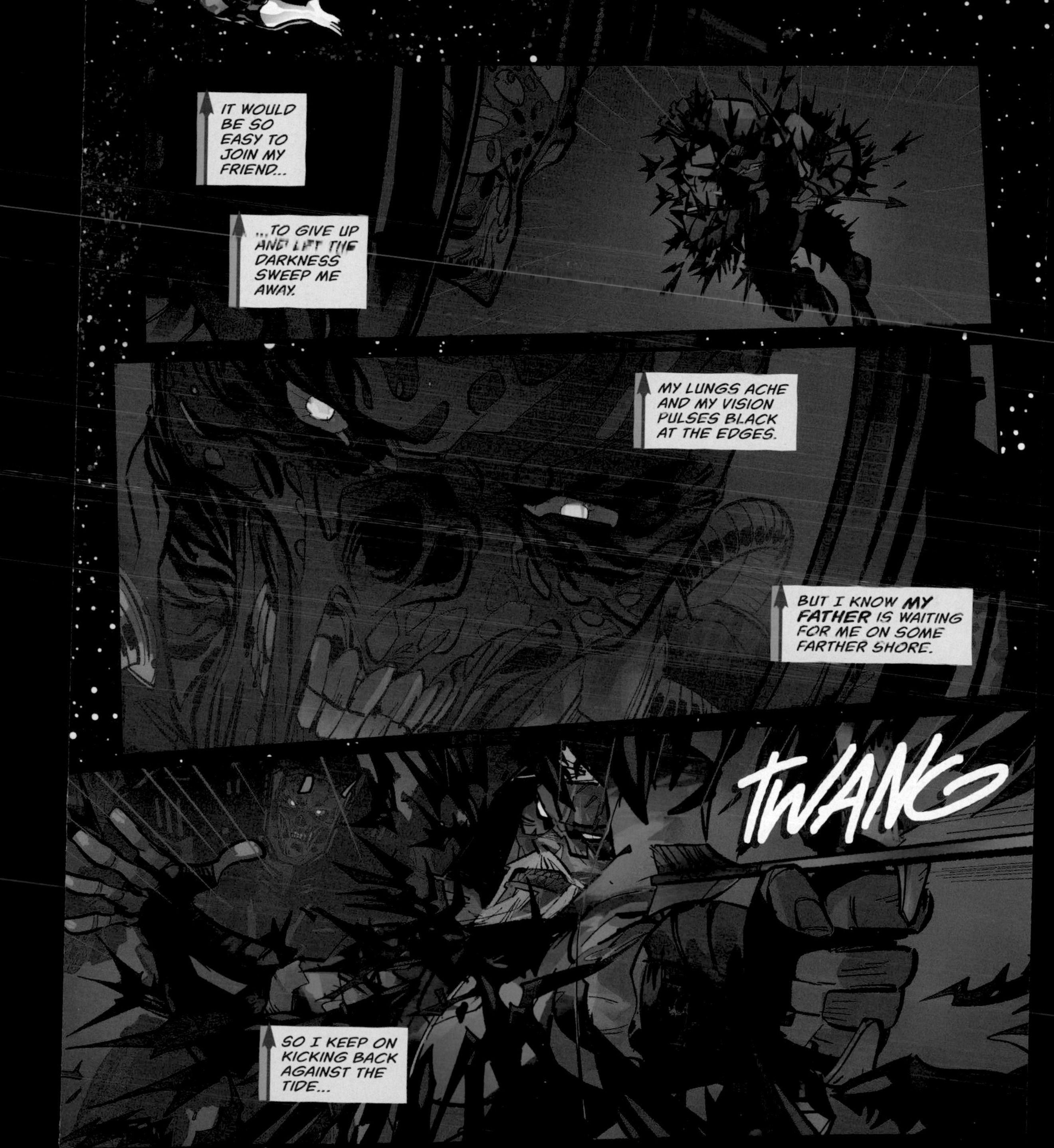
IT WOULD BE SO EASY TO JOIN MY FRIEND...
...TO GIVE UP AND LET THE DARKNESS SWEEP ME AWAY.
MY LUNGS ACHE AND MY VISION PULSES BLACK AT THE EDGES.
BUT I KNOW MY FATHER IS WAITING FOR ME ON SOME FARTHER SHORE.
TWANG
SO I KEEP ON KICKING BACK AGAINST THE TIDE...

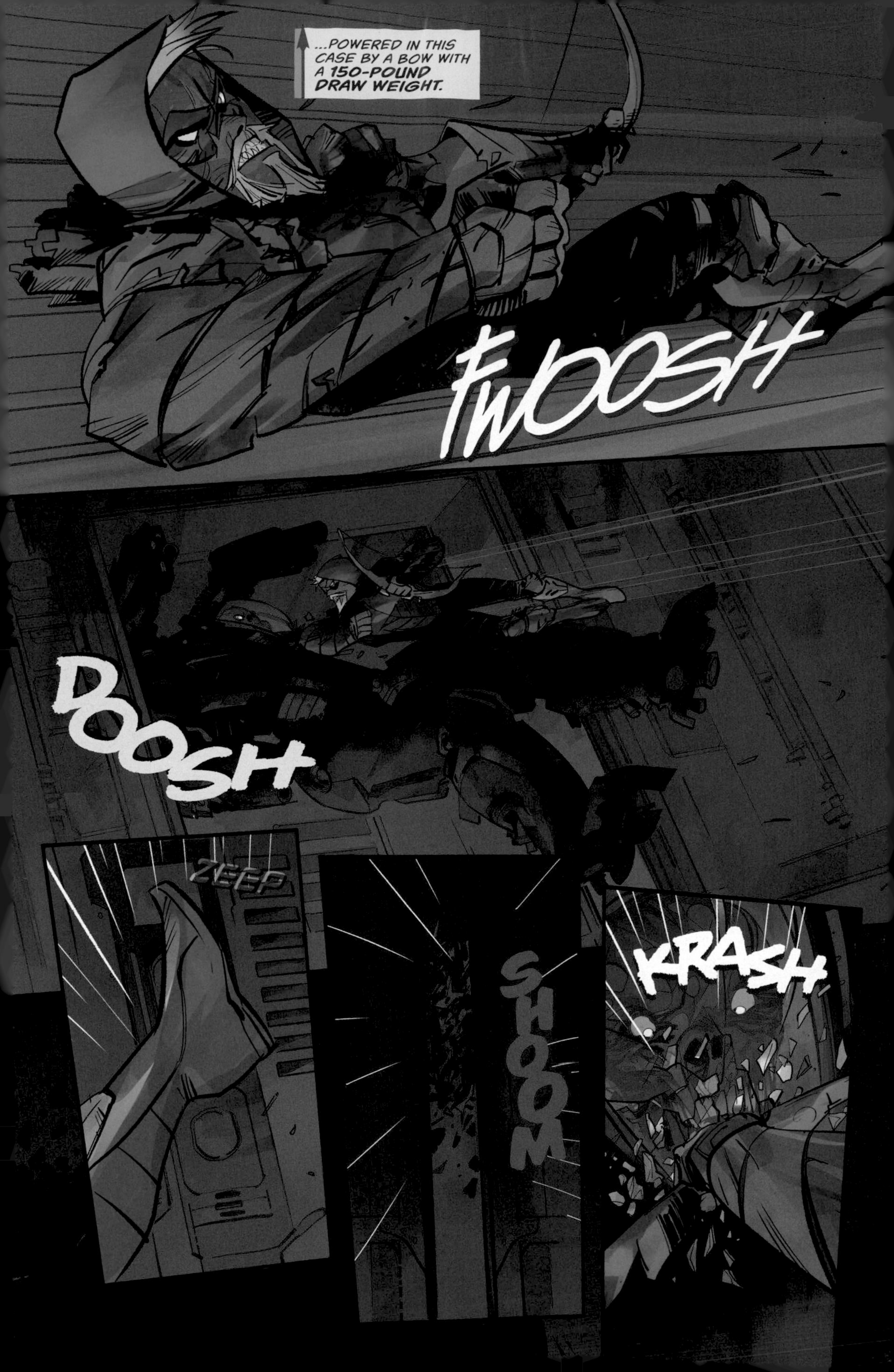
...POWERED IN THIS CASE BY A BOW WITH A 150-POUND DRAW WEIGHT.
FWOOSH
DOOSH
ZEEP
SHOOM
KRASH

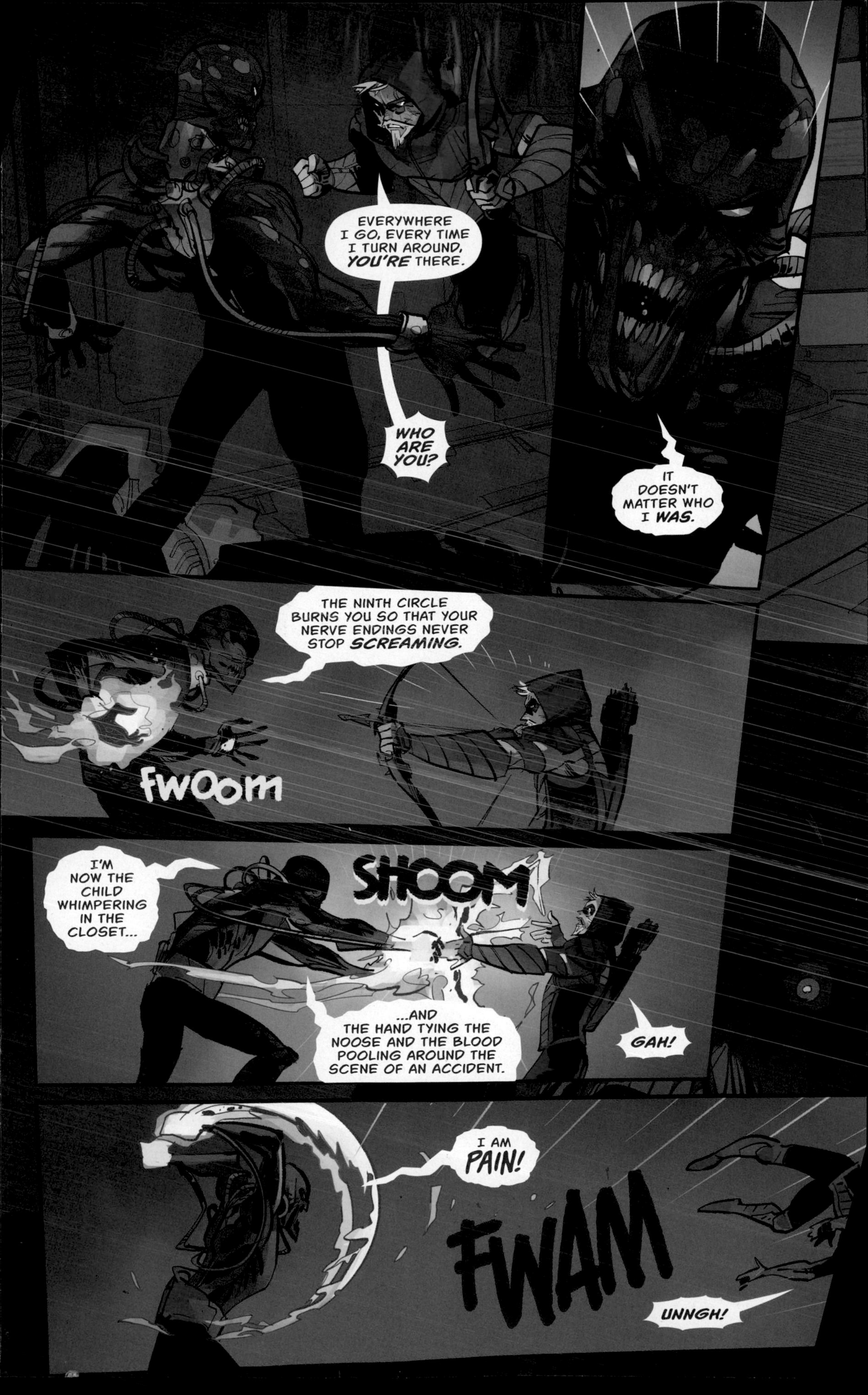
EVERYWHERE I GO, EVERY TIME I TURN AROUND, YOU'RE THERE.
WHO ARE YOU?
IT DOESN'T MATTER WHO I WAS.
THE NINTH CIRCLE BURNS YOU SO THAT YOUR NERVE ENDINGS NEVER STOP SCREAMING.
FWOOM
SHOOM
I'M NOW THE CHILD WHIMPERING IN THE CLOSET...
...AND THE HAND TYING THE NOOSE AND THE BLOOD POOLING AROUND THE SCENE OF AN ACCIDENT.
GAH!
I AM PAIN!
FWAM
UNNGH!

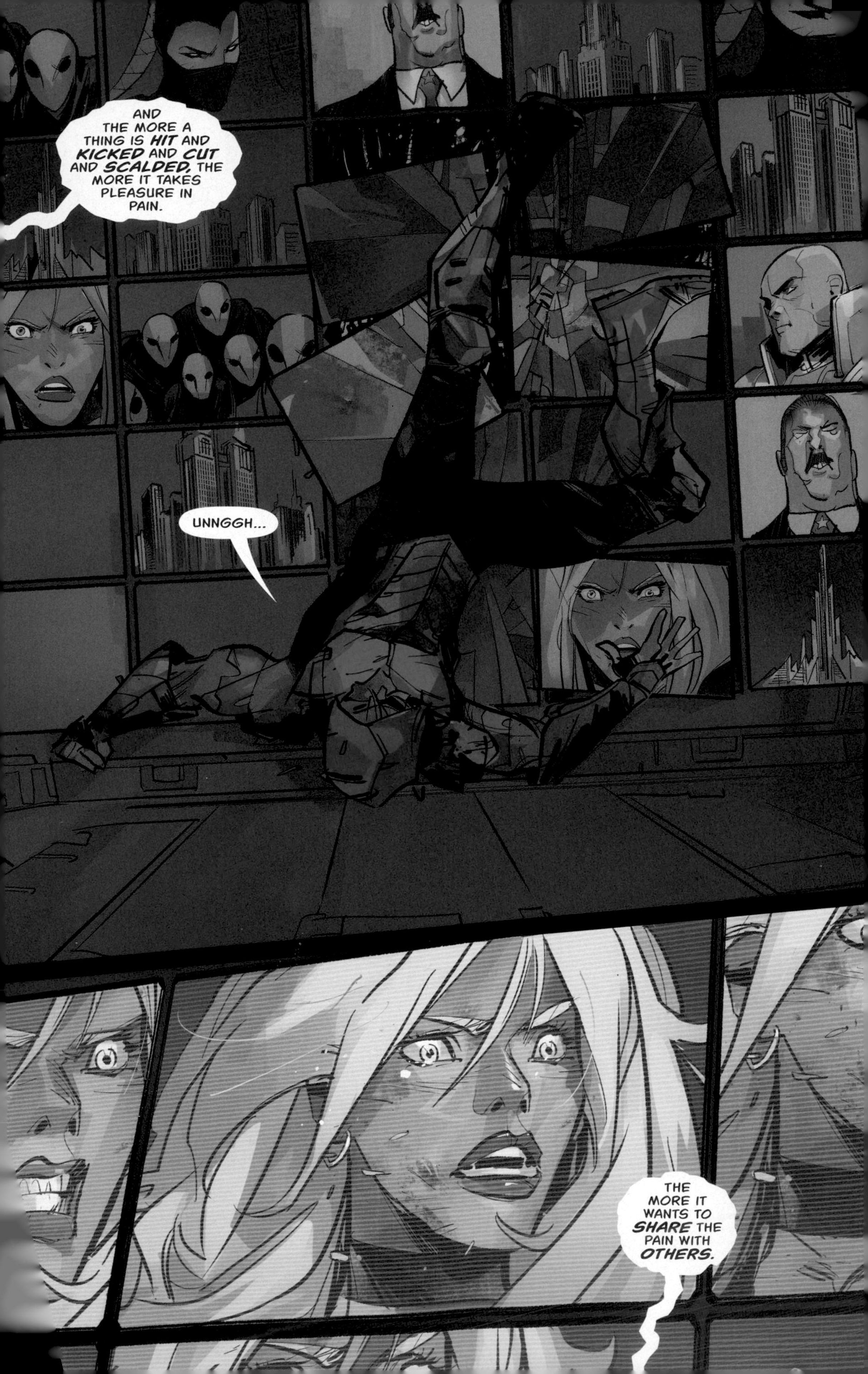
AND THE MORE A THING IS *HIT* AND *KICKED* AND *CUT* AND *SCALDED*, THE MORE IT TAKES PLEASURE IN PAIN.
UNNGGH...
THE MORE IT WANTS TO *SHARE* THE PAIN WITH *OTHERS*.

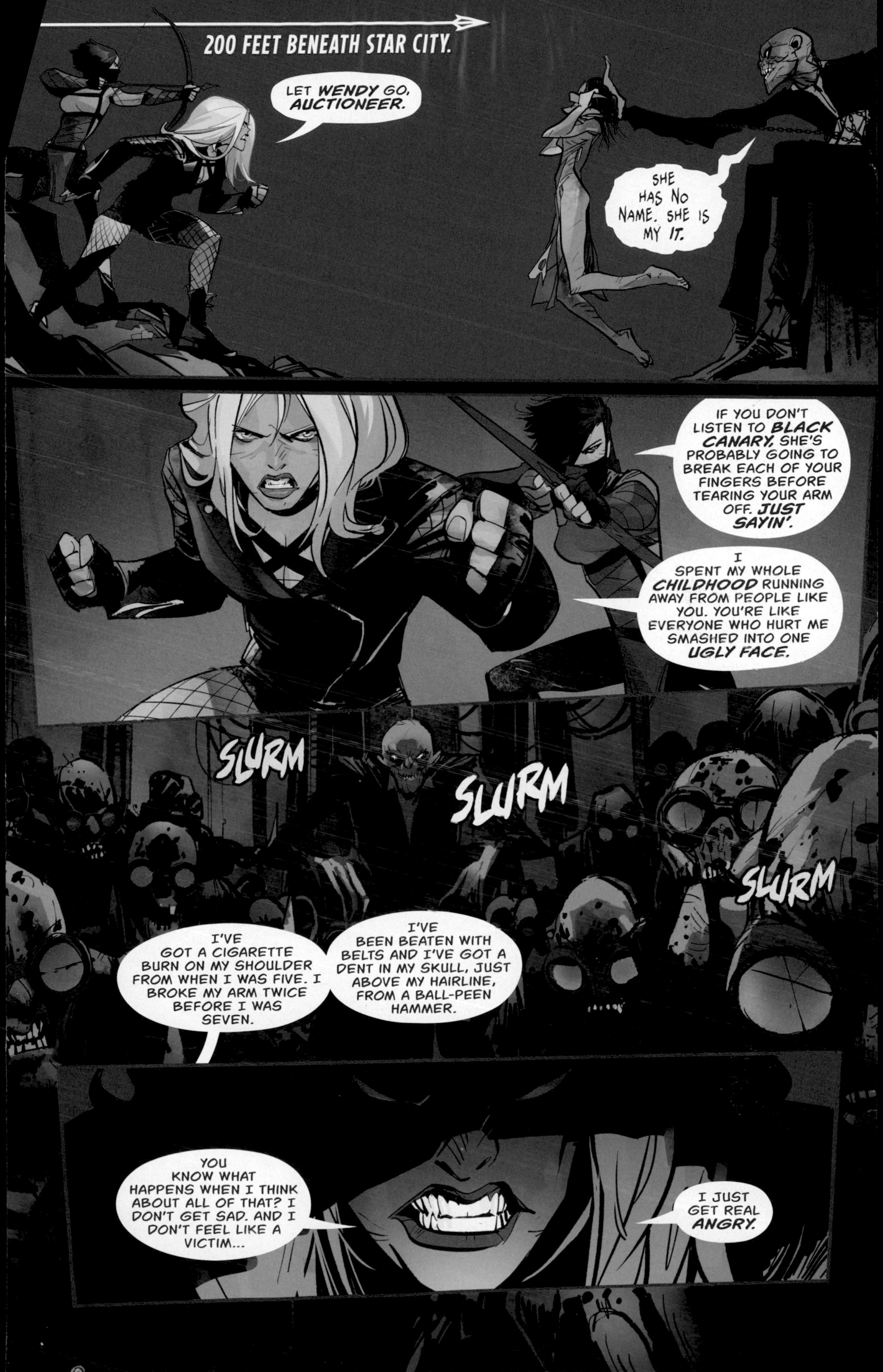
200 FEET BENEATH STAR CITY.
LET WENDY GO, AUCTIONEER.
SHE HAS NO NAME. SHE IS MY IT.
IF YOU DON'T LISTEN TO BLACK CANARY, SHE'S PROBABLY GOING TO BREAK EACH OF YOUR FINGERS BEFORE TEARING YOUR ARM OFF. JUST SAYIN'.
I SPENT MY WHOLE CHILDHOOD RUNNING AWAY FROM PEOPLE LIKE YOU. YOU'RE LIKE EVERYONE WHO HURT ME SMASHED INTO ONE UGLY FACE.
SLURM
SLURM
SLURM
I'VE GOT A CIGARETTE BURN ON MY SHOULDER FROM WHEN I WAS FIVE. I BROKE MY ARM TWICE BEFORE I WAS SEVEN.
I'VE BEEN BEATEN WITH BELTS AND I'VE GOT A DENT IN MY SKULL, JUST ABOVE MY HAIRLINE, FROM A BALL-PEEN HAMMER.
YOU KNOW WHAT HAPPENS WHEN I THINK ABOUT ALL OF THAT? I DON'T GET SAD. AND I DON'T FEEL LIKE A VICTIM...
I JUST GET REAL ANGRY.

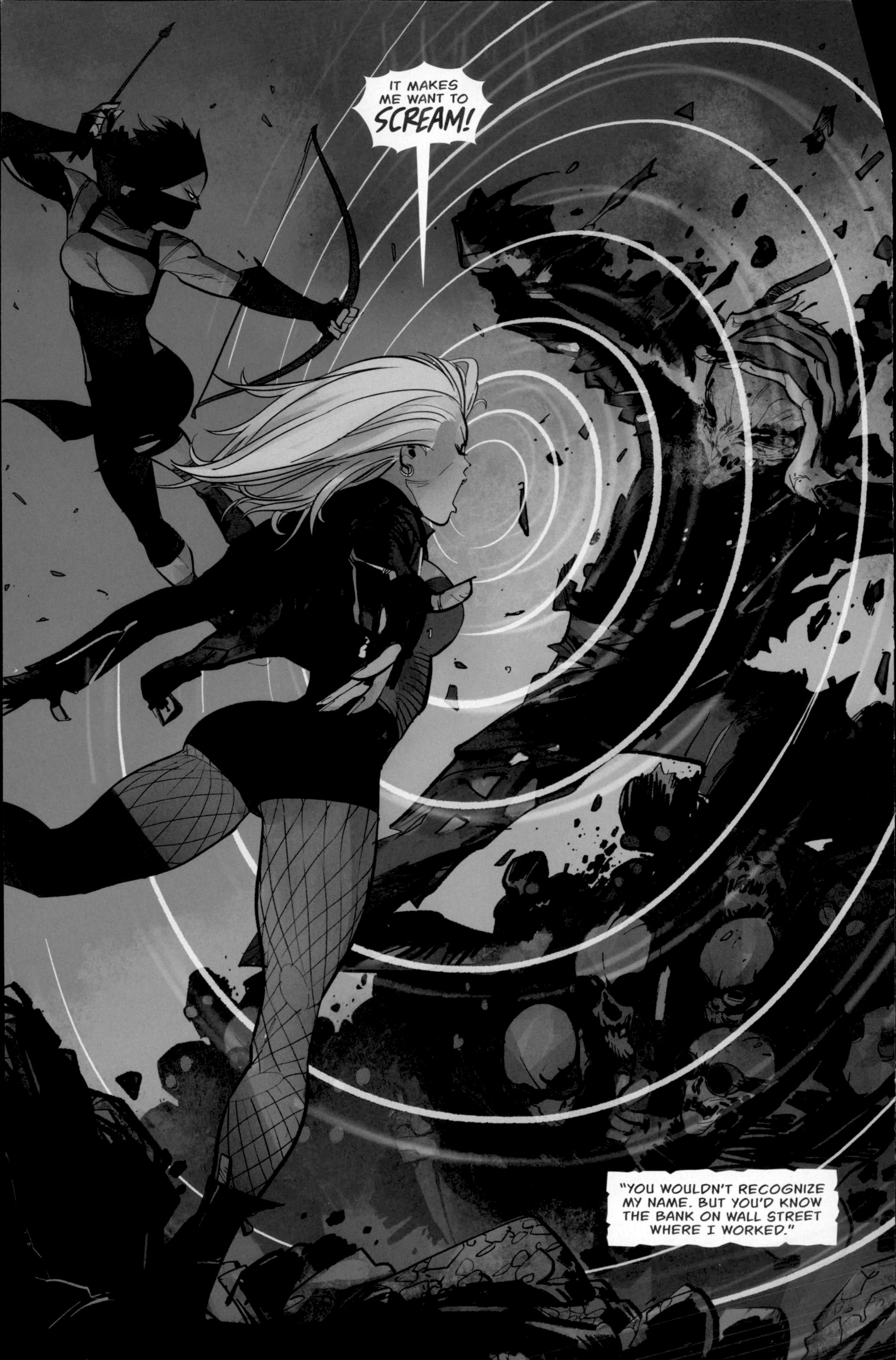
IT MAKES ME WANT TO SCREAM!
"YOU WOULDN'T RECOGNIZE MY NAME. BUT YOU'D KNOW THE BANK ON WALL STREET WHERE I WORKED."

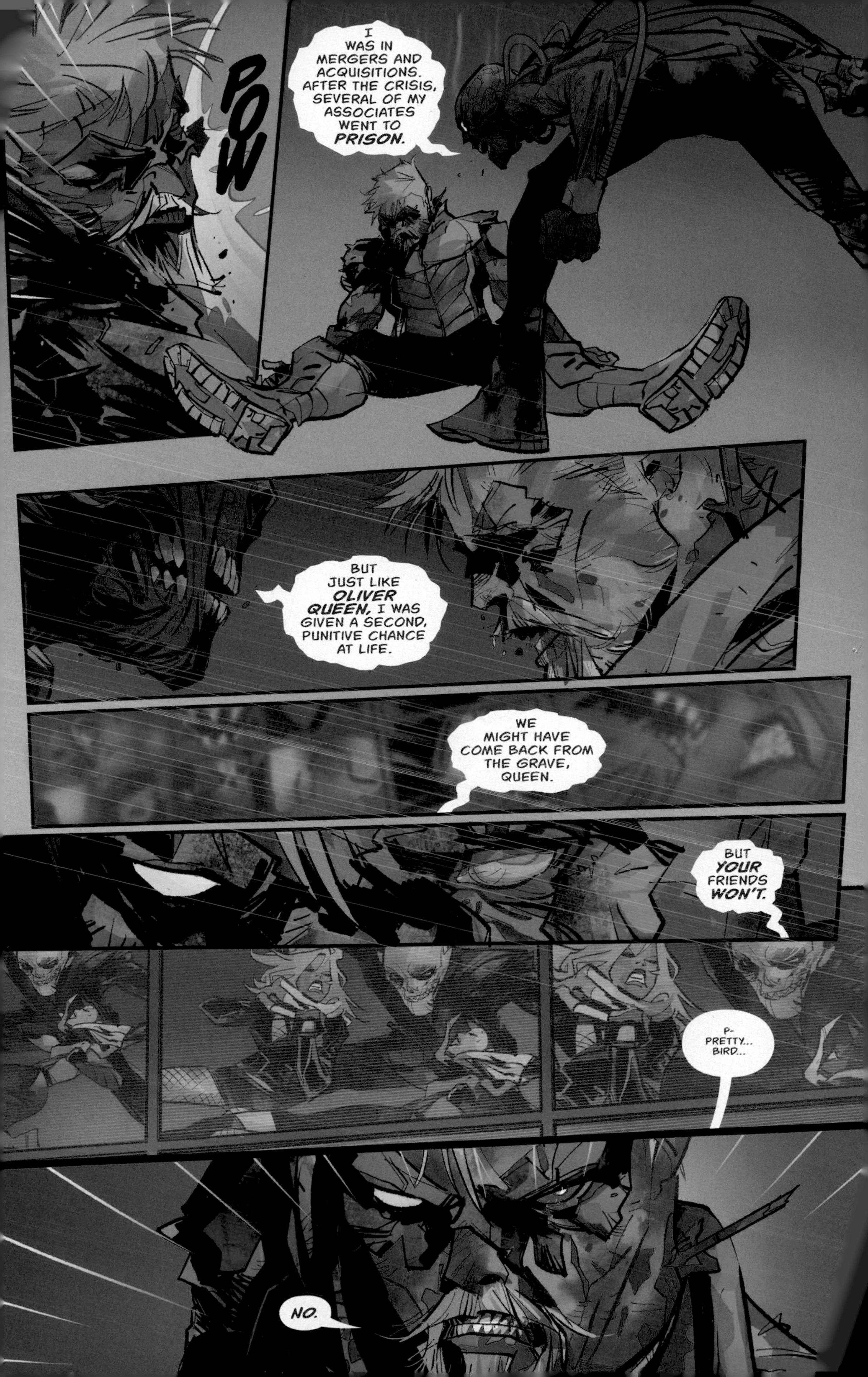

POW
I WAS IN MERGERS AND ACQUISITIONS. AFTER THE CRISIS, SEVERAL OF MY ASSOCIATES WENT TO PRISON.
BUT JUST LIKE OLIVER QUEEN, I WAS GIVEN A SECOND, PUNITIVE CHANCE AT LIFE.
WE MIGHT HAVE COME BACK FROM THE GRAVE, QUEEN.
BUT YOUR FRIENDS WON'T.
P-PRETTY... BIRD...
NO.

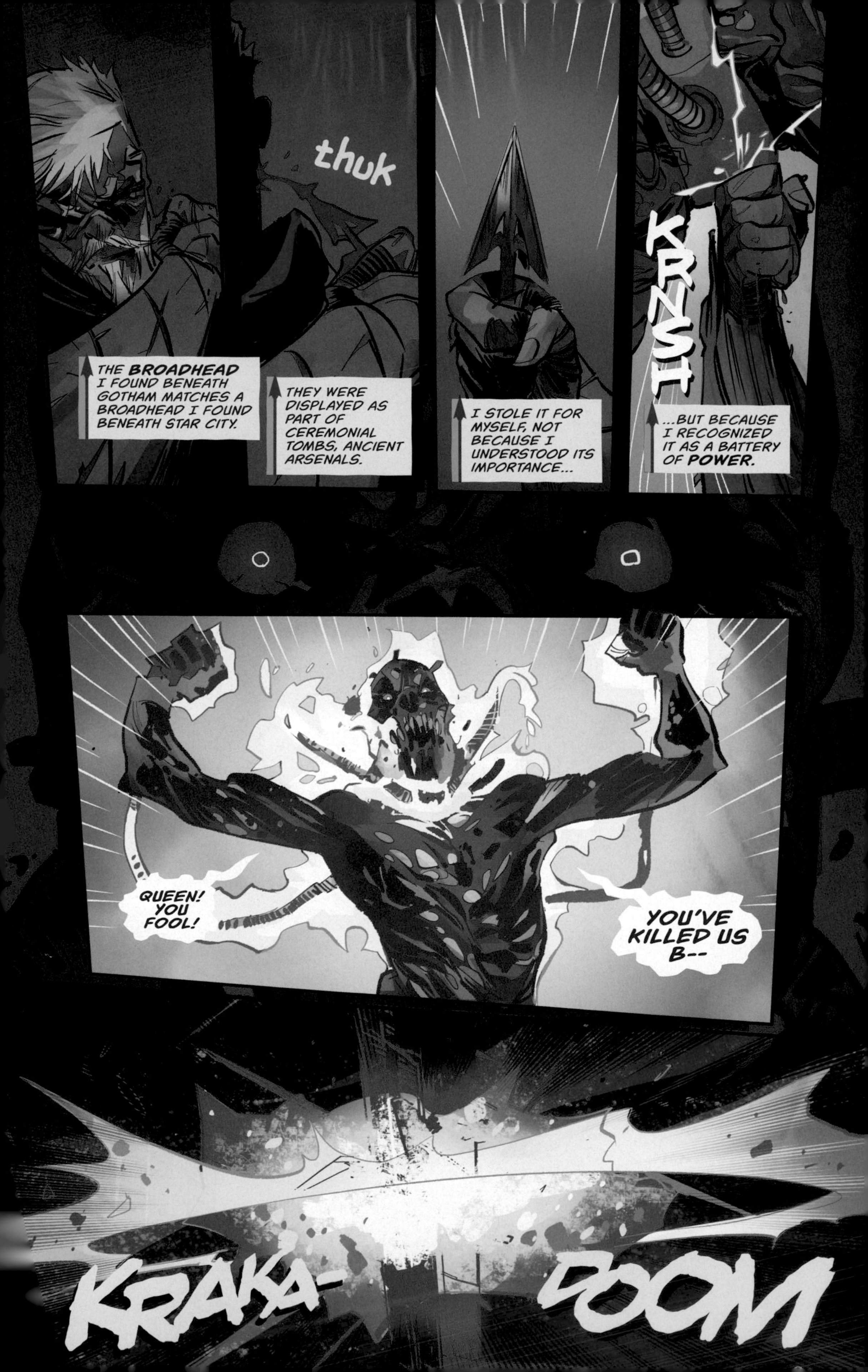
thuk
KRNSH
THE BROADHEAD I FOUND BENEATH GOTHAM MATCHES A BROADHEAD I FOUND BENEATH STAR CITY.
THEY WERE DISPLAYED AS PART OF CEREMONIAL TOMBS, ANCIENT ARSENALS.
I STOLE IT FOR MYSELF, NOT BECAUSE I UNDERSTOOD ITS IMPORTANCE...
...BUT BECAUSE I RECOGNIZED IT AS A BATTERY OF POWER.
QUEEN! YOU FOOL!
YOU'VE KILLED US B--
KRAKA-DOOM

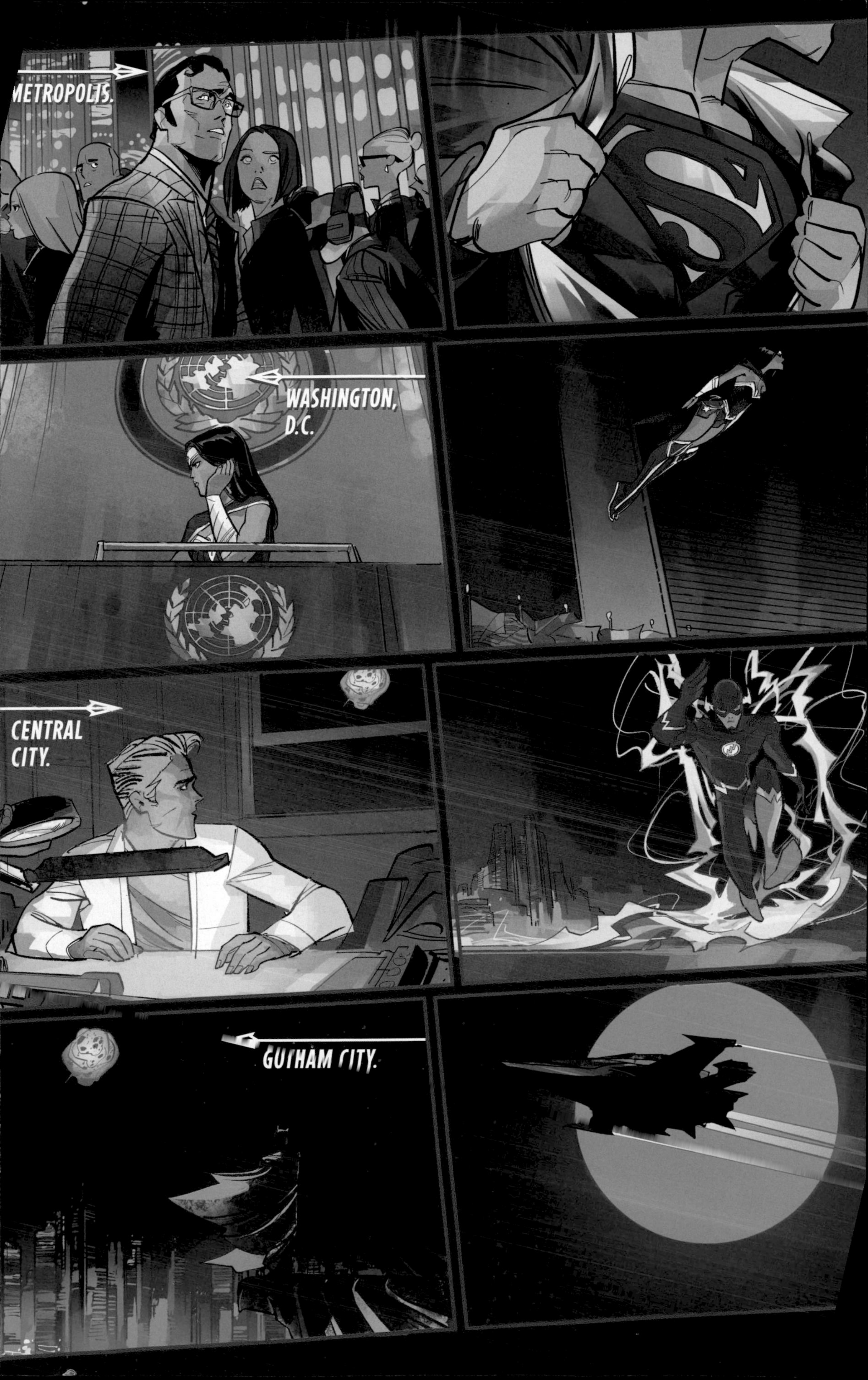
METROPOLIS.
WASHINGTON, D.C.
CENTRAL CITY.
GOTHAM CITY.

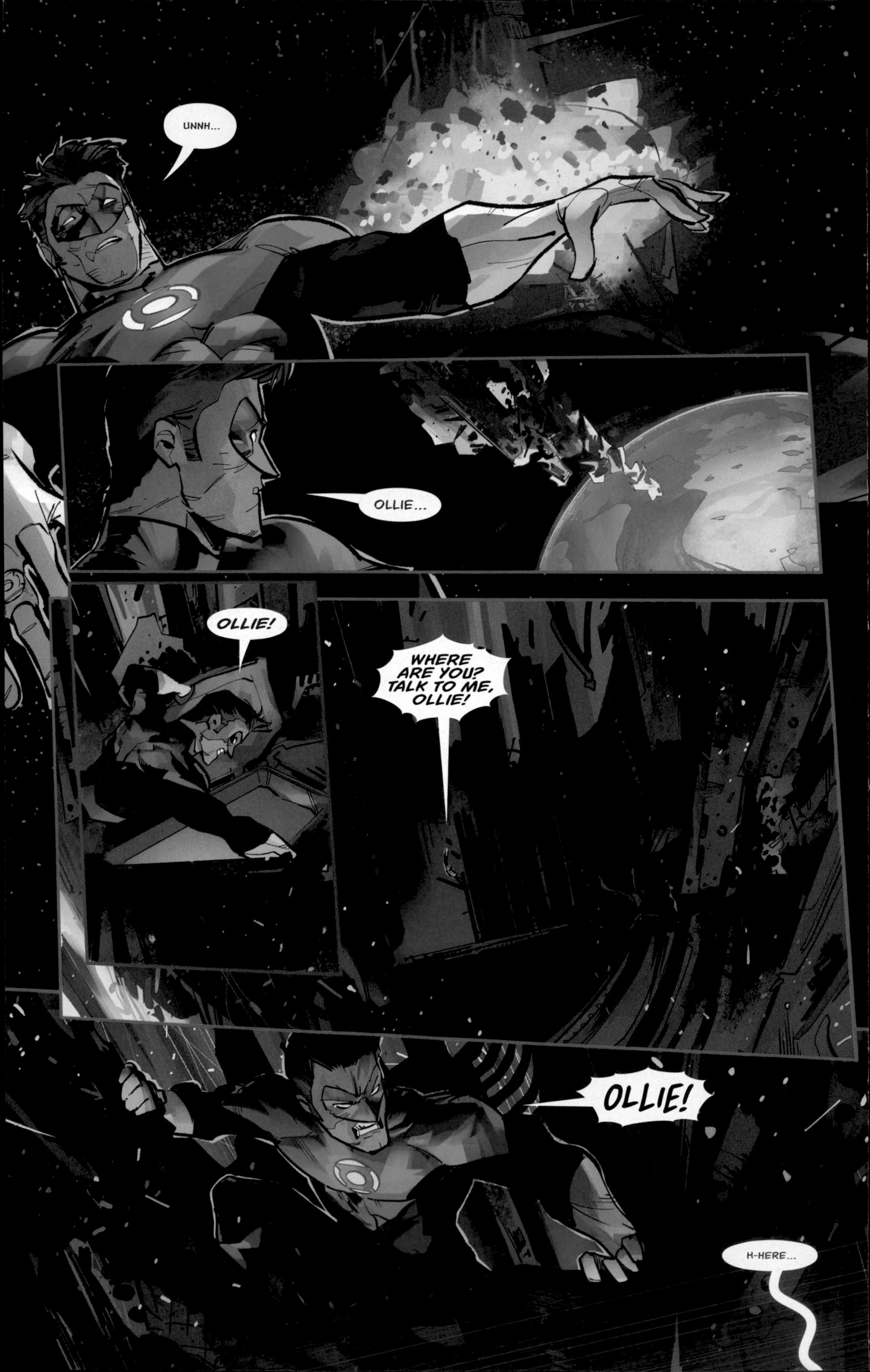
UNNH...
OLLIE...
OLLIE!
WHERE ARE YOU? TALK TO ME, OLLIE!
OLLIE!
H-HERE...

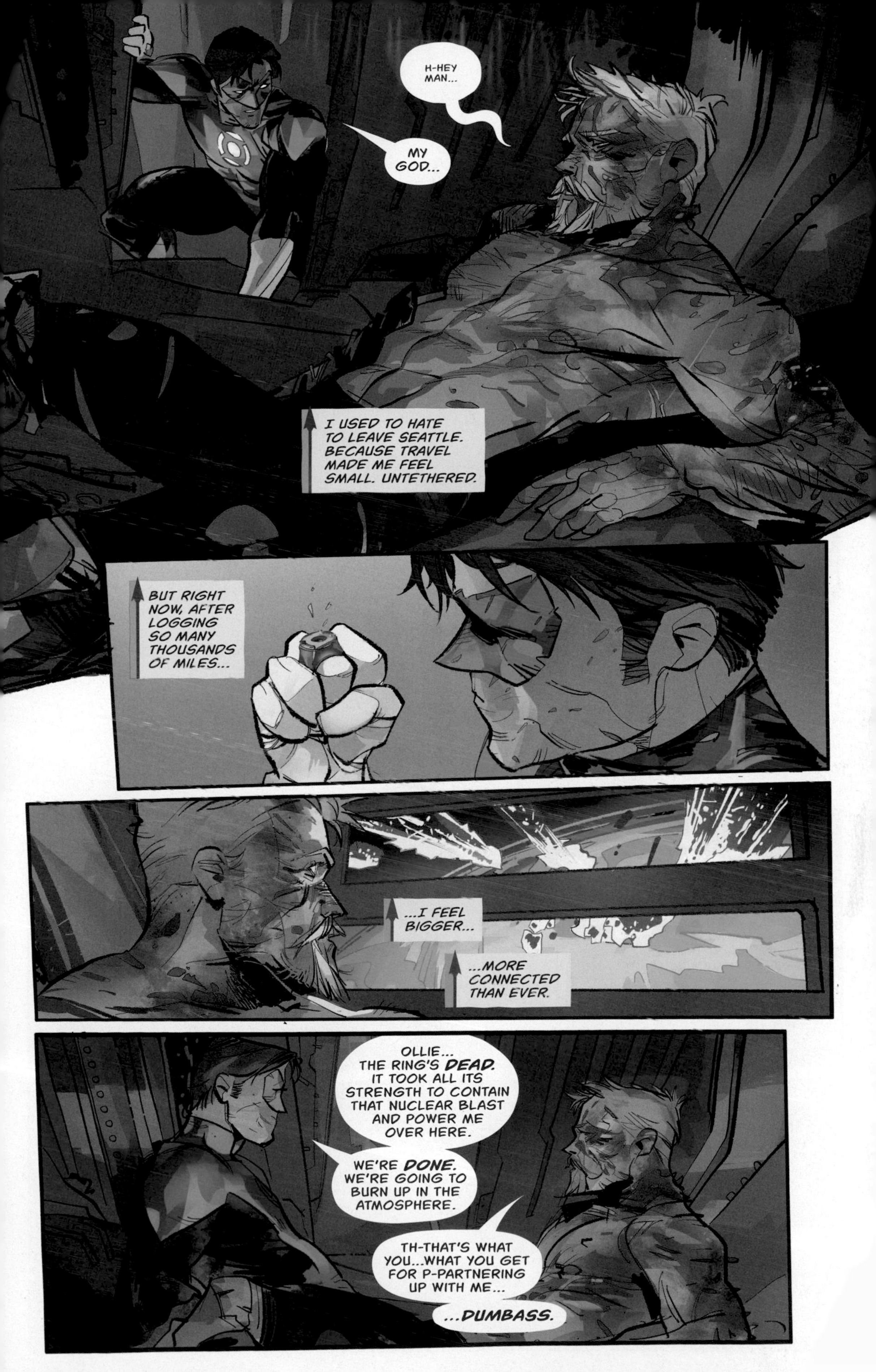
H-HEY MAN...
MY GOD...
I USED TO HATE TO LEAVE SEATTLE. BECAUSE TRAVEL MADE ME FEEL SMALL. UNTETHERED.
BUT RIGHT NOW, AFTER LOGGING SO MANY THOUSANDS OF MILES...
...I FEEL BIGGER...
...MORE CONNECTED THAN EVER.
OLLIE... THE RING'S DEAD. IT TOOK ALL ITS STRENGTH TO CONTAIN THAT NUCLEAR BLAST AND POWER ME OVER HERE.
WE'RE DONE. WE'RE GOING TO BURN UP IN THE ATMOSPHERE.
TH-THAT'S WHAT YOU...WHAT YOU GET FOR P-PARTNERING UP WITH ME...
...DUMBASS.

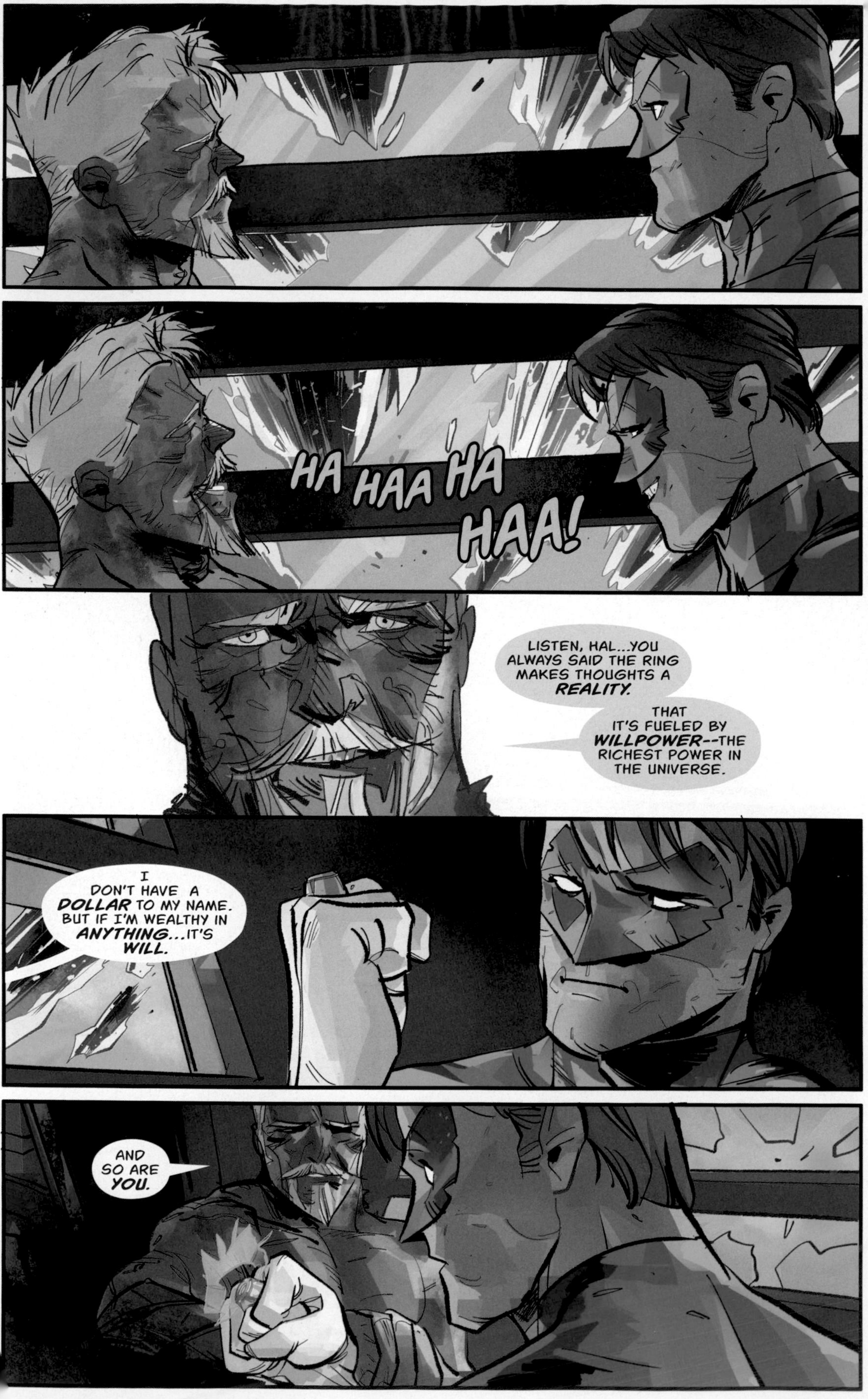
HA HAA HA HAA!
LISTEN, HAL...YOU ALWAYS SAID THE RING MAKES THOUGHTS A REALITY.
THAT IT'S FUELED BY WILLPOWER--THE RICHEST POWER IN THE UNIVERSE.
I DON'T HAVE A DOLLAR TO MY NAME. BUT IF I'M WEALTHY IN ANYTHING...IT'S WILL.
AND SO ARE YOU.

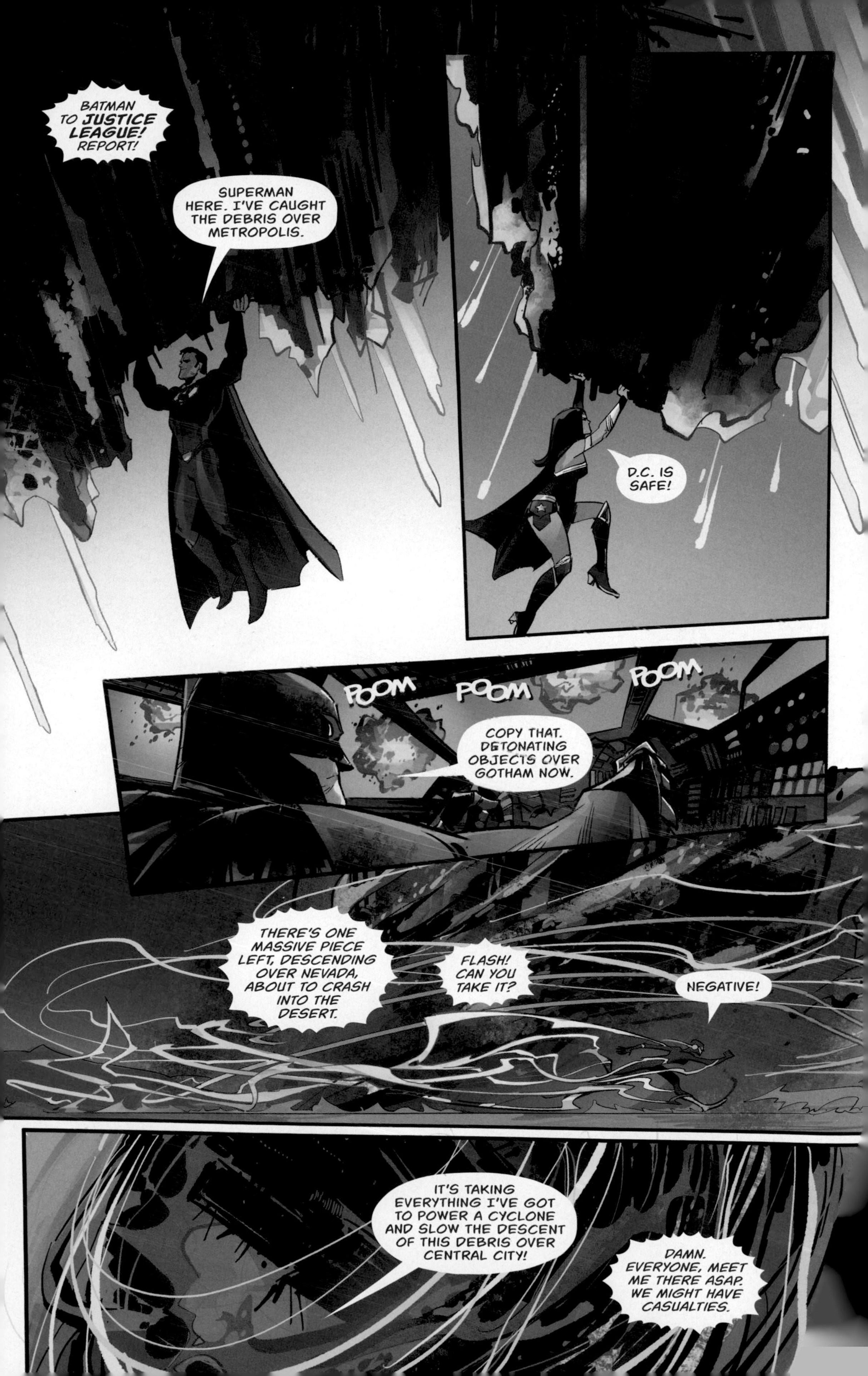
BATMAN TO JUSTICE LEAGUE! REPORT!
SUPERMAN HERE. I'VE CAUGHT THE DEBRIS OVER METROPOLIS.
D.C. IS SAFE!
POOM
POOM
POOM
COPY THAT. DETONATING OBJECTS OVER GOTHAM NOW.
THERE'S ONE MASSIVE PIECE LEFT, DESCENDING OVER NEVADA, ABOUT TO CRASH INTO THE DESERT.
FLASH! CAN YOU TAKE IT?
NEGATIVE!
IT'S TAKING EVERYTHING I'VE GOT TO POWER A CYCLONE AND SLOW THE DESCENT OF THIS DEBRIS OVER CENTRAL CITY!
DAMN. EVERYONE, MEET ME THERE ASAP. WE MIGHT HAVE CASUALTIES.

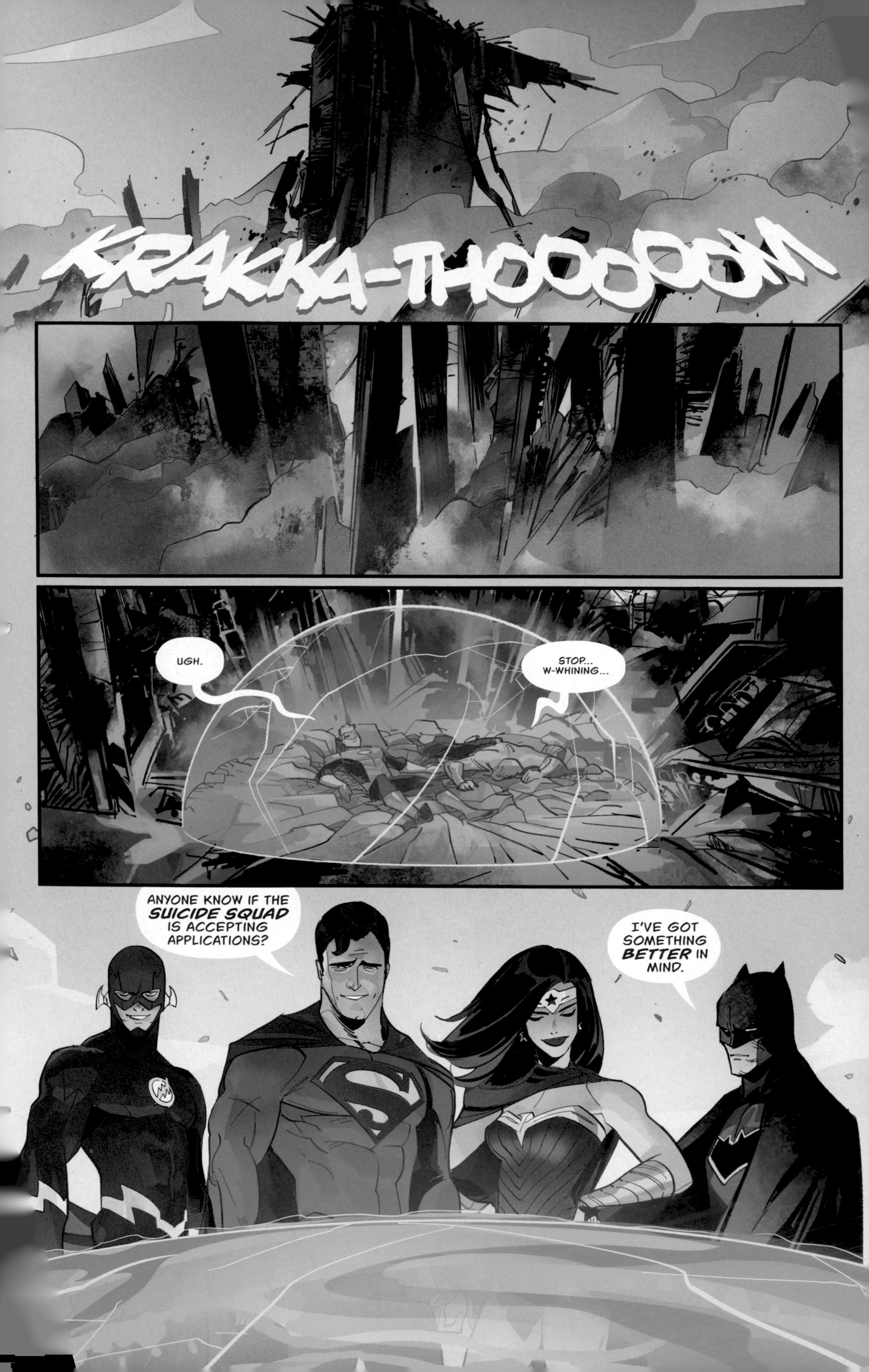
KRAKKA-THOOOOOOM
UGH.
STOP... W-WHINING...
ANYONE KNOW IF THE SUICIDE SQUAD IS ACCEPTING APPLICATIONS?
I'VE GOT SOMETHING BETTER IN MIND.

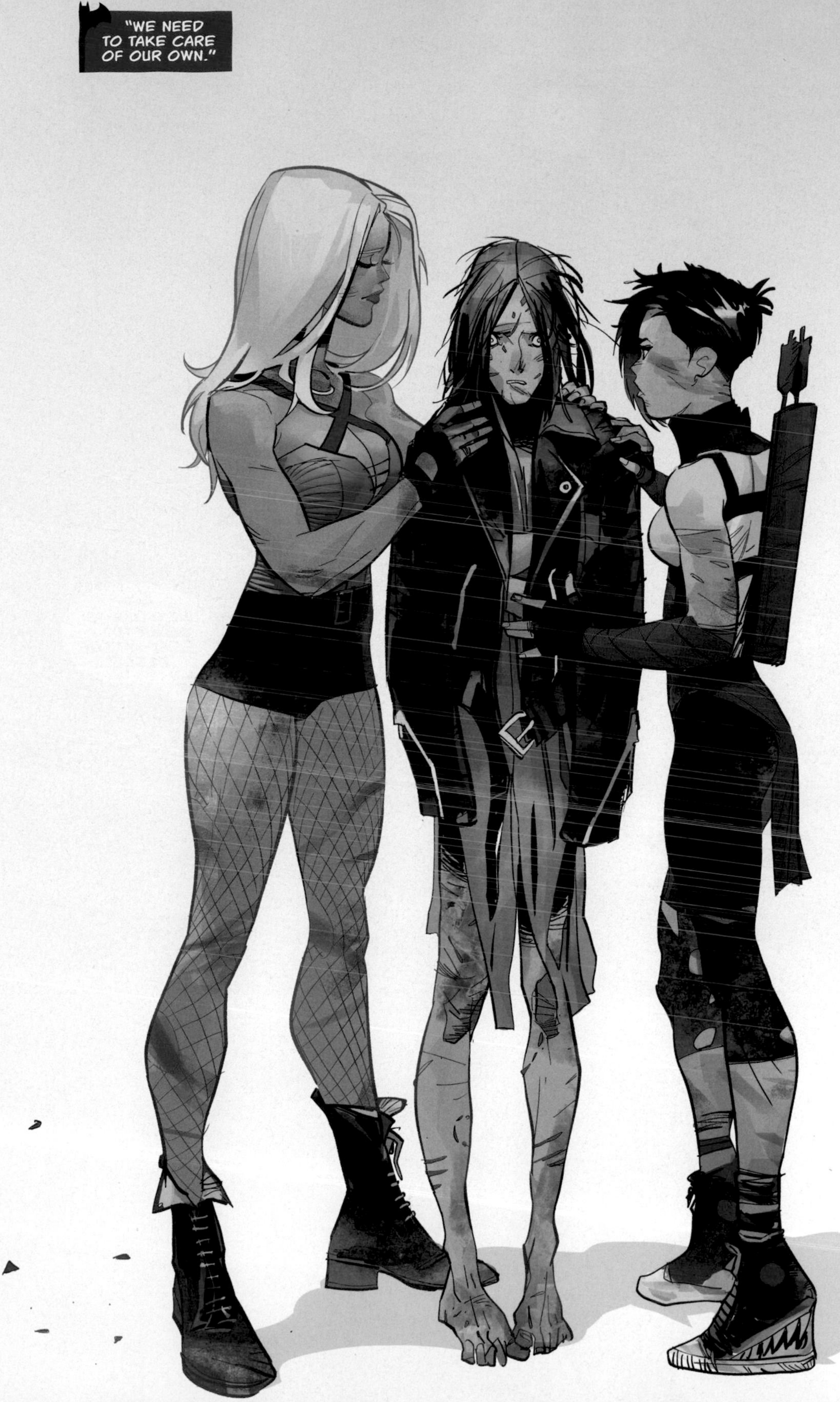
"WE NEED TO TAKE CARE OF OUR OWN."

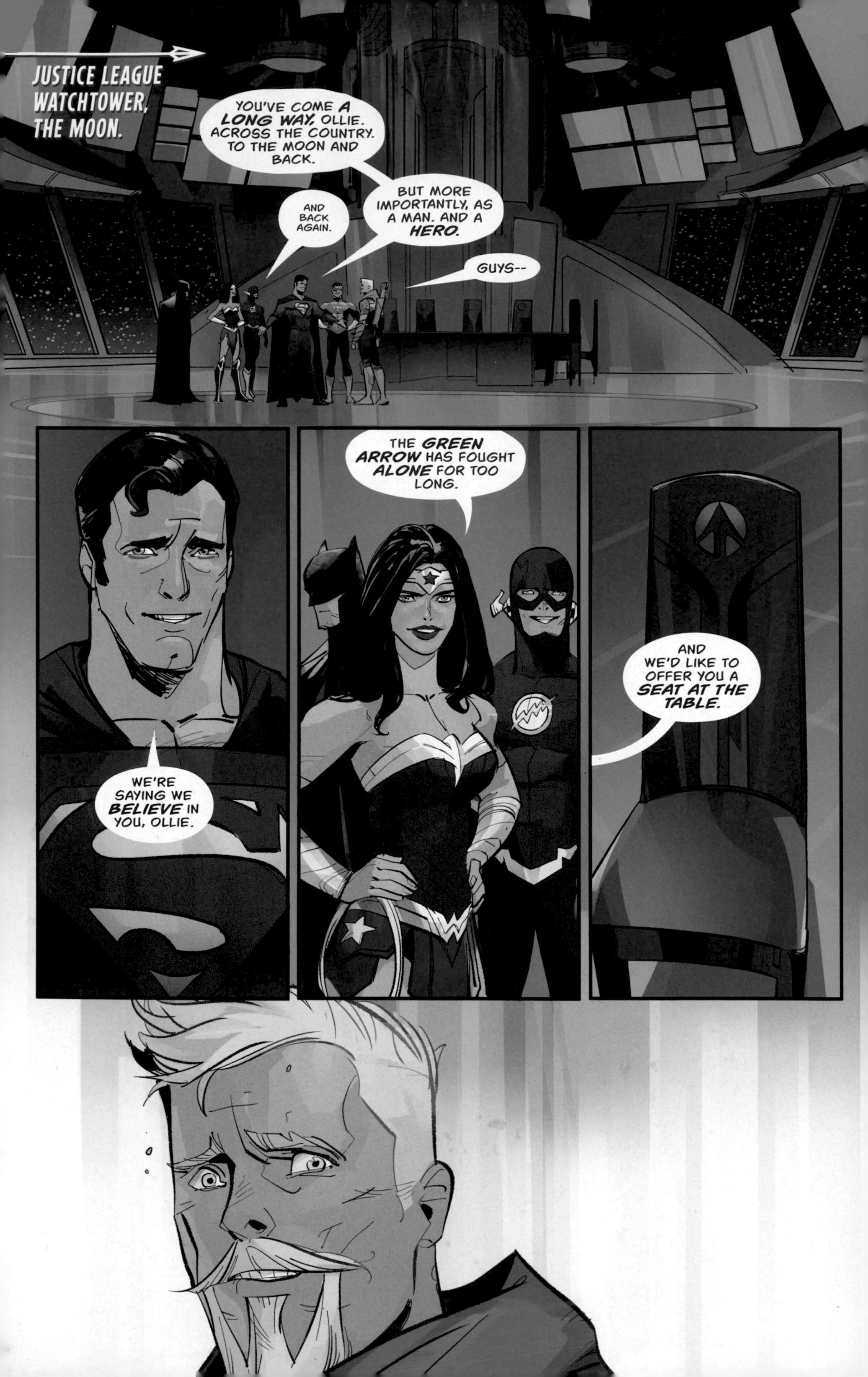
JUSTICE LEAGUE WATCHTOWER, THE MOON.
YOU'VE COME A LONG WAY, OLLIE. ACROSS THE COUNTRY. TO THE MOON AND BACK.
AND BACK AGAIN.
BUT MORE IMPORTANTLY, AS A MAN. AND A HERO.
GUYS--
WE'RE SAYING WE BELIEVE IN YOU, OLLIE.
THE GREEN ARROW HAS FOUGHT ALONE FOR TOO LONG.
AND WE'D LIKE TO OFFER YOU A SEAT AT THE TABLE.

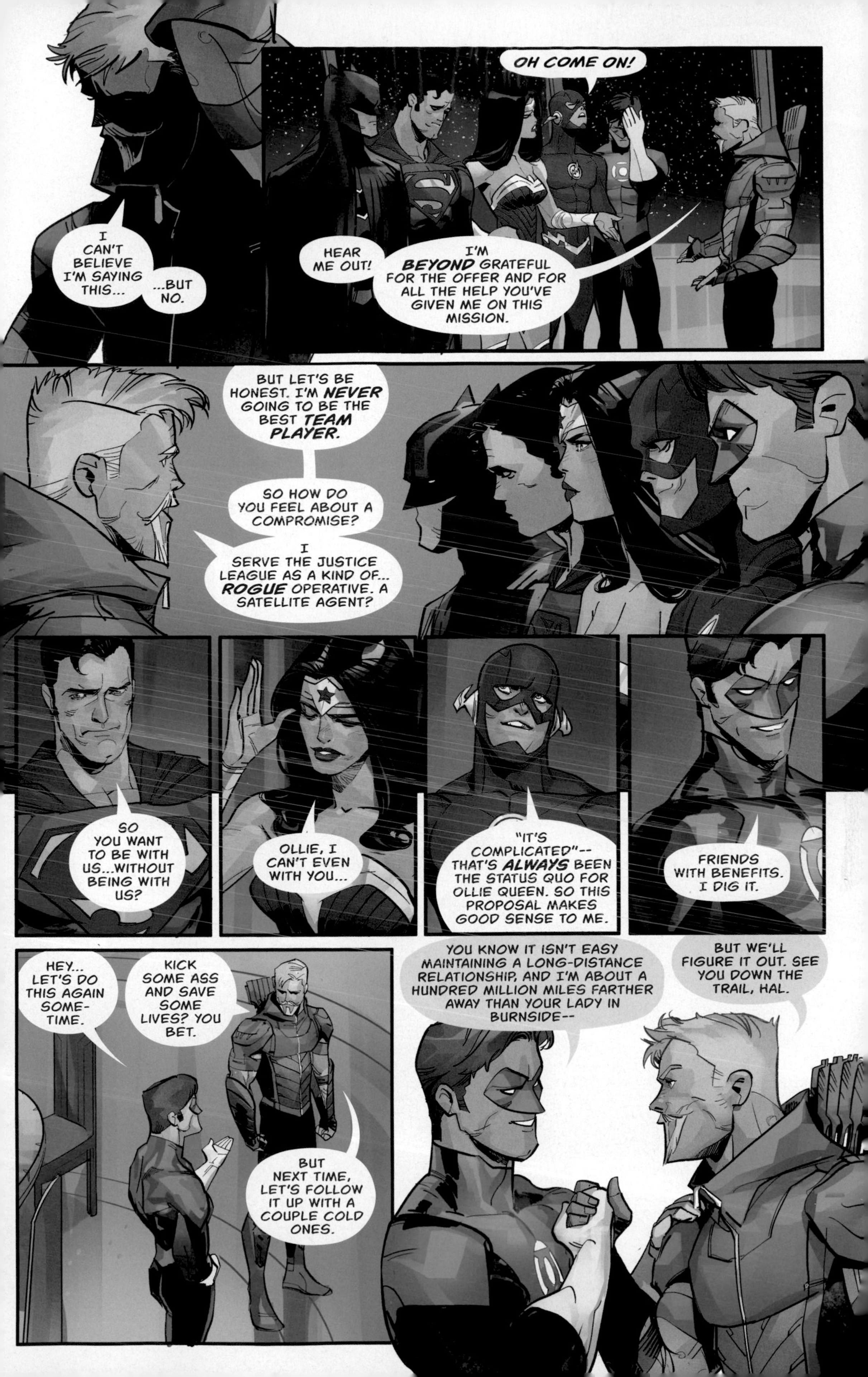
OH COME ON!
I CAN'T BELIEVE I'M SAYING THIS...
...BUT NO.
HEAR ME OUT!
I'M BEYOND GRATEFUL FOR THE OFFER AND FOR ALL THE HELP YOU'VE GIVEN ME ON THIS MISSION.
BUT LET'S BE HONEST. I'M NEVER GOING TO BE THE BEST TEAM PLAYER.
SO HOW DO YOU FEEL ABOUT A COMPROMISE?
I SERVE THE JUSTICE LEAGUE AS A KIND OF... ROGUE OPERATIVE. A SATELLITE AGENT?
SO YOU WANT TO BE WITH US...WITHOUT BEING WITH US?
OLLIE, I CAN'T EVEN WITH YOU...
"IT'S COMPLICATED"--THAT'S ALWAYS BEEN THE STATUS QUO FOR OLLIE QUEEN. SO THIS PROPOSAL MAKES GOOD SENSE TO ME.
FRIENDS WITH BENEFITS. I DIG IT.
HEY... LET'S DO THIS AGAIN SOME-TIME.
KICK SOME ASS AND SAVE SOME LIVES? YOU BET.
BUT NEXT TIME, LET'S FOLLOW IT UP WITH A COUPLE COLD ONES.
YOU KNOW IT ISN'T EASY MAINTAINING A LONG-DISTANCE RELATIONSHIP, AND I'M ABOUT A HUNDRED MILLION MILES FARTHER AWAY THAN YOUR LADY IN BURNSIDE--
BUT WE'LL FIGURE IT OUT. SEE YOU DOWN THE TRAIL, HAL.

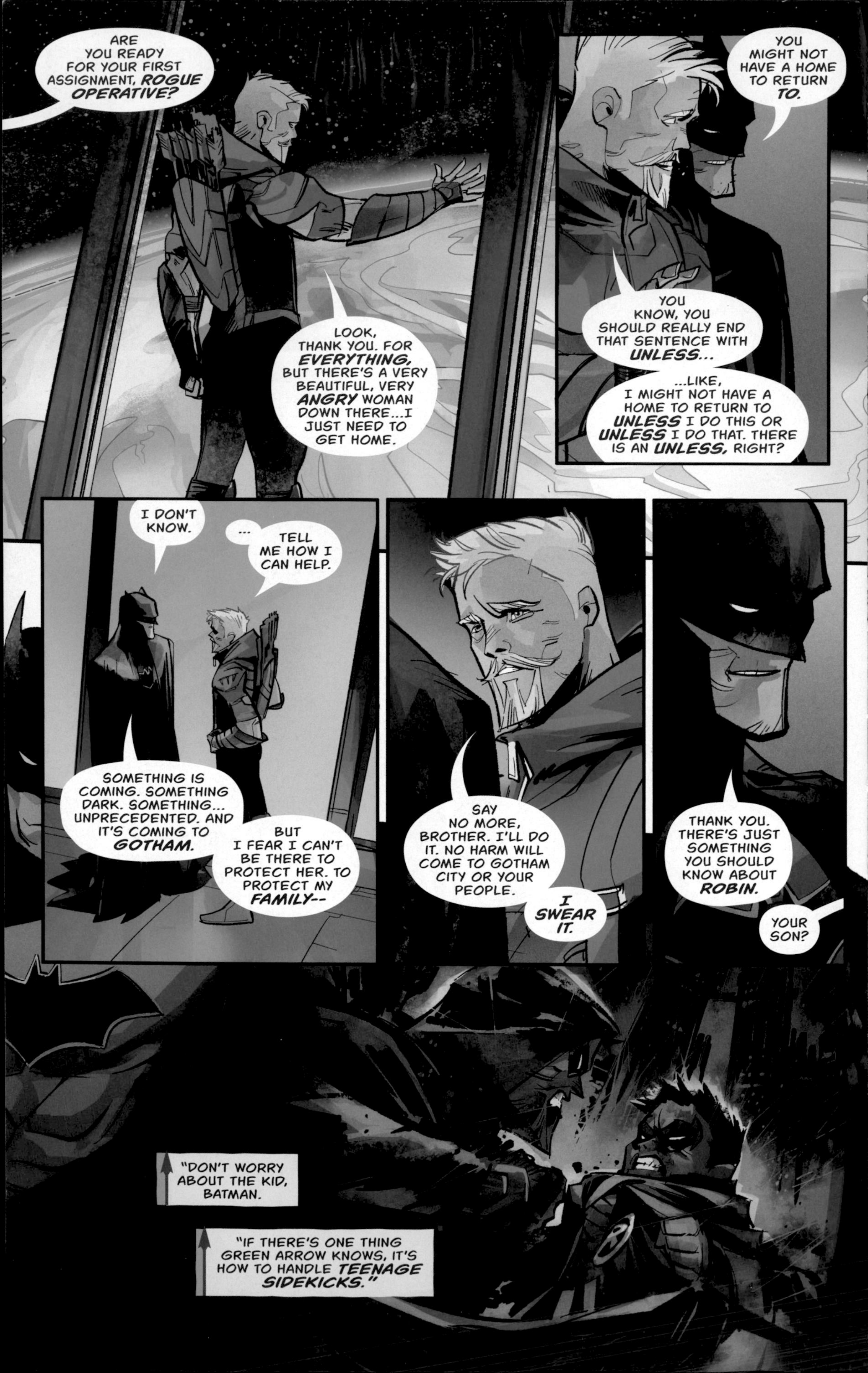
ARE YOU READY FOR YOUR FIRST ASSIGNMENT, ROGUE OPERATIVE?
LOOK, THANK YOU. FOR EVERYTHING, BUT THERE'S A VERY BEAUTIFUL, VERY ANGRY WOMAN DOWN THERE...I JUST NEED TO GET HOME.
YOU MIGHT NOT HAVE A HOME TO RETURN TO.
YOU KNOW, YOU SHOULD REALLY END THAT SENTENCE WITH UNLESS...
...LIKE, I MIGHT NOT HAVE A HOME TO RETURN TO UNLESS I DO THIS OR UNLESS I DO THAT. THERE IS AN UNLESS, RIGHT?
I DON'T KNOW.
...
TELL ME HOW I CAN HELP.
SOMETHING IS COMING. SOMETHING DARK. SOMETHING... UNPRECEDENTED. AND IT'S COMING TO GOTHAM.
BUT I FEAR I CAN'T BE THERE TO PROTECT HER. TO PROTECT MY FAMILY--
SAY NO MORE, BROTHER. I'LL DO IT. NO HARM WILL COME TO GOTHAM CITY OR YOUR PEOPLE.
I SWEAR IT.
THANK YOU. THERE'S JUST SOMETHING YOU SHOULD KNOW ABOUT ROBIN.
YOUR SON?
"DON'T WORRY ABOUT THE KID, BATMAN.
"IF THERE'S ONE THING GREEN ARROW KNOWS, IT'S HOW TO HANDLE TEENAGE SIDEKICKS."

GREEN ARROW #28 variant cover by MIKE GRELL and LOVERN KINDZIERSKI

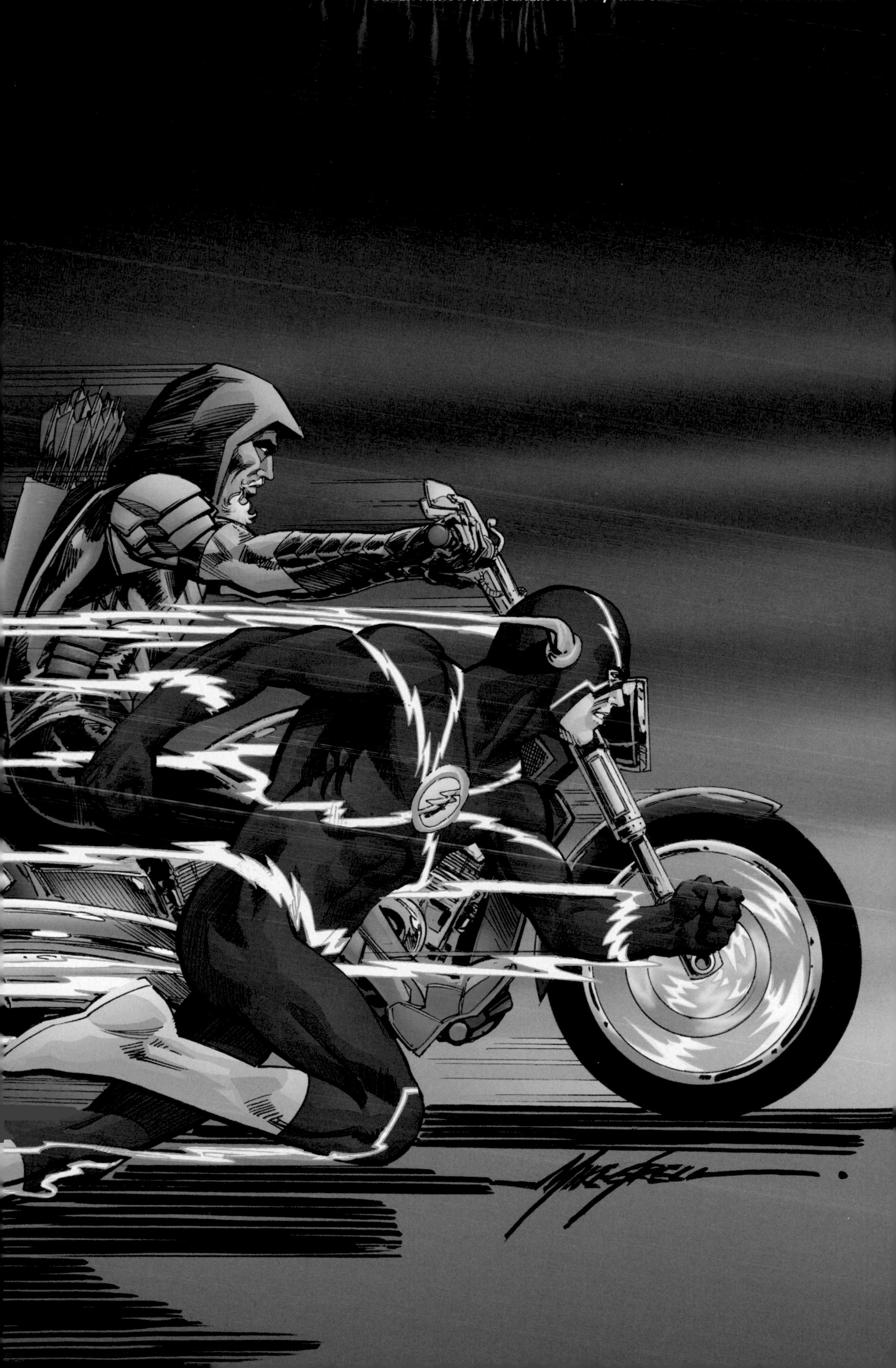

GREEN ARROW #27 variant cover by ESAD RIBIC

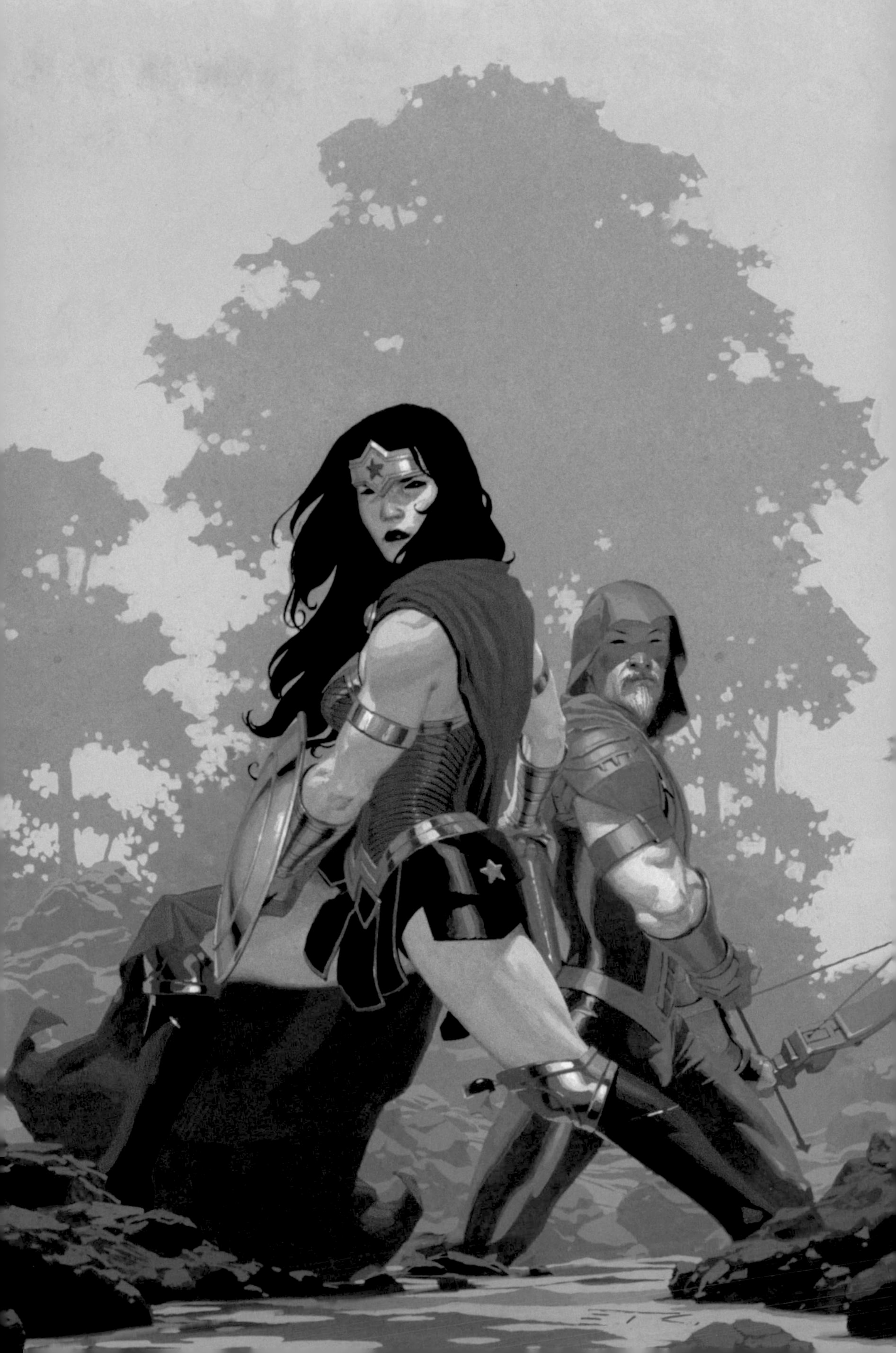

GREEN ARROW #29 variant cover by MIKE GRELL

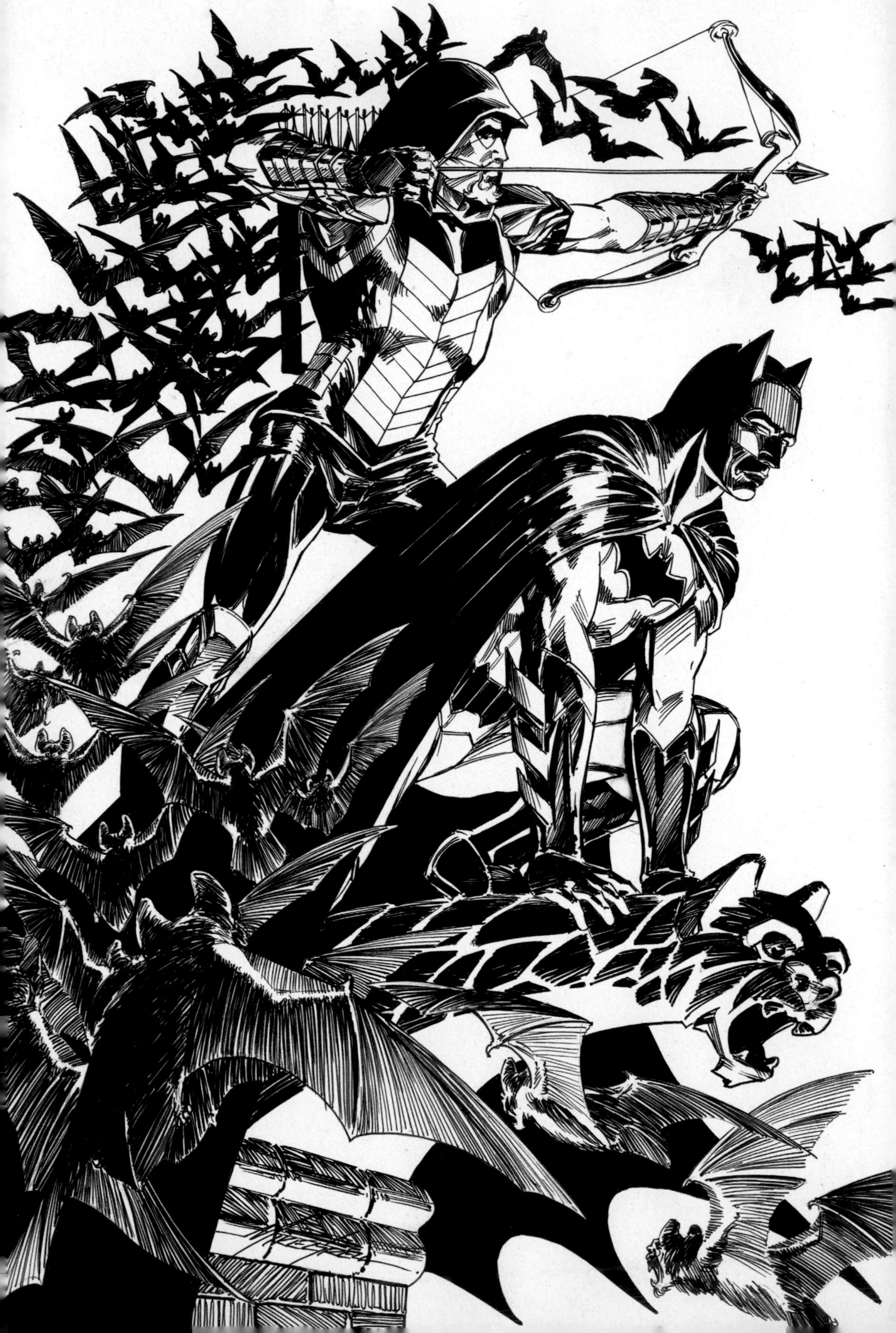

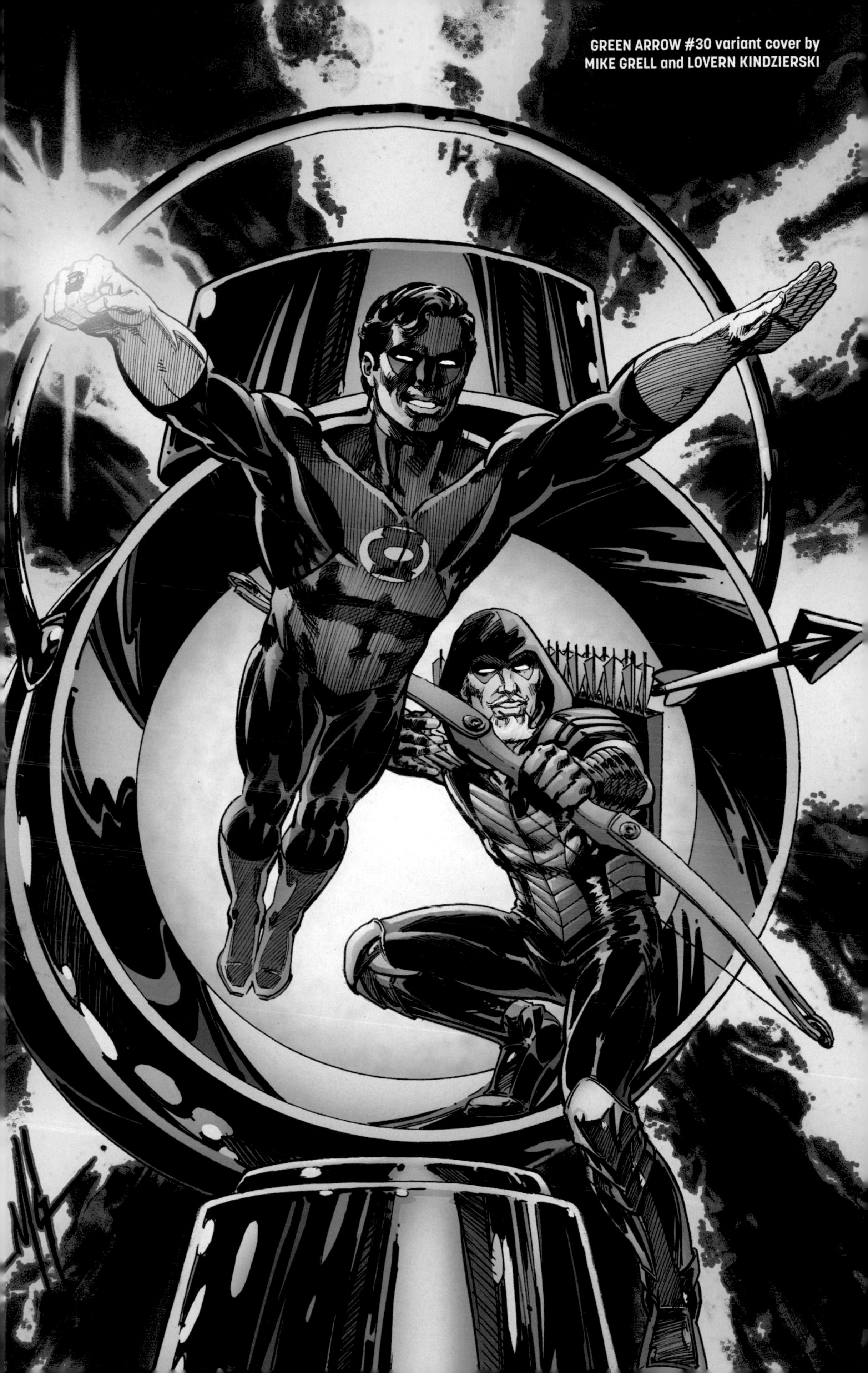

GREEN ARROW #30 variant cover by
MIKE GRELL and LOVERN KINDZIERSKI

GREEN ARROW #31 variant cover by MIKE GRELL and LOVERN KINDZIERSKI

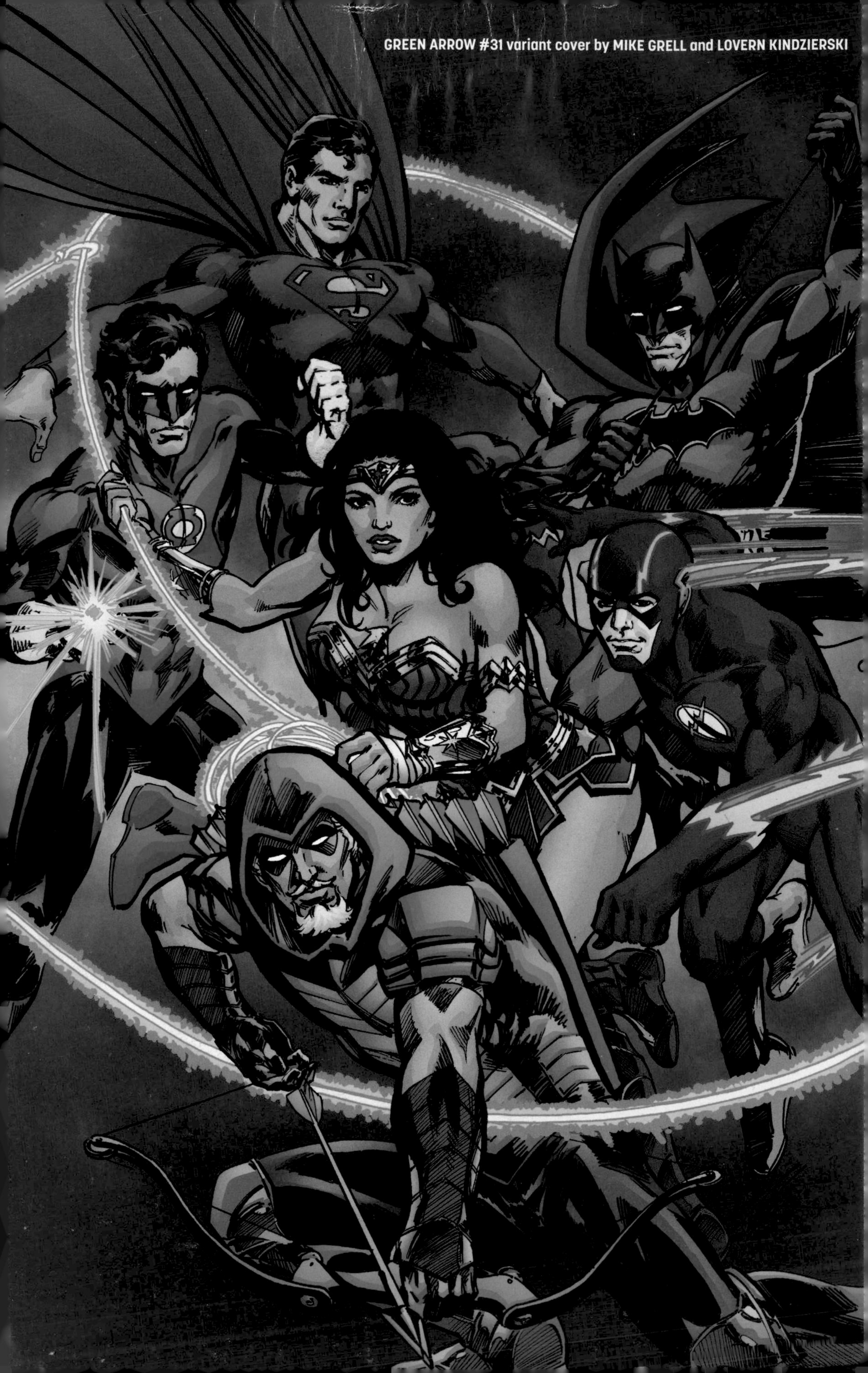